Speech Communication

Speech Communication: A Career-Education Approach

Second Edition

RAY E. NADEAU *Purdue University*

JOHN M. MUCHMORE *William Rainey Harper College*

ADDISON-WESLEY PUBLISHING COMPANY

Reading, Massachusetts • Menlo Park, California

London • Amsterdam • Don Mills, Ontario • Sydney

This book is in the
ADDISON-WESLEY SERIES IN SPEECH

Frederick W. Haberman
Consulting Editor

Chapter-opening photographs are by courtesy of the following:
Chapter 1, Tom Zannes; Chapters 2, 3, 4, 6, 9, Ray White; Chapter 5, Continental Airlines; Chapters 7, 10, Marshall Henrichs; Chapter 8, John Callahan.

Published simultaneously in Canada. Library of Congress Catalog Card No. 78-18640.

ISBN 0-201-05007-2
ABCDEFGHIJK-AL-798

Preface

LET'S BEGIN HERE . . .

This text examines speech communication in career settings. However, before you begin to review the contents of the book, we would like to share with you some of the thoughts we had as we wrote it. We think that career education is important. We know that most of you have very definite occupational goals and that you are making a strong commitment to achieving them. This text is designed to help you attain those goals. Further, we believe that the premise on which the first edition was based bears repeating: The more effective a communicator you are, the more success and satisfaction you will realize from your work.

We have chosen this career-education approach because we believe there is a critical relationship between your ability as a communicator and your success and satisfaction in your career. To make our basic message clearer, we have made extensive use of examples of the relationships between speech communication and careers, and we have drawn these examples from a wide variety of occupations. We are confident that the principles we present in this text have much broader application than in just your work activity, but we also know that you will be better able to make that broader application if we satisfactorily demonstrate just how significant speech communication is in one of your most important areas of commitment—your work.

WHAT'S NEW . . .

One of the most satisfying opportunities that authors have in revising a textbook is that they can retain all that was valuable in the first edition, add elements which subsequent experience has shown should be included, and eliminate those items that are outdated or no longer necessary. We have taken full advantage of this opportunity.

As you use this text, you will discover that we have first established how and why communication is so important to you in your career; then we have explained the basic elements of communication so that we will have a common vocabulary and understanding. Finally, we have demonstrated how you can apply these basic elements and the principles drawn from these elements in order to become a more effective communicator. We have placed these materials in an order consistent with that which you will encounter in your work experiences.

In each chapter you will find (1) an early indication of the objectives of the chapter as we explain "Where we're going," (2) materials necessary to achieve those objectives, (3) opportunities to apply the materials, under the heading, "Try this," and (4) occasions to evaluate the materials when we ask "What do you think?" In this edition, the objectives have been modified. They are not meant to be exclusively "behavioral" in the classic sense of the term. Instead, they are meant to alert you to some of the things that we believe are particularly important in the chapter. The other activities represent a combination of the old and the new.

WHAT'S INSIDE . . .

The first two chapters focus on why communication is crucially important to you and how it helps establish who you are.

The third through the sixth chapters examine the bases of communication; we place heavy stress on making those bases meaningful to you by demonstrating their application to varied occupations. (The fourth chapter introduces new material based on recent research in the area of nonverbal communication. Chapter six offers an expanded view of the listener and places increased emphasis on the mutual and shifting dependence that listener and speaker have on one another.)

Chapters seven through eleven move to a highly practical treatment of those communication skills which will be critical to you in your career. First, we directly address the challenge of getting a job by discussing data sheets and application letters. Then we carry you through one-to-one communication situations (interviews), one-with-several communication activities (groups), and one-to-many challenges (public communication). We believe that you will find the chapter discussions to be both logical and practical.

THANK YOU . . .

We want to thank you, the reader, for your willingness to examine the important role that communication plays or will play in your career and for your willingness to commit yourself to improving your own communication abilities.

Thanks are also due to other people who have made possible the book you are holding. Several of the materials used in the first edition and retained in this one were provided by others. For example, the job interview transcript and a number of speech outlines and photographs were originally furnished by Professor Owen Stallard and his students. The materials relating to nursing care had been provided by Professors Betty Blatchley, Anne Larowe, Mary Roy, and E. Stokes of the Department of Nursing, School of Technology, Purdue University, and by Jane Pruett and Karen Geyer of St. Elizabeth Hospital Medical Center, Lafayette, Indiana. All these contributions to the first edition continue to be relevant and have been retained. (Jennie Bishop was the primary typist of the first edition, and she has served in the same capacity for the second.)

A multitude of students have obviously contributed to our thinking. We are especially appreciative of the lessons that students like Penny Altman, Tony Zimmerman, Diane Norman, Carl Cassidy, and others have taught us through their dedication to both career and study. We acknowledge, too, the support of the career program coordinators who have been willing and anxious to share thoughts with us. We also thank Ray White and John Callahan of Harper College for their help with photography, and we are grateful to the "models" who contributed their services because of their awareness of the vital importance of speech-communication to occupational effectiveness.

In short, a text of this kind is not solely the work of one or, in this instance, two authors; it is a composite whole for which the writers provide the overall theme, organization, and elaboration, but many others (family, friends, students, colleagues, other authors, workers, et al.) provide essential materials and services.

To the many reviewers whose perceptive comments have contributed substantially to the text, to the members of the Addison-Wesley team, especially Damon Reed Gardner and Sue Zorn whose support and direction have been most helpful, and to all our "assistants," named and unnamed, we are extremely grateful.

West Lafayette, Indiana R. E. N.
Crystal Lake, Illinois J. M. M.
August 1978

Contents

1
Approaches to Career Communication

If you
need help, tell
a Policeman.
He
will help you.

1 Approaches to Career Communication

"I like work; it fascinates me. I can sit and look at it for hours."

J. K. Jerome

We have no idea what work you are doing now, or what career you have chosen, or what occupations you may be considering. We do know that very few can afford the luxury that Jerome describes. Sooner or later, everyone goes to work, pursues a career, chooses an occupation.

Under whatever circumstances you hold or intend to hold a job, you have discovered—or will soon discover—that human communication is important. You need it to get the job, to perform the job, to grow in the job, and sometimes to change the job. You will be able to accomplish all of these things more easily if you are able to communicate effectively. The purpose of this book is to help you understand communication and to help you develop skills in communicating successfully with those you come in contact in your chosen field and with others as well.

Here's where we're going

The following objectives should help you identify and understand the more important concepts in this chapter. If you read the chapter carefully and complete the suggested projects, you should be able to:

1. Prepare a paragraph of 50 to 75 words in which you give one or more examples of *social* communication. OR: Prepare a paragraph of 50 to 75 words in which you describe your *social* need to communicate with others.
2. Prepare a paragraph of 50 to 75 words describing your *practical* need to communicate with others. OR: Prepare a paragraph of 50 to 75 words in which you give examples of your having communicated for *practical* reasons.
3. Demonstrate an understanding of *nonverbal communication* by describing, in 50 to 75 words, a personal experience in which you responded to a nonverbal signal.
4. Prepare a paragraph of 50 to 75 words explaining how listening is communication. OR: Describe a conversation in which you felt the other person was not really listening to you. How did the other person's listening behavior affect you?
5. Show an understanding of "feeling with" another person by finding a brief example of "feeling with" in a novel, short story, TV program, or movie. Share it with the class.

YOUR NEED TO COMMUNICATE

Everyone wants to be with others, at least a part of the time. And everyone feels the need to talk with others. For example, you normally go to public places—movies, meetings, sports events—with somebody. In fact, you will sometimes decide not to go somewhere because you can't find someone to go along. It also happens that you sometimes "*have* to talk with somebody." You have something on your mind and you want to talk about it with a friend or with someone else you trust. Even if you don't have something special on your mind, sometimes you just want to talk with somebody about anything, including the weather.

You don't turn these "wants" and "needs" off when you go to work. Consider how you search for someone to join in the cafeteria. Do you remember how hard you looked for a friendly face so that you would have company in a meeting? And do you recall how you took your cup of coffee and returned to your work because there was no one around to share the moment?

Since you are a social being, you will be unhappy if you have to be alone for any length of time. Although you may be shy and have some fears about meeting people, you still would like to be with them. And as you can see, being with someone or not being with someone is a kind of communication in itself. If you agree that "a man is known by the company he keeps," you also agree that you don't have to be talking or listening to be "communicating."

Most of us have experienced a strong desire to belong to a special group of people—a club, a social organization, or just a collection of attractive people. If you can remember that sort of desire, you may also remember what happened when you were accepted—or rejected. If you were accepted, simply being around those persons may have made you feel better about yourself. In addition, other persons attribute meaning to that acceptance. The same is true in the case of rejection. Your feelings about yourself may be diminished, and others will react to both the rejection and the behavior you exhibit after the rejection.

Try this

1. To gain further understanding of the part *social communication* plays in life, tell the class—in three to five minutes—about a personal experience you had or about an experience someone else had.
2. To gain further experience in *social communication* or communication for pleasure, recommend—in three to five minutes—a television or radio program to the members of the class. Include at least two reasons why you feel they would enjoy the program.

You also need to communicate because communication is the only way you have to let people know who you are, what you know, and what you can do. It is common to find a skilled and talented person working at a second-rank job because he or she isn't able to "sell" his or her ideas to others. Knowing how to be a dental assistant won't help you much if the dentist doesn't feel that you can meet and talk in a friendly way with patients. And as a general rule, you'll also find that superiors who are very good at their work are very good at communicating. An education is valuable, and your being able to communicate can greatly increase the value of your education.

Look around at the people you know in your community. You'll find plenty of proof that the good communicator enjoys some practical advantages and some social advantages as well. If you have any doubt about the importance communication will play in your future, consider Alvin Toffler's view of the world to come. He emphasizes that ". . . all students should be grounded in certain common skills for human communication and social integration."[1]

If you agree that communication skills will be important to your career but believe that once you've chosen that career and trained for it your worries

1. Alvin Toffler, *Future Shock* (New York: Random House, 1970), p. 366.

are over, you may be wrong. The U.S. Department of Labor reports that "career changes are made by a 'striking number of U.S. workers.' "[2] The Department estimates that a third of all American workers will change their careers over a five-year period.

A good communicator enjoys advantages now and will almost certainly be better equipped to deal with the rapid change that we may anticipate.

SOME WAYS TO COMMUNICATE

Once you accept your *need* to communicate, you will be interested in *ways* to communicate. In a discussion of ways to communicate, you will encounter listening and speaking. Just as important is the interaction between listening and speaking. If you speak and we listen there is an interaction. If we speak and you listen, there is a similar interaction. This interaction is critical to successful communication.

Figure 1.1 represents a common conception of the communicative process. The speaker has an idea, "encodes" it by selecting what he or she considers to be appropriate verbal and/or nonverbal forms of expression, and sends that encoded message to the listener. The listener receives it through the senses of hearing, sight, etc., and, giving his or her own meaning to it (decoding), responds verbally and/or nonverbally and thereby provides feedback, which tells or should tell the speaker how the message is being received.

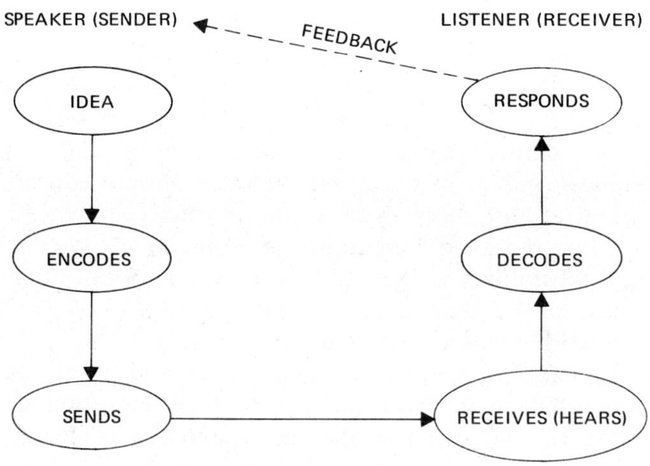

Figure 1.1

2. *Wall Street Journal,* February 8, 1977, p. 1.

Activities like those above *are* a part of communication, but we know now that the process cannot be so neatly divided into an orderly series of steps. As a result of the work of researchers over recent years, we now see communication as a very complex process (described in detail in Part 2 of this text), one that is constantly ongoing, continuously interactive, sometimes intentional, and sometimes unintentional. The two most fundamental parts, however, are listening and speaking.

Listening[3]

Research indicates that most occupations call for a great deal of listening. Doctors and clergymen, for example, may spend 80 to 85 percent of their working time engaged in listening. Managers, supervisors, salesmen, and teachers will be engaged in listening activities 40 to 60 percent of the working time.[4] A poor listener will be at a disadvantage.

Examine these typical answers to the question, "What can I get out of better listening?"[5]

More information upon which to base my decisions

A better knowledge of the people with whom I work

Fewer foul-ups

A more accurate view of myself and the way I affect others

A chance to learn more

Better speakers to listen to—if I listen better they'll be stimulated to speak more effectively

Fewer complaints and grievances

Better communication

People more willing to act favorably on what I say

More cooperation

More self-control

A better understanding of the things that I talk about

A lot of things that I'd rather not hear

And maybe the knowledge that those things that I'd rather not hear aren't really as bad as I imagined they would be

3. See Thomas E. Anastasi, Jr., and Sidney A. Dimond, *Listening on the Job* (Reading, Mass.: Addison-Wesley, 1972). The writers depended largely on this work for the discussion of listening. In the present text, see Chapter 6 for additional insights into the behavior of the listener.

4. See Anastasi and Dimond, p. 8.

5. Answers selected from Anastasi and Dimond, p. 10.

And, on the other hand, maybe they were worse than I had imagined

Truth

I don't know—I've never really listened enough to know what might happen

Don't be misled. Listening is not just hearing. Not all of those who "hear" listen. Listening is a valuable skill that you can develop. You might begin to develop these skills by taking into account certain physical factors and habits.[6]

Recognize the need to find a good place to listen. The more distractions, the more difficult it is to listen. If the radio is too loud, turn it down. If the room is too warm, lower the thermostat.

Pay attention to the speaker—the other person. One of the most common listening errors is that of thinking about what we are going to say rather than listening to what the other person is saying.

"Listen" to the whole person. Pay attention to behavior, to movement, to tone of voice, types of emphasis, and volume.

Paraphrase and summarize. These are things that you should do both silently and aloud. As the speaker progresses, you will want to occasionally review what has been said. When you have a moment of confusion, stop the other person and check: "If I heard you correctly, you said . . . ."

Try this

1. Examine your powers of concentration. Sit for a few moments in a relatively quiet room. Listen for sounds you've never heard before.
2. Join your friends in a listening exercise. Before an individual may speak, he or she must repeat what the preceding speaker has said—to that person's satisfaction.[7]

The first of these exercises should demonstrate to you just how much we tune out—when we fail to concentrate. When you are listening to others, your effectiveness will increase if you plan your listening—if you concentrate on listening for a specific purpose. The second exercise should show you how often

6. For a more complete discussion of these and other listening skills, see Chapter 6. You may also wish to consult either Carl Weaver, *Human Listening: Processes and Behavior* New York: Bobbs-Merrill, 1972), or Ralph G. Nichols and Leonard Stevens, *Are You Listening?* (New York: McGraw-Hill, 1957).

7. Carl Rogers describes this and a number of other helpful activities in Carl R. Rogers and F. J. Roethlisberger, "Barriers and Gateways to Communication," *Harvard Business Review*, July-August 1952, pp. 46-52. Copyright © 1952 by the President and Fellows of Harvard College; all rights reserved.

we fail to listen carefully to the other speaker and instead allow our attention to focus on our own thoughts.

Listening is an active process. The real listener actively cooperates with a speaker. You cooperate by giving the speaker your entire attention, by looking interested, by showing that you believe that the speaker has something worthwhile to say, and by respecting the speaker as a person.

Listening takes effort but it pays off in at least three ways. First, there is real satisfaction in relating directly to another human being. We are all in this daily struggle together, and we feel the need for help and encouragement in almost everything we do. Listening to others tells them that you accept them as they are and that you feel they have the right to express their ideas. There is no room for fault-finding in this kind of listening. Good listening is the kind of feedback that encourages and supports the speaker all the way.

Not only does listening help you to "relate to" someone else, but it helps you "feel with" that person and become a more sensitive human being at the same time. You've often heard someone say, "I know how you feel," or "I feel the same way you do." Sometimes those statements actually have something to do with feeling; more often than not, the speaker simply means that he or she understands your position or agrees with you on some subject. On the other hand, the kind of feeling that we're talking about here is real—it involves emotion, affection, compassion, sympathy, and any other intense feeling that can be shared with another human being. Some call this having the same "in-feeling" as someone else; the modern word "empathy" (*em* = in, *pathy* = feeling) derives that meaning from the ancient Greek. A good listener is willing to forget his or her own problems in a sincere effort to see and feel things through the eyes of the speaker. This, again, takes effort. If you can really put yourself in somebody else's place (instead of just talking about it) and share in his or her feelings, you are successfully "feeling with" that person, whether you're speaking or listening.

The ability to empathize can be a very helpful tool in your occupation. When you have a clear sense of how others regard your occupation, when you know what goes through their heads when they encounter you, your own communicative efforts can be more purposeful.

George Kirkham was a professor of criminology who decided that he needed to know more about the policeman's job. He became a policeman for more than six months. He learned about abuse, threats, and violence. He saw the kind of human misery and tragedy which are a part of the policeman's everyday life. He concluded that the policeman is asked to be too much—to be a curbside psychiatrist, marriage counselor, social worker, and even minister and doctor.[8] Kirkham has returned to teaching criminology but one thing is

8. Kirkham's experience is described in *U.S. News and World Report*, April 22, 1974, pp. 70–72.

sure: he now teaches from a new position of experience and understanding. He has learned to "listen" in the fullest sense. He is able to "listen" from the other person's perspective.

Kirkham demonstrated that he could learn to empathize with the law enforcement officer. The law enforcement officer can also increase his or her effectiveness by learning to empathize. The Riverside, California, police department has developed a program of cultural studies which includes time spent living-in with some of the city's Mexican-American families. The purpose of the program is to create better relations between the members of the police department and the city's 18,000 Mexican Americans.[9]

These are unusual examples of trying to develop an ability to empathize. However, both of them support the importance of being able to "feel with" another human being. If you can learn to "feel with" another without actually having to experience the other's life, you will be a very valuable person in both your social and career relationships.

Finally, and more selfishly, active listening pays off because you learn something from it. If nothing else, you learn how someone else feels about a subject. Further, you almost always pick up some information, either about a subject or about how one person can relate to another in a friendly and human way. Or you can learn something about what to do and what not to do in trying to communicate with one or more listeners.

When you find that you are one of a number of people listening to a speaker in a small gathering or even in a public meeting, you can *listen actively.* A responsive audience helps any speaker to do his or her best. On the other side of the coin, an audience that appears to be bored can "kill" the best speaker. Active listening in a public setting can be just as rewarding an experience as active listening in a person-to-person or small-group situation.

Questions like these can help you become an active listener.

To Help the Speaker

Is my listening *encouraging* the person talking to me?

Am I trying hard enough to get the *speaker's* meaning?

Do I see how the speaker *feels* about what he or she is saying?

To Help Myself

Am I adding anything to my stock of information?

Any new ideas coming my way?

By watching this person in action, can I learn something about good (or bad) communication?

---

9. *Time,* April 21, 1975, pp. 33–34.

Learn to listen actively. You'll discover that it's a fine way to get to know others and to contribute to your own personal growth as well.

Try this

1. To become more aware of the need to adapt what you say to your listeners, write a paragraph of 50 to 75 words giving at least two reasons why it was easy to listen to a speaker you have recently heard.
2. The goal here is to gain experience in active listening. Break up into groups of three, select one of the following statements and discuss it.[10]

   The best jobs are (or are not) in small companies.

   The specialist in any field has (or has not) the best chance to get ahead.

   All you get in a government job is security.

   Women teachers do (or don't) meet many unmarried men.

   You can't earn much money working in a bank.

   You can't earn much money working for somebody else.

   A salesperson has to be (or doesn't have to be) extremely aggressive to do well.

   An outsider has little chance in a family-owned business.

   There isn't (or is) much opportunity for women in government (or teaching, or business, or . . .).

   There is (or isn't) a good future in a secretarial job (or in some other job you name).

In any one group, student 1 chooses a question or statement and talks about it to student 2, while student 3 acts as observer and referee. Student 2, the listener, takes part in the conversation but only to ask questions which will help him or her to understand student 1. After five minutes, student 2 takes over and summarizes, in his or her own words and without notes, what student 1 has said. If the summary is thought to be incorrect on any detail, either student 1 or the referee may interrupt to clear up any misunderstanding. Then the second round begins: Student 2 becomes the speaker, chooses a question or statement, and starts talking to student 3 with student 1 as referee. In the third five-minute session, student 3 is the speaker, student 1 the listener, and student 2 the referee. Following the three rounds of conversations, the three students talk about what happened along these lines: Did anyone find it hard to be the listener? Why? Did anyone find it hard to summarize what had been

---

10. The statements in this series are adapted from *A College Student's Guide to Career Planning,* by Frank S. Endicott. Copyright 1967 by Frank S. Endicott, published by Rand McNally & Co.

said? Why? Did listening, questioning, and repeating bring the listener closer to understanding the speaker? Was the speaker satisfied with the summary offered by the listener? Why or why not? Was the listening experience worth carrying over into other conversations?

What do you think?

What is the difference between listening and hearing? If there is a difference, why use the word *actively* with listening? Do you know any good listeners? Have you ever listened because you didn't want to offend or hurt someone? Did you get anything out of it? Does the pretending make sense? Have you ever tried to talk with someone who was watching a favorite TV program? Did you get that person's full attention? Or did he or she continue to glance at the program? What did that person's listening or not listening do to you? Were you encouraged or discouraged? Have you ever had the experience of going to a party and having someone constantly look over your shoulder as he or she "talked" to you? What did you feel like doing? What did you do? What do you do for somebody's self-confidence when you listen carefully to everything he or she says? What happens if you half-listen or don't listen at all? Does a small band or orchestra do a better job if the audience claps and responds? What does band playing have to do with active listening? Is there any excuse for putting people down? When? Do you think some active listening to young adults would make them a little more sure of themselves? Would they be happier? Possibly more successful now and in the future? Is it possible to "feel with" someone who doesn't give you a chance to say anything? Or if you're speaking and the listener can hardly wait to break in, is he or she listening? Do you believe that people should conceal their feelings? When? Why?

Speaking

We sometimes think of speaking as simply the sending of word-messages that we prepare in the mind and then "let out." However, as you have probably concluded, the process of communication isn't all that simple. For purposes of demonstration, consider just one added element, namely, using the tone of your voice to change the meaning a listener would normally attach to a word, phrase, or sentence. For example, the words "Come to me" can be said angrily, soothingly, sarcastically, coaxingly, and in many other ways, each suggesting different meanings to the listener. For another example, you can say "Friend!" in a way that to the listener carries the idea of "Enemy!" So it is that words or verbal communication take on added, different, or contradictory meanings from your tone and from what the listener thinks he or she hears in your tone. As you have already suspected, there is more to speaking than just words.

In studying communication, we should also become familiar with nonverbal "speaking." In the discussion of listening, we suggested that "looking sympathetic" tells the speaker something about how you feel about him or her. That way of "looking" is really nonverbal or not-with-words communication. You've heard someone say, "If looks could kill, I'd be dead." That person received the message but it did not have to be expressed in words. Much of the communication of both the speaker and the listener is nonverbal; for example, there's a message in the way people dress as well as in the other ways they present themselves to others. More on this subject in a later chapter, but, again, to become a good communicator, you have to be aware that (1) communication without words is a part of face-to-face communication with words and (2) sometimes communication without words exists by itself.

Our earlier discussion of social communication suggests that few of us like to remain anonymous. Certainly, you have had moments when you hoped that no one knew your name. Most of the time, however, you want to get to know others—to know their names and what they do. We make that assumption—that you would like to get acquainted or get better acquainted with other students in your class. We also assume that you want to know more about communication, the process that plays such an important part in your life. The following activities should help satisfy those "wants."

Try this

1. Talking about yourself

Join two or three other students in the class.[11] (Don't join with those whom you know.) In no more than two minutes tell the others in your group some things about yourself. You talk; they listen *without interrupting*. Each of the others, in turn does the same thing. Stay comfortable. We're not interested in *True Confessions*. Tell the others your name, what kinds of interests you have, a little about your family, some of your favorite things and some of the things that you don't like.

Then, talker 1 (the student who was the first to talk about himself or herself) listens without interrupting for no more than three minutes as the others in the small group tell him or her (1) what they actually heard and (2) any conclusions they drew from what he or she said or didn't say. In turn, talkers 2 and 3 (and 4 if there was a fourth member) become listeners as the others tell them what they heard and what they concluded.

Finally, there may be time for general class discussion of some of the interesting things that happened in particular groups.

---

11. Adapted from J. William Pfeiffer and John E. Jones (eds.), *A Handbook of Structured Experiences for Human Relations Training,* Vol. I (Rev.), p. 1. (La Jolla, Calif.: University Associates, 1974.) Used with permission.

2. Introducing another student

Speaking: In no more than two minutes, introduce another student to the members of the class. Give them the kinds of information mentioned in "Talking about yourself." Finish with the student's name, at which signal he or she should stand up to be recognized.

The student just introduced can then introduce a third student, or can "return the favor" by introducing the student who introduced him or her. In other words, these introductions can be arranged in pairs or on the domino plan, whereby student 1 introduces student 2, who introduces student 3, and so on.

Listening: From time to time, the instructor or a student chairman should break the expected pattern by having a student in another part of the class repeat the introduction he has just heard, or repeat the next to last introduction, etc. The student who knows that he may be asked to introduce any student for a second time is going to be a better listener, and he is also going to be better acquainted with everyone in the room.

SUMMARY

Your ability to communicate will be an important factor both in your social contacts and your work relationships. This chapter describes the importance of both speaking and listening to the communication process. In addition, the chapter emphasizes the significance of both verbal and nonverbal communication.

The communication process is a complex process involving many factors. Study and practice will allow you to become a more effective participant in the process.

2
Deciding Who You Are

2
Deciding Who You Are

". . . I can look back and say, 'I helped put out a fire. I helped save somebody. It shows I did something on earth.' "

Fireman Tom Patrick in Studs Terkel's *Working*

People frequently fail to realize how important their career is in determining who they are. Likewise, they often fail to see that their own perceptions of "self" may limit career options or, if those perceptions are positive, open new career possibilities.

Consider your own case. You may have given a lot of thought to the type of work you want to do. On the other hand, you may have selected your career by accident or as a result of outside pressures. This chapter examines the challenge of deciding who you are and determining how your occupational role will affect that decision.

In the first chapter you encountered opportunities to *"Try this."* You will find similar opportunities in this and following chapters. You may find it helpful to complete these tasks in a notebook, your own "communication journal." You will be able to refer to them later and see if your perceptions change during the class. The journal is yours, and you need not share it with others unless you want to.

Here's where we're going

If you read this chapter carefully and respond to the challenges, you should be able to:

1. Name a particular occupation and list five ways in which you believe choosing it could contribute positively to one's self concept.
2. Prepare a paragraph of 50 to 75 words explaining how a choice you made in the past had some effect in shaping the person you are now.
3. Prepare a paragraph of 50 to 75 words showing how the decision to enter a particular occupation might change you.
4. Write a definition of *perception* and write a short paragraph in which you give an example or examples of *perception* drawn from your own experiences or observations.
5. Write a definition of *selective perception* and write a short paragraph in which you give an illustration of selective perception.
6. Write a definition of *self-concept* and write a paragraph explaining how it did or could influence your career choice.

YOU AND YOUR CAREER CHOICE

Since this chapter will focus on both deciding who you are and the role that your occupation, work or career will have in that decision, it will be helpful to arrive at definitions. You have noticed that the terms *work, career, occupation* are being used interchangeably. There may be slight differences in meaning, but all three of the terms describe a similar activity.

In the government publication, *Work in America,*[1] *work* is defined as "an activity that produces something of value for other people." *Career* and *occupation* are words describing a long term commitment to a particular kind of *work.* The most significant thing about this definition of work is that it recognizes that a commitment to homemaking or to volunteer activities can be a *career* just as much as medicine. Furthermore, if you like a job, it can be very satisfying; if you don't like it, it can be frustrating, wearing, tiring. Fireman Tom Patrick engages in a specialized kind of *work.* He has been thoroughly trained and has committed his life to a career as a firefighter. He certainly produces something of value to others.

Equally important, the job produces something of value to him—"It shows I did something on earth."[2] He is lucky to have achieved that feeling. He is much more fortunate than the steelworker Terkel interviewed. ". . . I am nothing. After 40 years of workin' at the steel mill, I am just a number."[3]

1. *Work In America: Report of a Special Task Force to the Secretary of Health, Education and Welfare.* Cambridge, Mass.: MIT Press, 1973.
2. Studs Terkel, *Working.* New York: Pantheon Books, 1974, p. 589.
3. Ibid., p. 557.

YOU AND YOUR BACKGROUND

Your work does make a significant contribution to who you are, but other factors affect your concept of yourself—and their influence precedes that of your choice of a job.

Maybe you've noticed that a self-confident person communicates more readily and more easily than someone who is ill at ease and uncertain of himself. What makes a person self-confident? Some say it's knowing who you are, as well as knowing what you can and can't do, and having some definite job or career goal in mind.

If in one way or another you get to know yourself pretty well, you may come fairly close to seeing your strengths and weaknesses and very close to accepting yourself as you really are—and others will also come closer to knowing the real you. With that seeing and accepting of yourself will come a kind of I'm-willing-to-face-the-facts self-confidence. The self-confident person is good at communication because he or she doesn't consider it necessary to pretend to be something or somebody else and is therefore more at ease with himself or herself and with others.

If it is a good idea to face the facts about ourselves, what are some of the facts *you* face? To begin with, you were probably born white-American—or black-American—or Mexican-American—or Puerto-Rican American—or Oriental-American—or American-Indian—or some other kind of American. You were brought up as a Protestant—or as a Jew—or as a Catholic—or as a Muslim—or as a Hindu—or in some other faith—or in no faith. Your parents, if living, are married, unmarried, or separated—well-off, not so well-off, or poor—educated, not so well-educated, or uneducated. If your parents are white, Catholic, just getting by financially, and not so well-educated, you are now one kind of person. If your parents are black, Baptist, and wage earners with high school educations, you are another kind of person. Your parents, along with your general background and education, had a lot to do with the kind of person you are today.

In other words, for reasons which will become progressively clearer in the next section of this chapter and in succeeding chapters, *you are one of a kind,* a unique human being. You are different from everyone else in this world and different from everyone else in your own family. If you have an identical twin, that twin is almost but not quite the same in physical characteristics only. You have different attitudes, different feelings, different interests, different prejudices, different abilities, different standards, etc. When you say something, what you say and how you say it is *the product* of your past experiences; when you listen to someone, what he or she says is *screened and interpreted* through your past experiences. No one ever has the same set of experiences as someone else, and, as we shall later emphasize, the experiences we have are colored or selected by earlier experiences. For one example of many, you see things you are interested in more readily than you see other things. If you like old cars, you'll see more old cars than other people do; the same is true of antiques, dogs, birds, and other objects or living things. If you like sports, you'll read about them and attend sports events. If you like music, you'll listen to records and attend musical events. What you like—and what you dislike—you'll talk about; how you talk about it will depend on your total background as well as on your most recently selected experiences.

YOU AND YOUR SELF-CONCEPT

However important to your future your background may be, even more important is *your evaluation of yourself as a person in the light of that background* and all the experiences that are a part of it.

The "self-concept is the person's total appraisal of his or her appearance, background and origins, abilities and resources, attitudes and feelings which culminate as a directing force in behavior."[4] That means that your total awareness of yourself, together with what you think and feel, "guides, controls, and regulates" what you say and do.

No one need tell you that life brings with it some successes and some failures. You also know that when you succeed, you "feel good," and when you fail, you "don't feel so good." If, on balance, you've had a fair share of successes in accomplishing what you set out to do, your opinion of yourself is probably high enough to encourage you to continue trying to reach new goals. If you've had a goodly number of setbacks, your opinion of yourself may make you think twice before undertaking something you consider difficult. In other words, a series of successes is likely to build up your self-concept; a series of failures is likely to wear it down. In any event, you learn who and what you are through all the successful and unsuccessful experiences you encounter, especially those you have during your earlier years.

Of major consequence, of course, are your experiences with people. What you think about yourself depends heavily on what you think others think of you. And what others think of you is mostly inference on your part. You draw conclusions about yourself from what people say or from what they are reported to have said. You draw conclusions from the way they look at you and from how they relate to you. You decide, sometimes on flimsy evidence, that someone likes you or doesn't like you.

---

4. Wallace D. LaBenne and Bert I. Greene, *Educational Implications of Self-Concept Theory* (Pacific Palisades, Cal.: Goodyear, 1969), p. 10. Much of the discussion of the self-concept in this chapter is based on LaBenne and Greene, pp. 10–20, 122–123.

Your total view of yourself, based on your experiences generally and on your experiences with people, *governs what you decide to do and not do.* For example, if you don't swim well, you're not going to enter a swimming race, and if your clarinet playing is limited to band music, you won't be applying for a job with a symphony. On the other hand, if you did well in journalism in high school, you might be encouraged to try writing for the college paper, and if you're good at figures, you might want to work toward becoming an accountant. If you find it easy to meet people and associate with them, you might decide to go into a field calling for that ability; if you are retiring and shy, you might decide to take a job that does not require "meeting the public."

And so it goes—successes build self-confidence and failures wear it down. The important thing is to "accentuate the positive." When you do something well, take advantage of that successful experience and follow it up with other efforts in the same or a related area. If you fail—and we all fail from time to time—the defeat should be interpreted only as " 'I have failed,' not 'I am a failure.' "[5]

What is it that leads one person to say "I have failed" and another to say "I am a failure"? One *perceives* an incident in one way, the other perceives it in another. Perception (more about this in Chapter 6) is the process of making sense out of past experience. For example, the first time a small child is rejected by a busy parent, the child may not understand rejection. The child will examine the actions of the parent and give meaning to them. The child will learn that certain behavior means rejection.

You may enter a situation which many people fear. Many of us are afraid of the dentist's office. This fear grew out of our experiences in such an office. If you have been fortunate and have had a sympathetic and highly skilled dentist who has worked to remove fear from the dental experience, you will not perceive the visit to the office as being nearly so threatening as others might.

Additionally, perceptions differ widely because one's self-concept, itself the product of all past experiences and perceptions of them, provides the selective perception or lens through which one views any new experience. If you believe that you are strong and able to deal with pain, you may perceive the visit as simply a necessary step in a good health program.

To put it another way, we are incapable of absorbing all the stimuli bombarding us, and since we are conditioned by our past to notice certain things and ignore others, our perceptions become selective; we subconsciously and unconsciously select what we are going to be aware of.

When failure occurs, somebody with a weak self-concept has a tendency, on the basis of his or her past experiences, to look at the dark side and make

5. LaBenne and Greene, p. 12.

some sweeping generalization like "Everybody is against me," or "I knew I couldn't do it." The individual who has experienced several rejections by personnel officers may quit applying because, "Ah, they wouldn't hire someone like me." The individual with a strong self-concept, again on the basis of his or her past experiences, has tendency to minimize failure and say something like, "Clearly they didn't need someone who is as well qualified as I am."

You may be puzzled as to how the matter of self-concept can relate to your career. Consider the two extremes that we just identified—the individual with the strong self-concept and the individual with the weak self-concept. If you allow yourself to view yourself as a failure, it is likely that you will seek out a career without challenges. You will avoid responsibility. The net effect will be to confirm the anticipated failure. In avoiding risk and responsibility you will avoid failure, but your success will be so limited that you will not receive the kind of rewards that will make you feel better. The raises and new positions will go to others, and you will feel more a failure.

If, on the other hand, you develop a strong self-concept, you will accept challenges, seek out new opportunities, get the raises and new positions and reinforce your already strong self-concept.

Consider the individual who prefers a different set of rewards. Fireman Patrick is realizing a reward from his awareness that he is helping other people. He feels better about himself because he knows what he does is important.

We've mentioned the possibility that an individual may make several career changes during his or her life. Gail Sheehy has discovered that one of the most frequent reasons for a midlife career change is a desire to help others to bring more meaning into their own lives.[6]

The 45-year-old salesman who becomes a priest is demonstrating how a changing self-concept leads one to make a change. Likewise, the fact that the change satisfies the individual's need indicates the effect that career has on self-concept.

The point of all this is that you do have some control over the building of a solid and positive self-concept. You have to (1) take realistic stock of yourself and your abilities, (2) recognize that the occasional failure is not the end of the world, and (3) make some plans for personal growth which will increase the number of your successes and cut down on the failures. Stated another way, the first step toward a positive and satisfying self-concept is "the ability to recognize and accept with understanding one's own weaknesses and strengths."[7]

---

6. Gail Sheehy, *Passages: Predictable Crises of Adult Life* (New York: E. P. Dutton, 1974).
7. LaBenne and Green, p. 122.

TAKING STOCK OF YOURSELF

The person you are today is clearly a mix of many things: your general background, your family situation, your education up to now, the choices you've made and those you didn't make, the experiences you've had, and the people you've met. You look at the world around you through your own special glasses, the lenses of which were made by everything that ever happened to you. As we noted earlier, nobody else, including members of your own family, sees things exactly as you do because nobody else has had the same background and experiences as you. The listening exercises in the first chapter demonstrated that the same principle applies to our hearing.

You may not be satisfied with the person you are today or with the life you see around you. You can waste a lot of time and energy in envy of others and in griping about "lack of a chance to get ahead," or you can decide to do something about it. You can resent your racial or religious heritage, or you can decide to take pride in it. You can drift along, kill time, drop out of school, and blame everything and everybody but yourself, or you can decide to train yourself for one or more specific lines of work. You can fall victim to cultural stereotypes and believe that only men can be physicians, that nursing is an occupation for females, that girls should learn how to type because there is always a need for secretaries and that it would be a waste of time for a male to learn shorthand.[8] You can accept unfortunate racial stereotypes that suggest that certain minorities cannot handle complicated work—that "they" may be capable of only manual labor.

Or, you can recognize that interest, ability, and talent are individual qualities not determined by sex, race, or religion, and you can select and pursue an occupation based on what you want—not on what some mysterious *they* says you should do. You can believe that "some have it made" and get ahead through the people they know (and some of this *does* happen), or you can believe that every human being without exception has some special worth, some special ability, and some special talent.

Try this

Sit back and think for a few minutes, then write one sentence that demonstrates something unique about you. It's difficult but, once you come to recog-

8. For those who are interested in just how dramatically cultural, ethnic, and racial stereotypes have affected persons and the occupational roles that they are prepared to assume, Margaret Hennig and Ann Jardim's *The Managerial Woman* (Garden City, New York: Anchor Press/Doubleday, 1977) offers a very revealing discussion.

nize that you are "one of a kind," you can come closer to finding out what that kind is by asking yourself some questions like these:

Where did I come from? How did I get to be the way I am?

Why do I like some people and why don't I like others?

What are my prejudices? Do I try to understand and accept others? Or do I more often look for reasons to reject them?

Do I face the facts about myself? What handicaps do I have? Can anything be done about any of them?

What advantages do I have? Do I have any special talent or talents? How do I know?

How can I make the most of what ability I have? What am I aiming at?

Am I willing to start from *here* to get to *there?*

In addition to trying to answer the general questions above, you may find it useful to ask yourself some of the more specific questions below.[9] Since everyone has had experiences different from those of anyone else, some questions will be appropriate to you and some will not. The questions are intended to help you determine your strong points as well as your shortcomings, with the idea of bringing your self-concept into sharper focus and establishing or strengthening a positive view of yourself.

Your Social Self

Do I feel comfortable with other students of my age?
Do I believe that my manners are inferior?
Am I uncomfortable about my background?
Am I afraid to meet new people?
Can I start a conversation?
Am I able to enter into a conversation which others have begun?
Do I feel comfortable with persons older than myself?
Do I belong to a group? Do I approve of the group I belong to? Do I want to belong to another group?
Am I ashamed of my house, my family, my neighborhood, or my appearance?
Am I afraid of not being able to belong?
Am I rejected by specific groups?

9. Except for minor editing, questions in this section are in the 1968 curriculum study written by William E. Buys, Charles V. Carlson, Hite Compton, and Allan D. Frank. Their report appears in *The Speech Teacher* **27**, November 1968, pp. 307–310.

Your Student Self

Do I like the school or college I am attending?
What is my attitude toward the instructors?
Is earning good grades important to me?
If I choose not to accomplish an assignment, do I accept the consequences?
Do I respect intellectual achievement?
What does it mean to be educated?
Am I afraid in the classroom? Am I afraid of instructors?
Do I like to read? Have I been made to feel inferior because I can't read well? Do my friends think me strange if I choose to read and think?
Does my family think that being educated is important?
Can I be successful without going through school?

Your Political Self

Have I ever registered a complaint with the student council or with some administrative officer?
Do I keep informed about local, national, and world events?
What community problems am I particularly interested in? How could I get more involved?
Do I really understand the political process? What are my rights? What responsibilities do they bring?
Have I participated in a political demonstration, such as a teach-in, sit-in, march? How did I feel? Do I feel these demonstrations are an effective means for change?
Do I belong to a group that makes decisions democratically? Do I speak out? How do I feel when the vote is "against" me?
Have I worked in a local or national political campaign?
Have I contributed time or effort to any social or political reform groups of any kind?

Your Economic Self

How do I want to earn a living?
What jobs have I enjoyed?
Have I looked for jobs without being told?
Do I need a job?
What are my earning abilities?
What is my answer when someone asks, "What do you want to be?" or "What do you want to do with your life?"

Must I prepare for what I want to do by going to college?
Must I decide now upon a choice?
Do I want to work as hard as my parents do?
Could I be a "bum"? What do I think a "bum" is?
Does it take only time to develop a talent? Can I try to be an artist?

Your Moral Self

Do I have a standard of "rules for right living"? Do I follow it?
Is my standard derived from my family's standard?
Do standards of ethics change?
Is the moral person one who accepts without thinking the standards of his or her society?
Am I my brother's keeper?
Does time affect my responsibilities?
Do I have contracts to honor?
Do I feel that "the end justifies the means"?
Do I respect the law and its representatives?
What is the function of law? Does it benefit me?

Your Changing Self

In what ways am I growing and changing?
Do the members of my family change? Do I expect them to change? Do I resent their changing?
Have my interests changed? In the sports that I play, in the books I read, in the movies I like, in the TV programs I watch?
Have my attitudes changed toward others?
Do I believe that truth may be relative?
Am I frightened by change?
Does any living thing remain static?

Even when you have worked out answers to most of the questions above, they may not be the best answers. Your own feeling about how you look may not be shared by others. We have already noted one of the real ironies of life: much of what you feel about yourself is based on how you think others feel about you. Too often we misread what others think about us and jump to conclusions without asking or checking. You may have assumed that the instructor's frown meant that she thought you couldn't learn or that the doctor's detailed questions meant that she thought you were really ill. In reality, the instructor's frown might mean that she is disappointed that she can't offer you a greater challenge, or the doctor's detailed questions may mean that she is almost certain that there is nothing wrong because you have none of the standard symptoms. Maybe you misinterpreted the instructor's smile. You interpreted it as an indication of pride in your comments, when it was an effort at kindness to keep you from being embarrassed at being wrong.

What you believe you can learn and do may not be in line with what you can really learn and do. On the other hand, you could be selling yourself short. So, in addition to talking with yourself about "the real you" and about what others say about "the real you," another step to take is talking with a trusted counselor, advisor, or friend. Discussing the answers you give to yourself with someone having a different point of view is a way to get some checks on your answers. Still another step is to take whatever aptitude tests are available to you through your school or college counseling office. Finally, after you think you really know yourself pretty well, the point to remember is that you are capable of change, you are capable of personal growth.

MAKING PLANS FOR PERSONAL GROWTH

What directions should your personal growth take? If you have already chosen what you hope will be your life's work and if you're already working toward that goal, much of your growth problem is already solved. Still, if you haven't yet chosen a vocation or career, you are not alone in that situation. And if you're having second thoughts about your present goals, you have a lot of company there, too. If you haven't made a career decision yet, or if you're questioning the decision you made, the important thing now is to work at solving that problem. Among the ways to go about it are these:

1. Ask your librarian for the reference books describing jobs and groups of jobs. You'll be given such titles as the *Dictionary of Occupational Titles, The Job Guide for Young Workers,* and the *Occupational Handbook.*
2. Take the aptitude tests available through your college and, taking into consideration your own likes and dislikes plus the information the books give about where the openings are going to be, choose an occupation or a group of related occupations. (If you can't get into one, you can get into another.) Here are some basic questions you may want to consider.[10]

   What high school subjects interested me most? In what subjects did I do my best work? Why?

   In what college courses am I most interested? In what courses have I achieved the best grades? Why?

10. Questions adapted from *A College Student's Guide to Career Planning*, by Frank S. Endicott. Copyright 1967 by Frank S. Endicott, published by Rand McNally & Co.

What kinds of activities in or out of school have given me satisfaction? Why?

Have some types of work interested me more than others? What are they? Why have these experiences appealed to me?

If I looked over the list of courses offered here, crossing out those in which I think I would be interested, what pattern would result?

From what I know about my interests and abilities, what fields of work seem most likely to fit a person like me?

3. Visit or observe individuals holding down jobs of the kind you believe you might like. Record some of the comments made and/or your observations and feelings about the jobs as you saw them "on location."

And while you are working on that solution, keep in mind the earlier observation that most of us will probably change our careers during our lives. You're not only solving a current problem. You're developing a method for dealing with the same challenge when it arises again.

Try this

Start preparing for "your chosen place in the work world" by selecting one or more of the plans above for making a career decision and carrying it out. Keep a record of your discoveries for future reference.

YOU AND YOUR COMMUNICATING SELF

In order to think about anything, including yourself, you need a system of symbols which enables you to make things stand for other things. One such system is obviously language; the word "horse" calls to mind whatever your image of "horse" may be. You can think about the horse without having an animal of that species or a picture of it in front of you. If you didn't have your language available to you with its "treasure chest" of structure and symbols, thinking would be impossible. This book, like other books, is full of printed words or symbols. They have meaning for you only because, over the years, you have learned the appropriate word or language symbol system. (You have also learned the traffic-light-and-sign symbol system, the road-map symbol system, etc.)

The symbol, then, is something turned over to us by society with some meaning or value already attached to it, although subject to our own special interpretation. The symbol *represents* experiences, activities, and things which are not right there before us.

The written note on a sheet of music represents a sound—we are able to see something that is heard. A number stands for a quantity. We are able to talk about the population of Chicago without inviting three million people over. If you see a ring on the third finger of the left hand of an adult, you know that he or she is probably married.

In the absence of the actual things, our supply of symbols makes it possible for us to think and communicate about them. Humans have the ability to symbolize, and this makes it possible to record the past, discuss the present, and predict or plan for the future. When you think about your past experiences, or about your present problems, or about what you hope to accomplish in the future, you are using the symbolic system inherited from society in general and modified by your past and present experiences.

*Intra*personal communication is the kind that takes place when you are using your learned system of symbols to carry on a conversation *within* yourself. One part of you makes suggestions, comes up with plans, considers alternatives, gives you ideas, and is generally creative. The other part of you is your "personal brake" or critical self; it says things like "Yes, but. . . , " "Not so fast," and "You may be sorry." George Herbert Mead, psychologist and philosopher, called the creative self the *I* and the critical self the *me*. "The *I* proposes, the *me* criticizes, the whole person acts."[11] For example, in connection with your development of a positive self-concept, it is this ability to carry on a conversation with yourself which makes it possible for you to look at yourself, evaluate your special talents, criticize your actions, compare yourself with others, and decide what you can reasonably hope to achieve in the future.

When you're talking to yourself and trying to determine what to do and what not to do, the answers to the questions raised depend to some extent on what role or part you happen to be playing at the time.

The fact that you are in this class means that you sometimes assume the role of student. If you are a full-time student, you may also be a part-time employee, an active church member, and a member of a veteran's organization. The full-time student will probably organize the other roles around the student role.

If, on the other hand, you are a full-time nurse taking the occasional college course when you can work it into your schedule, your primary identity can hardly be that of "student." In other words, you may assume a number of roles in your lifetime, but certain of them are more important to you. Once you select a career and begin to actively pursue it, you will find that your occupational role is an extremely critical one. It will combine with your family roles (husband, wife, father, mother) to govern a large portion of your behavior. One of the important things to realize is that your occupational role is one that you will achieve. If you want to be a policeman, you have to learn what a policeman is supposed to do and then learn to do it. If you want to be a good policeman and a good father, you will have to learn both those roles. If you want to be a good doctor and a

---

11. From *Roles of Man: An Introduction to the Social Sciences* by Deena and Michael Weinstein, p. 5 (see pp. 4–10 for a concise exposition of the Mead analysis). Copyright © 1972 by the Dryden Press, Inc. Reprinted by permission of The Dryden Press, Inc.,

good mother, you will have to learn a different set of role behaviors. If you don't decide what you want to do, you will be unable to develop a set of effective role behaviors. In communicating with yourself, it is easier if you keep your primary roles in focus; if you are really a student, succeeding or failing in that role is often a matter of simple priorities. You take care of that role first and try to organize all other interests around it.

In talking with yourself, it is also crucial to remember that what your *I* says and what your *me* says spring from your total past, and, as a result, your judgment is colored with the special tint of your own perceptions. Therefore, as we said before, it is a good idea to check out your thinking and conclusions through talking with and listening to others. If you've done your "homework," if you are realistic, if you find and present the facts, if you have a fairly accurate view of yourself in relation to them, and if you recognize the present focus of your life, you cannot help but have a solid feeling of self-awareness and self-acceptance. That self-acceptance is a vital step toward a more satisfying life, toward better communication with yourself, and certainly toward better communication with others.

What do you think?

The questions below may serve as a base for general class discussions, or groups of four or five students may use them as the base for informal small-group "buzz" sessions:

Is there something to be proud of in every person's background? Is our future determined by our past? To what extent? Does everyone change over the period of a year? In what ways? To what extent can the change or changes be controlled? Is it possible not to change?

Is it true that each person in this world is truly unique? Why is it hard for a person to get to know himself or herself? What are the advantages to trying to pin down one's qualities and abilities? Is it possible to be anything but yourself over a period of time? Is any personal strain or tension a part of pretending to be someone you're not? The self-concept is said to "guide, control, and regulate" what a person says and does; can that statement be defended? What is perception? What is selective perception? What do they have to do with the self-concept?

Do you think it is all right to talk about yourself? Do other people really want to know how you feel about things? Is talking about yourself a way to relate to others? In trying to get acquainted with someone, how much talking about yourself do you think you ought to do? Can talking about yourself help you arrive at a realistic view of yourself? Under what circumstances?

What is meant by the statement that "language is a symbolic system?" What other symbolic systems can you think of? If you were kept "in solitary" all your life, would you be capable of thinking? What is *intra*personal communication? Does the Mead theory of the *I* and the *me* talking with each other make sense?

SUMMARY

This chapter has emphasized the importance of coming to recognize just who you are. That recognition is critical to your selection of a career just as it is critical to your everyday activity. Perhaps the most concise comment is that of a New York community college student:

> *Once a cat knows what he is, where he is from,*
> *and how he got there, the frustration ends*
> *and the progress begins.*

Louis Eliza, student New York Community College

3
Communication: Encoding and Decoding

3

Communication: Encoding and Decoding

"I noticed nothing . . . the sound of my own voice drowned out all the things that I should've been hearing and seeing."

Officer Bumper Morgan in Joseph Wambaugh's *Blue Knight*

In this chapter we will continue our earlier discussion of the communication process. The intent of the chapter will be to comment in greater depth on the varied components of the process with particular emphasis on coding and encoding. Additionally, we will try to demonstrate how the process relates to an individual's career. Bumper Morgan is a fictional police officer, but his comment is not fiction. Your communication in your career may well be just as important to you as communication in a social context—sometimes it may be more important because your life may depend upon your being successful.

Here's where we're going

Careful study and discussion of this chapter should allow you to:

1. Exhibit an understanding of the term *speech-communication* by repeating the chapter definition of speech-communication and by explaining each of the key terms in that definition.

In Chapter 1 you were introduced to the general process of communication. Let's now examine a more specific definition of speech-communication: *Speech-communication is the interactive process by which speaker and listener, through the encoding and decoding of verbal and nonverbal messages, exert intentional and unintentional influences on one another's behavior.*

You've already encountered the terms *encoding* and *decoding,* but let us review them. *Encoding* is the step we take when we translate our ideas into a code. In communication, *encoding* occurs when we select the verbal and nonverbal forms of expression that we will employ to recreate our message in the minds of our listeners. *Decoding* is that step in which a listener receives a message and attaches his or her own meaning to it.

This chapter is a continuation of the earlier discussion of the communication process, with discussion in greater depth of the varied components of that process and with an emphasis on coding and the factors affecting it. When you engage in an intrapersonal activity, your choice of language and of nonverbal signals is less critical. You will know what you mean even if the words and actions would make no sense at all to others. As soon as one of those *others* becomes a part of the communication activity and as soon as you want to have an effect on one of those others, encoding and decoding become critical factors.

What happens when two or more people engage in human communication? Too often the first impulse is to say that one of them sends a message to the other and that the other person responds. If this is your impulse, check it because it's wrong. The danger in talking about communication in that way is that communication is made to sound like some kind of I-act-and-then-you-react pattern. What actually happens is that streams of message stimuli are continuously passing from speaker to listener and from listener to speaker. Talking or not talking, whenever two individuals are together in the same area or room, both are knowingly or unknowingly sending and receiving messages.

When we freeze the communication process and talk about the separate elements of communication, we do it out of necessity. Keep in mind that a process is a continuous activity—an ongoing experience that's constantly changing. As a participant in that process, you are constantly receiving new stimuli—new messages and you are constantly monitoring and altering your own communication effort. In order to understand the process we halt it and examine it part by part.

YOUR PERSONAL SCREEN

Whether you are a message source or a message receiver, your ability to encode and decode is based in large part on your personal screen. As already suggested in Chapter 2, you are the sum total of everything which has happened to you since the day of your birth. Your past directly influences the ideas you will want to express in the first place, and it also affects the way in which you will phrase or encode those ideas. In other words, you have a personal filtering or screening apparatus which lets some ideas in, keeps others out, governs the strength of your feeling about them, and determines your particular mode of expression.

Perhaps the most obvious kinds of examples of your personal screening process exist in your physical abilities. You may have good vision, good hearing, an acute sense of smell and a highly sensitive sense of touch. Or, your abilities in any of these areas may be limited. In any group of people, you will discover different levels of physical ability.

If you don't hear as well as one of your friends, your filtering mechanism will eliminate sounds that your friend will hear. Have you ever heard someone say, "What was that?" and had to answer, "Gee, I didn't hear anything."

In addition to differing physical abilities, individuals have different attitudes. If you have been raised in a home free from prejudice, you may be astounded that others judge on the basis of facial shapes, nose sizes, hair quality, and skin color. For others, prejudice will be an important factor in their screening process. Your family, your education, your personality, your sex, your preferences, your prejudices, your likes and dislikes, your attitudes, your peculiarities—all these elements are a part of your total makeup and a part of the filtering mechanism which controls what you notice, what you don't notice, and how you make sense out of the new experiences you are constantly encountering. In addition, you are probably aware that your screen (mood, feeling, etc.) is constantly subject to change, sometimes from minute to minute.

When we talk about career communication, it is important to emphasize one more aspect of your personal screen. You will have specific training in preparation for your career. This training will make (or has already made) you more aware, more concerned, and more knowledgeable about the career and issues concerning it than those who do not have that training. Law enforcement officers will know more about law and crime. Dental hygienists will know more about dental health. Computer operators will have a greater appreciation of those "Do not fold, mutilate or spindle" cards. English teachers will notice mispelled words, and home economists will be much quicker to detect the odor of overcooked food. Your career decision and the training that it requires will have a major effect on the communication activities that you undertake in your career.

ENCODING

Let's assume that you have an idea that you want to send to a listener in order that the listener might share that same idea. The idea itself, the words you choose to describe the idea and the way you look and act when you express it depend on your total background, on all the qualities mentioned in the paragraphs above, and on all the other qualities that go to make up the total you. When you encode or put a message together, you are a part of the message, and the message makes sense to you because you know what it is supposed to mean.

What do you think?

Do you have any special habits of gesture? Do you think they help you communicate your ideas to others? Do you use some of the same expressions (ways of putting words together) as your parents? Would you say that you also have some of their attitudes and prejudices? In talking about a problem in one of your courses, would you use the same language to discuss it with a friend that you would use in taking it up with the instructor? In other words, would you encode the message differently? Do some of the students in the class have bigger vocabularies than others? How do you account for the differences? Have you heard some of the students use technical terms that you did not understand? Do some of them talk about their jobs? If they do, are you surprised at how involved they are? Are you completely in the dark about the things they say?

THE NOISE-DISTRACTION SCREEN

In addition to being filtered through your personal screen, your message has to pass through two more filters or screens before it reaches the mind of the listener. The first of these screens is usually called "noise."

We are using the phrase "noise distraction" in its broadest sense. "Noise distraction" is anything that reduces the ability of a listener to receive a message. There are real noises (jackhammers ringing telephones, sirens, banging doors, whirring air conditioners, and clanging pipes) and there are figurative noises, all the other interferences, interruptions, disturbances, and distractions which get in the way of the message.

Whether you're talking with a friend on a downtown sidewalk, discussing something with one of your parents in your home, or getting direction on some assignment from an instructor, outside and inside noises, disturbances, and distractions have an effect on your effort to communicate. Traffic noises may make it hard to understand each other in the downtown example, a blaring TV may make it difficult to talk with a parent, and the instructor's hurry to get to another class may cause him or her to "cut you short." Noise and mood situations in the classroom are apparent to you, and you're well aware that a class at nine in the morning is more alert than one meeting at one in the afternoon. In the second instance, both the instructor and the students have a tougher job in communicating.

And do you recall an instructor wearing something so unusual—a wild tie, a bright blouse, odd shoes—that you found yourself staring at the item of apparel and forgetting to listen to what the instructor was saying? This sort of distraction is a different kind of "noise" but it is important to recognize its effect on messages. Studies have demonstrated that clothing and uniforms can affect a message,[1] that even the type of automobile you drive can become a source of "noise distraction,"[2] and that an "ugly" room can change the response of a listener.[3]

As a message passes through existing "noise," it is often changed or distorted enough so that the message reaching the listener is quite different from the message the speaker had created in his or her mind.

Try this

1. During the course of a class, make a list of the things that distract you—take your attention away from the business of the class. (Be careful. If you are too obvious in making the list, you may become a distraction for others.)
2. Drive down a street, exercising your normal degree of care. When you return to your room or home, think back over that street and list ten distractions that you noticed.

What do you think?

Would you consider failure to speak loudly enough to be heard easily a kind of "noise"? How about the listener's being a little deaf—is that "noise"? Do you listen very well when you are uncomfortably hot? "Noise"? Does your mind wander sometimes during a class? How do you account for some other thoughts coming between the lecture of the instructor and you? Is it possible for a certain noise (soft music, for example) to get in the way of the conversation of one couple and be romantic background to another? In other words, could it be that what is noise to some is an aid to the communication of others?

---

1. John Muchmore, "The Uniform: Its Effect," *Police Chief,* January 1975, pp. 70–71.
2. Anthony N. Doob and Alan Gross, "Status of Frustrator as an Inhibitor of Horn Honking Responses," *Journal of Social Psychology,* December 1968, pp. 213–218.
3. A. H. Maslow and N. L. Mintz, "Effects of Esthetic Surroundings: Initial Effects of Three Esthetic Conditions Upon Perceiving 'Energy and Well-being' in Faces," *Journal of Psychology* **41,** 247–254.

THE LISTENER'S PERSONAL SCREEN

In addition to passing through the screen of "noise," the message also has to pass through the listener's personal screen. Like your personal screen, this listener screen will reflect the listener's cultural experiences, education, personality, sex, prejudices, physical abilities, general background, and everything else that goes to make up the listener's person.

DECODING

No matter what you intend to say, there is no way to guarantee what the listener will hear. The way the idea ends up in the listener's mind will depend not only on your ability to encode but also on the listener's ability to decode. If the listener doesn't like you and is unwilling to try to understand you, even the simplest of messages may be misunderstood. For example, your saying something as simple as "Shut the door, please," could run into problems. First, you have to speak loudly enough and clearly enough to break through the physical noise screen; your roommate may be doing math homework and not hear you. Or if you can see your roommate through the door playing favorite records in the next room, your message going through *his* or *her* personal screen may be changed to "You're making so much noise that I can't hear myself think." What a message really means, then, *depends on what the listener thinks it means.* The listener decodes or translates your message in a way that makes sense *to him or her.*

What do you think?

Do you listen more carefully to one member of your family than to another? Why? Do you "turn off" some people? Why? How? Does your acceptance of a message ever depend on how a person looks and acts? How well do you hear when someone you don't like is talking to you? Does the word "home" mean exactly the same thing for you as it does for every other student in the class? How about words like "democracy" and "truth"? What were the circumstances when you last said, "What I meant was. . . "? What screen blocked understanding? Was it general "noise" or the listener's personal screen? Or both? Does the smell of the dental office make your palms begin to sweat? Does the appearance of a uniformed officer have an effect on you? Are there objects that get in the way of communication?

FEEDBACK

You need to *know* what you're doing if you expect to *control* what you're doing. Feedback is the collection of signals that are "fed back" to you as you communicate. These "signals" tell you what you're doing. You can look at a person as you speak and get some idea of what he or she feels about what you're saying. You can also adjust what you're saying to fit what you see in your listener's face and any other signs (such as a raised fist). A second source of feedback is the sound of your own voice. You hear it and adjust it to fit the situation. For instance, you adjust voice volume to overcome street noise, and you decide on just how much volume is necessary through the feedback you get from hearing yourself. A third source of feedback is inside your body. You don't have to look down to find out where your feet are, and you don't have to look at your raised arm and pointed finger to know that your arm is raised and the finger pointed. The position of your body at one time and the expression on your face are known to you through feedback. Your movements may be ever so slight when you are talking with one person; they may be more sweeping and definite when you are talking with many. You control the differences through inside or internal feedback. Perhaps the most obvious source of feedback is actual verbal feedback. "Yes." "No." "That's a great idea!" "I don't have the slightest idea what you're talking about."

What do you think?

Do you think people who have never heard of feedback actually use it? Examples? Do you believe feedback can help you in communication? Have you ever begun asking someone for a favor and then decided to drop the matter? Did feedback have anything to do with your decision? What recent instances of feedback can you remember from your conversations with others? Did you do any adjusting? If the pitch of your voice goes up when you're tense or nervous, how do you know the pitch is higher than normal? When you sing, are you using feedback to help you carry the tune? What are the advantages, if any, of knowing about feedback? If you've worked as a salesperson, have you ever felt yourself reacting physically to a customer's request—a blush, a raise of your eyebrows? As a customer have you ever been embarrassed by a facial reaction or vocal quality that a salesperson has exhibited?

AND BACK THROUGH YOUR PERSONAL SCREEN

Feedback from the listener and from the speaker's own voice has to go back through the personal filter or screen of the speaker. The listener may be too polite to say, "Shove off," and the speaker, checking the feedback from somebody who seems to be listening with interest, may make the mistake of thinking he or she is coming on strong. Or a listener may agree with a speaker on a subject ("Communism is a threat to us" or "Communism is not a threat to us") but resents being cornered about it during his or her lunch hour. The speaker may conclude that the listener opposes his or her viewpoint, although all the listener wants is peace. Or the listener may feed back a direct question, "Who says so?" If the speaker is easily angered, he or she may react with anger; if the speaker is a more stable type, he or she may simply say, "That's a good question" and give some proof.

INTENTIONAL OR UNINTENTIONAL INFLUENCE?

One additional point should be made: The speaker may be talking in order to exert a specific influence on the listener (for example, an appliance salesperson trying to sell a product), or the speaker may be talking to an old friend with no purpose in mind except the pleasure of the conversation. In the first instance, the speaker is *intentionally* trying to influence the prospect; in the second, the speaker has no conscious intent to exert influence, although he or she may *unintentionally* have something to do with the immediate or later behavior of the listening friend. For example, the speaker could mention a good bargain he or she got from a local store, and the friend might later go downtown to try to get the same bargain. You should also recognize that a speaker can be affecting a listener on both an intentional and unintentional level at the same time. It is possible for the law enforcement officer to be intentionally trying to create respect for law while unintentionally creating disrespect for that same law. It is possible for a salesperson to be *intentionally* trying to sell while at the same time *unintentionally* driving the prospect away with a "hard sell" method. So we assume that, intentionally or unintentionally, the speaker-communicator causes the listener-communicator to react and/or act in some way. This listener-communicator is at the same time, *intentionally* and *unintentionally,* affecting the speaker's behavior.

We have now broadly outlined encoding, decoding, and other elements of the speech-communication process. It cannot be emphasized too often that "the listener-communicator" is also communicating *at the same time* as "the speaker-communicator," and, in conversations and conferences (as well as in speaker-audience situations where, for example, questions are asked), the roles are often switched back and forth. You are often a listener-communicator for a part of the time and a speaker-communicator for a part of the time. In most occupations, particularly service occupations, the ability to function as a listener-communicator will often be just as important—and sometimes more so—than the ability to function as a speaker-communicator.

Although we have been discussing elements of communication in a certain sequence, remember always that human communication should not be described in terms of any kind of action-followed-by-reaction pattern and that

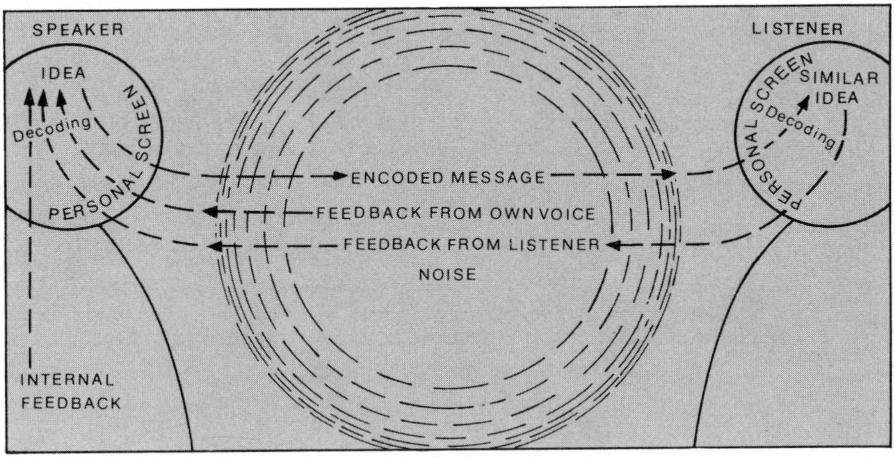

Figure 3.1

"streams of message stimuli" are continuously passing between those participating in the communicative transaction. With those reservations in mind and to the extent that a diagram can indicate what goes on in a very complicated process, Fig. 3.1 may serve as a review of some elements present in communication.

In review, Speech-communication may be defined as *the interactive process by which speaker and listener, through the encoding and decoding of verbal and nonverbal messages, exert intentional and unintentional influences on one another's behavior.*

The intended meanings of the words in this definition should be clear from the earlier discussion. The word *process* is used, as we noted before, to emphasize that communication is continuous. Communication is *interactive,* that is, it is dependent upon its participants for its existence and its meaning. Likewise, when two or more people are together, they are communicating. With this in mind, we should add that the speech-communication process is so continuous that it is often very hard to tell where it begins and where it ends. When you say "No, thanks" to an offer of a cigarette, your answer is based on earlier experience. After you say "No," there may be no further talk about cigarettes, but both you and the person who made the offer are drawing some conclusions and making some adjustments to each other's behavior.

For another example of continuing process, when does a public lecture begin? With the letters and calls to get the speaker to make an appearance? With talking about what the speaker might say when he or she gets there? With the introduction of the speaker at the time of the lecture? When does the lecture end? When the speaker stops speaking? After news stories and talk about the lecture have died down? And still one more example, when you decide to buy a car, when does the sales transaction begin? When you shake the salesperson's hand? Or have you already begun to react as a result of the parking lot? The condition of the building? The speed and manner in which you were greeted? When does the transaction end? After you've signed on the dotted line? Or after you've discovered just how good the service department really is? Speech-communication, then, is so complicated a process that it is even hard to decide when it begins or ends.

When you are talking with yourself about some matter or problem, you are both *speaker* and *listener* by turns. Otherwise, the meaning of those two words is clear. We closely associate *encoding* and *decoding* with speaker and listener because we think of the first as assembling a message in code form (verbal and/or nonverbal), and we think of the second—the listener—as receiving that message and decoding it; that is, the listener gives it the meaning or meanings dictated by his or her background as well as present mood and feelings. We should remember, of course, that the listener is doing some encoding of his own; he can—and often does—put what he thinks of an incoming message into recognizable code (smile, frown, nod, blank stare, etc.).

The words *verbal* and *nonverbal* express the idea that human communication takes place *with* words, *without* words, or with words supported by or contradicted by other indicators of meaning such as gestures. (The next chapter explores this subject in greater detail.)

Intentional and *unintentional* carry conventional meanings. You can intentionally try to influence the behavior of someone through making plans to do so and then communicating with him or her in the effort to accomplish your objective. You can unintentionally influence behavior in many ways; for example, your regional dialect—if you have one—can influence the kind of treatment you get from some official or casual acquaintance.

As for *influence on behavior,* we know that communication between people affects (influences) what they say or do (behavior). Communication may also affect what people think, but we are here concerned only with behavior we become aware of through the senses, primarily seeing and hearing. If you ask a client to do something, and he or she does it, you have influenced that client's behavior. If, as a landscape architect, you tell a customer to use more fertilizer and he or she does, you have influenced that customer's behavior. On the other hand, if the client or customer decides not to do what you have suggested, and the reason for that decision is based on their feelings that you didn't *sound* knowledgeable or appear to be secure, then you have influenced the customer or client in an unintentional manner. And at the same time you're telling that client or that customer to take a particular course of action, the way he or she responds or looks will affect or influence what you do next.

SUMMARY

In this chapter we have been discussing encoding, decoding, and other elements in the process of speech-communication. In oversimplification of this very complex interaction, we first discussed the speaker-communicator's personal screen and the part it plays in the encoding of the speaker-communicator's idea in a message form. We discovered that the encoded message has to pass through the additional screens of noise distraction and the personal background through which the listener-communicator interprets or decodes the message. Simultaneously, in the effort to improve communication, the speaker-communicator is trying to take advantage of feedback—screened through noises and his or her own background—from the listener, from the sound of his or her own voice, and from within himself or herself. The point was also made that we influence behavior sometimes intentionally and sometimes unintentionally. It was noted that it is difficult to find a clear-cut beginning or end to communication; strange as it may seem, we send messages when we're silent, and we receive messages when we're talking. Finally, throughout the chapter we have tried to demonstrate the application of each of these concepts in a career setting and to emphasize that the application in those settings may be critical.

4
Communication: Verbal and Nonverbal

4

Communication: Verbal and Nonverbal

"Some [waitresses] don't care. When the plate is [put] down, you can hear the sound. I try not to have that sound. I want my hands to be right when I serve. I pick up the glass, I want it to be just right. . . . I like it to look nice all the way. To be a waitress, it's an art."

Waitress Dolores Dante in Studs Terkel's *Working*

Dolores Dante's description of the art of being a good waitress is important because it reveals the part that nonverbal communication plays in an occupational setting. She has identified some of the behaviors which help create the "good waitress." Additionally, Ms. Dante's comments demonstrate how an occupation can contribute to positive self-concept as well as how positive feelings about oneself can make the occupational role more important and more satisfying. In any event, a waitress like Ms. Dante doesn't have to say anything to communicate how she feels about her job. Because nonverbal communication is so important a part of communication in general, this chapter will place a special emphasis on that nonverbal component.

Here's where we're going

As a result of examining the materials in the chapter, you should be able to:

1. Display an understanding of the terms *verbal* and *nonverbal* as they are applied to communication by preparing definitions for each of those terms.
2. List and define the categories of nonverbal communication.

3. Demonstrate an understanding of nonverbal communication by describing a message that you have communicated nonverbally and explaining how your nonverbal behaviors contributed to that message.
4. Show an awareness of how nonverbal communication can clarify, modify, or change meaning by: first, writing a brief sentence; second, reading the sentence aloud with a conscious effort to make minimal use of nonverbal behaviors; and third, reading the sentence aloud a second time and employing appropriate nonverbal help.
5. Demonstrate an ability to identify nonverbal factors by selecting a photograph of a person from a magazine and by selecting and describing nonverbal items in the picture that allow you to make judgments about the person in the photo.
6. Display an understanding of *paralanguage* by selecting five words and showing how the meaning of those words can be changed by vocal changes.
7. Display an understanding of how nonverbal communication might apply in a career setting by selecting a particular career and identifying and explaining the possible effect in that setting of at least one example of each of the categories of nonverbal communication.

The title of this text includes the term *speech-communication.* Some readers may take this to mean that we are concerned only with communication that is accomplished by using the spoken word. Nothing could be further from the truth. We *are* concerned with words or the verbal component of communication. In addition, we are concerned with the nonverbal component of communication, that is, the *manner* in which the words are presented and the effect that the *surroundings* have on the message. Words seldom constitute messages by themselves. For that reason, a discussion about speech-communication needs to consider both verbal and nonverbal factors or it would be an incomplete discussion.

VERBAL COMMUNICATION

We learn the power of words very early in our lives. Children quickly learn that a particular combination of sounds will get better results than crying, and so they learn words and learn to put them into a certain order. This is the point at which children acquire the basic tool that allows them to exercise some control over their environment. Because of the apparent ease with which children learn to speak, many persons take verbal activity for granted. They see it as a simple and natural act, and they cease to concern themselves with it.

They see the word as the thing, and believe that merely encoding a message in words will ensure communication. You know better. You have discovered that even though words have accepted meanings—meanings with which most of us agree—those same words have additional and different meanings to different people. *Webster's New Collegiate Dictionary,* in part, defines *fat* as an adjective.

> *"1. notable for having an unusual amount of fat: a: PLUMP b: OBESE . . . 2a: well filled out: BIG b: well stocked: ABUNDANT . . . "*[1]

For the individual who has been slender all his or her life, *fat* contains no threat and is easily understood. For the unfortunate person who is overweight or who constantly fights a weight problem, the word is a threatening one—it has a meaning that far exceeds the denotative meaning that the dictionary reports. *Fat* connotes or suggests all sorts of unpleasant things to the latter individual. The slender person has no sense of just how much impact the word has.

Semantics, the study of meanings, is a complex study. We will limit our attention to it by offering two bits of summary advice. First, the words you use *are* important. Don't make the mistake of feeling that it doesn't matter what words you use as long as "you get your point across." The words you choose affect that meaning. The receiver may understand the meaning and, in addition, make judgments about you because of the words. If the judgments are positive, you are fortunate. If they are negative, both the immediate and long-term communication relationship may be destroyed or weakened. Second, having a "good vocabulary" doesn't mean knowing a lot of big words. It means that you are able to select and employ the most effective word in a particular situation.

Verbal communication is the product of words. Those words must somehow be transmitted to the receiver. There must be some sort of carrier, some sort of medium in order that the receiver may see or hear or, in the case of the blind, feel or hear the words. The carrier goes beyond the word—beyond the verbal. If the words are written in ink on a dirty sheet of torn paper, our reaction to them will be far different than it will be if they are clearly and sharply typed on a white stationery of fine quality.

On the other hand, if the words are spoken, the tone of voice, the rate of speech, and the level of volume then become factors in determining the meaning of those words. These vocal qualities—including moments when we hesitate or are nonfluent, or when we laugh, yawn, or grunt—fall into the category of *paralanguage,* an "alongside language" that goes along with words

1. *Webster's Seventh New Collegiate Dictionary* (Springfield, Mass.: G. & C. Merriam Company, 1970), p. 303.

but affects the meaning of them as perceived by the listener. Albert Mehrabian has developed a formula which asserts that 38 percent of message effect may be attributed to these vocal qualities.[2] Although the vocal signals of paralanguage are often categorized as nonverbal communication,[3] they are so tightly linked to words that we have chosen to examine them as a part of verbal communication.

Try this

As a listener, how do you react in the following situations?

A speaker speaks in a near monotone and at a constant rate of speed. Do you think that she is:

1. Excited about her topic?
2. Afraid of the listeners and the situation?
3. Bored by the experience?

A speaker speaks at a very rapid rate and at a high pitch. Do you think that he is:

1. Bored by the experience?
2. Angry and intensely involved with the topic?
3. Afraid of the group?

A speaker constantly hesitates and repeats. Do you think that he is:

1. Secure with his message?
2. Bored by the experience?
3. An expert in his field?

If you wonder how these concerns relate to a career setting, think back to the last time you heard someone who had memorized a sales presentation and how easy it was for you to resist making a purchase. Do you recall how upset you were by a high-pressure salesperson, and do you remember how worried you became when the nurse sounded frightened?

You know from your own experience that it is possible to say "no" and mean "yes." Or to say "yes" and mean "no." You can say, "I'm certainly eager to get to my next class," and mean exactly the opposite. When the flying instructor says, "Don't solo with my jacket in the plane," that verbal instruction is only a part of the message. You can read any sentence or even a

2. Albert Mehrabian, *Silent Messages* (Belmont, Calif.: Wadsworth, 1971), p. 43.

3. For an excellent summary of research on nonverbal communication, see Starkey Duncan's "Nonverbal Communication," *Psychological Bulletin* **72,** 1969, pp. 118–137.

newspaper headline and give it several meanings through variations in tone and emphasis. For instance, "I am going to St. Louis" can be said in such a way as to indicate that (1) you are going there, (2) you are determined to go, (3) you are going to St. Louis in preference to some other city, (4) you are going to and not from that city, (5) you're going there but you don't relish the idea, (6) you're overjoyed at the prospect of going there, (7) anyone who thinks you are going there is out of his or her mind, and so on.

Those who know you are prepared to deal with switches in your tone of voice. They understand you when you are being sarcastic. They know that you do not laugh and smile a lot—or that you do. When you are performing in your occupational role, the relationships are often much shorter, and the individuals you encounter know you not as an individual but as a person offering some service. The visiting salesperson is not prepared to sympathize with a receptionist who is angry because of a personal problem. Instead, the receptionist is always expected to receive the salesperson with courtesy and efficiency—with a voice that sounds as if the visitor is welcome.

NONVERBAL COMMUNICATION

The discussion of paralanguage demonstrated that there is more to "language" than just words. Perhaps this has made you more aware of the fact that much of our nonverbal communication goes hand in hand with verbal communication. To the extent that nonverbal communication can be "translated" into word language, we have seen that even nonverbal communication does depend on words.

However, in the following discussion, you will find several categories of communication which are more obviously and clearly in the nonverbal or nonword class. The categories are used for convenience. Just as the distinction between "verbal" and "nonverbal paralanguage" blurs, so is there some overlap in the categories below.

Kinesic Language[4]

Gestures and other forms of bodily action (facial and eye movements, posture, etc.) are often used *in direct support of verbal communication*. These physical responses are normally placed in the category of kinesics, the study of message-sending and message-modification through how we look and act.

---

4. The nonverbal categories used in this text combine those of Duncan (footnote 3) and Jurgen Reusch and Weldon Kees, *Nonverbal Communication* (Berkeley: University of California Press, 1956), pp. 26–41. Copyright © 1956 by The Regents of the University of California; reprinted by permission of the University of California Press.

Gestures. There are three general purposes for which gestures are used:

For emphasizing ideas. Along with verbal emphasis in the form of vocal cues (volume, tone, rate, etc.), ideas can be emphasized—or modified—by pounding on a table; raising the arms in despair, sweeping them outward to thrust aside whatever it is that the speaker is thrusting aside that day, vigorously raising the hand as if to stop excessive spending, clenching the fist to indicate a willingness to fight corruption, or raising both arms to convey ignorance of what to do—all these gestures and many more are used to stress the importance of what a speaker is saying to one person or to many.

For describing. We all use our hands to help us in the process of verbal description. With or without speaking, people hold up their hands to show—and sometimes to exaggerate—the length of the fish they've caught. Pilots use their hands to describe aerial maneuvers. An accident witness describes—with the help of his or her hands—the tumbling of a car down an incline. "It's about this size," we tell somebody as we outline the size in the air by drawing circles, squares, cubes, and other shapes with our hands and arms.

For directing attention. Gesturing for this purpose "comes naturally." Somebody stops you on the street and asks directions to some address or location. You tell him or her where it is and you point in one or more directions to reinforce your word messages. Or you may be using a map of some kind in a conversation and you point out places and routes as you go along. Or you see an interesting story in the newspaper and you point it out as you call it to someone's attention.

Try this

Identify and use the gesture which seems to best fit the following words and phrases:

1. "Over there."
2. "Come here!"
3. "More food!"

You probably found that an appropriate gesture came to your mind immediately. Some of these gestures are used so regularly and so consistently that they have a universal meaning. If you delivered them in such a manner as to convey that meaning, you must have felt your whole body become a part of the gesture. In fact, if your whole body wasn't involved, you may have felt that the gesture was stiff and artificial.

Bodily action. Birdwhistell's research has emphasized that the entire body becomes a part of your message. He tells the old joke, "She couldn't talk at all if you made her hold her body still.''[5] It is literally true, as he says, that some people would have difficulty talking if they had no freedom of body movement. Anyone who is freely gesturing is, of course, using more of his or her body than just hands and arms. With the hand-and-arm gestures go nods and other movements of the head, smiles, frowns, and other expressions in the face, winks and blinks of the eye, thrusts of the chin, and changes in body position and stance, some indicating stress, some indicating relaxation. People generally speak and listen as ''animated wholes,'' and, although a speaker's hand and arm gestures may be the most obvious supporters of his or her ideas, the rest of the speaker's body is always involved in the effort to direct attention, describe, and emphasize.

One's facial expression is also an excellent indicator of the mental and emotional state of the speaker as well as of the listener. In the United States, eye contact has become an extremely important factor in your communication. The law officer who investigates the activities of a successful ''con-man'' is often told that the con-man seemed honest—''He looked me straight in the eye.'' The importance of eye contact has been supported by both experience and research,[6] and should be regarded as an important factor in communication.

Posture also provides a listener with information. Here too, we have a series of expressions: ''She has the weight of the world on her shoulders.'' ''Stands like a man.'' ''He is cowering with guilt.''

When you enter an occupational situation you will want to keep in mind the effect that these bodily movements, facial cues, and muscle responses have on communication. You often know by looking at people whether they are enthusiastic about what they're doing or whether they are bored, discouraged, happy, tired, or angry. Their mood carries over in their communicating and either reinforces it, has no appreciable effect on it, or affects it adversely. Listeners are quick to sense a person's mood from his or her appearance, and, unless they have reasons to resist, may adopt that mood as their own. In other words, it is important for you to realize that your clients, your customers, your bosses, and your fellow workers will attach meaning to your physical behavior. It is also important to realize that these people will be aware of inconsistencies between your verbal behavior and your nonverbal behavior and will have to decide which of them is communicating the correct message. If the nurse's hand is shaking as he or she prepares to give you an injection, how will you react? If the law enforcement officer backs away while ordering someone to leave, how will they react? If a secretary slumps into a chair, is he or she really ready to take dictation?

---

5. Ray L. Birdwhistell, *Kinesics and Context* (Philadelphia: University of Pennsylvania Press, 1970), p. 103.

6. Steven A. Beebe, ''Eye Contact: A Nonverbal Determinant of Speaker Credibility,'' *Speech Teacher* **23**, January 1974, pp. 21–25.

Object Language

One class of objects or things, *visual aids*, may be used in direct support of your speaking; you may already be familiar with such aids to speaking as graphs and drawings enlarged photographs, models of objects (or the objects themselves), mock-ups, and diagrams. Since visual aids are discussed in Chapter 10 (in the section on the informative briefing), a detailed discussion is omitted here.

A second class of things in object language consists of items like wigs, hiking shoes, cigarettes, one's home or living quarters, and so on. Those things we have in, on, or near our person and those we own or borrow—all have a language of their own; although we may not use them in direct support of communication, they say something about us and are very much a part of the impression we make on others.

You've heard, of course, that "clothes make the man" or "the woman." How you dress has much to do with the favorable or unfavorable impressions you can make in communication situations of all kinds. If everyone at a meeting is wearing jacket and tie, you won't score any points by showing up in a sweatshirt. Inappropriate dress always carries a message for the others present: "I either don't know what I ought to wear or I am deliberately ignoring accepted standards."

The right "uniform" makes you one of the group and helps gain acceptance for your ideas as well. There are certain occupations which are distinguished by their unique uniforms. The military depends heavily on consistency of uniform. Law enforcement agencies employ uniforms in order to furnish identification and establish an image. Some writers have gone so far as to contend that even in plain clothes the FBI agent maintains a kind of uniform. Tom Wolfe writes about the agents' compulsions to wear "shiny black shoes."[7] The health professions have adopted uniforms as have those in service occupations such as bankers, beauticians, and hair stylists. A variety of studies have supported the fact that people respond to uniforms.[8] We have come to expect certain behaviors from individuals wearing uniforms and if they do not conform to our expectations, we are troubled; we don't trust them. Likewise, if the uniform is not complete and there is something out of place we are troubled.

In the class of "dress" are clothing, hair styles, cosmetics, lotions, perfumes, membership pins and rings, and anything else that is a part of or fits on your person. You communicate your background and your awareness of what is acceptable through what you wear and how you wear it. For instance, business and professional people like to have job applicants show some understanding of dress requirements for the job interview (and for the job). If a job applicant appears on

7. Tom Wolfe, *The Electric Kool-Aid Acid Test* (New York: Bantam, 1969), pp. 1–14.
8. See, for example, John Muchmore, "The Uniform: Its Effect," *Police Chief,* January 1975.

the scene in unsuitable (to the interviewer) clothes, and doesn't seem to have mastered the basics of good manners, he or she is treated to some routine questions and the familiar "Don't call me, I'll call you."

People look at you and decode some messages from your appearance, and you do the same looking at others. If you see that a middle-aged usher in church has a heavily weathered face, you assume that he spends much of his time outdoors. If he is also very muscular, you assume that he works at hard physical labor. If he seems to be dressed in his "Sunday best," you assume that he wears other clothing during the week. If you notice in addition that his hands are rough and gnarled, the total message he gives off to you could be "I farm or ranch for my living." Once you get that particular message, you may further conclude that this usher is conservative in his politics. If you happen to get into a conversation with him at a later time, you are more than likely to tailor your initial comments to fit your preconceived notions about his occupation and his political views. In other words, your decoding of nonverbal messages predetermines what some of your verbal messages are going to be.

You see a speaker on the stand waiting for his or her turn to speak. From the speaker's hairstyle, facial expression, clothing, way of sitting, and the title of the talk on the program, you just about decide whether or not you're going to be at all interested. (Meanwhile, the speaker has been looking at you and your friends and receiving some messages about you and what reception he or she can reasonably anticipate.) Before the speaker has said a word, your decoding of the nonverbal messages almost dictates what your general attitude is going to be, at least at the first part of the talk. All of this may be wrong—but it does occur. Political candidates are very aware of just how critical dress and appearance can be, and the stories of just how far their concern can go become almost humorous.[9]

Just as personal grooming and habits of dress can help or hinder anyone's getting a message across, other items or objects associated with an individual also transmit messages. For example, plastering your wall with pinups says one thing about your tastes; plastering it with travel posters says something else. When a new acquaintance repeatedly finds you poring over books, the message you convey is that you like to read, or that you really hit the books. If your acquaintance consistently finds you slouched in front of the TV, the message could be that you are a TV hound, and he or she may wonder when you get anything done.

Your life-style is, of course, your own business. All we are saying here is that appearances are an important part of nonverbal communication. These appearances are so important that new professions have grown up around them. A column on "Looking Right!" which deals with men's clothing and accessories frequently appears in newspapers. Shortly before Christmas, the column focuses

9. In Joe McGinnis, *The Selling of the President, 1968* (New York: Trident, 1969), there is a clear indication of just how important clothes, space, make-up, color, and other factors have become.

on items that would be appropriate gifts. "Executives, like members of any other group, wear uniforms and use recognizable status symbols. If someone you love is in the business world, the right gifts can help him or her succeed. (The wrong item can, of course, do some damage.)"[10] In New York City, Dorothy Sarnoff has made a new career coaching people to career success.[11] The message is clear. In attempting to communicate with people, you build up or break down your image by sending them nonverbal messages which are acceptable or unacceptable to them.

Sign Language

You are certainly aware of the signs that are so much a part of our environment. Many of these signs depend on the printed word (STOP, GO, EAT HERE, BIG SALE, etc.) and may be considered verbal communication. Many others are able to communicate without words.

The pictographs that have become so familiar along our federal highways and in our public buildings furnish good examples of how easy it is to communicate without words. You will probably recognize meaning in the following signs.

You may also recognize that certain signs—without words—have come to designate products and services. McDonald's golden arches are now serving worldwide as a symbol of fast food. The barber's pole and the pharmacist's mortar and pestle symbolize their occupations.

Another kind of sign language that you know about is the sign language pioneers used to communicate with Indians; modern explorers still use sign language to communicate with tribesmen in remote areas. You may have used it yourself to relate to someone who didn't know the language or languages you speak. And there is Ameslan, the sign language used by the deaf, which has a vast vocabulary and is capable of all the subtlety and precision of verbal speech. It too, incidentally, can be used for communication among people who do not know one another's spoken language. Sign language can exist by itself, as in the preceding examples, or in situations in which you prefer it to speaking. For instance, if someone asks you how many eggs you want for breakfast, you may continue

10. John T. Molloy, "Looking Right!" *Chicago Daily News,* November 30, 1976, p. 15.
11. Jerry Bowles, "I Improved My Image," *Esquire,* August 1974, pp. 66–69f.

reading the morning paper and just hold up one or two fingers. "Do you want more coffee?" can be answered by a shake or nod of the head. If you step on somebody's toes in a crowded bus, an apologetic smile says, "I'm sorry."

Activity Language

Quite apart from the gestures and general bodily action which we see people using to support their ideas, and quite apart from inferences we draw about the mental or emotional state of speaker or listener, *activities or actions are sometimes message-sending in themselves.* For example, workers who have been generally relaxed and not too busy will suddenly become industrious as a supervisor approaches the work area. The encoded message is "We're very good workers and there is certainly plenty to do around here. You're lucky to have us on the job."

Individuals also do things to attract attention and make impressions. The student who stops by after a class to ask some questions may actually be interested in the answers; but he or she may also be hoping that the instructor will get the message and decode it as follows: "Here is a bright and enterprising student."

Of course, people don't always decode "activity messages" in the same way or in the way you would like them to. The instructor in the paragraph above might think, "Another snow artist!" For another typical situation, picture an elderly man running around your block every night. Depending on who happens to be doing the observing, the following could be the decoded messages: "That old man must be nuts." "That fine old man certainly keeps himself trim." "Here comes Rip Van Winkle again." "Wonder who chases him out of the house every night?"

Perhaps this is one of the most important cautions concerning not only "activity language" but all nonverbal communication. Here, even more than in the case of language, you as the communicator, are at the mercy of the receiver. The receiver's past experiences, biases, cultural background and perceptual abilities will determine the meaning of your nonverbal communication. In your occupation you will need to be as careful as possible to eliminate nonverbal behaviors which might be misunderstood, but you also need to keep in mind the fact that, despite your care, you may be misunderstood.

Besides the activities in which groups and individuals engage to send unstated messages, all human beings in this world have a capacity for feeling. If you reach out and touch someone you care for, there is a message in touch which needs no words. If you put your arm around anyone who is hurt in some way, you don't have to say, "I'm concerned." If you refuse to feel *with* or *for* someone, there is obviously a message in the refusal. (Occasionally, outright refusal is replaced by what Birdwhistell classes as the message of "untalk," the use of no words whatever in unfortunate situations involving total silence between two people you would normally expect to be communicating.)

Before going on to other forms of nonverbal communication, we conclude from the brief explanations above that gestures and bodily action frequently accompany verbal communication and are a part of the total message. The activity may be planned or unplanned; all that is necessary is that "the listener" observe the activity and draw conclusions from it. This potential for "accidental" communication emphasizes the need to be consistent, to be concerned and to be committed to the value of your work.

Schedule and Space Language

Members of the armed forces are always told, "Be where you're supposed to be when you're supposed to be there." Some cultures place little emphasis on being on time for an appointment; that isn't true of ours. Arriving late is generally frowned on, and those who make a habit of it send nonverbal messages which at best won't help them progress and may get them fired.

Infringement on somebody's space is regarded with as leary an eye as late-arrival infringements on somebody's time. In attending a particular class have you ever taken the seat that has been occupied by another student for several of the previous periods of that class? Even if you succeed, that student will probably send you some "look messages" asking, "What's the idea of taking *my* seat?" and try to beat you to that seat the next time class meets. You can make yourself extremely unpopular by ignoring seats that have been "reserved" in classes and elsewhere.

For another example of nonverbal space communication, let's say that you are a girl sitting alone at a twelve-chair table in the library. It would probably surprise you to have some boy you didn't know take a chair next to you; in our culture, if the newcomer sat at the same table at all, you would expect him to sit some distance away. If he did sit close by, his message might be, "Let's get acquainted." If you looked annoyed, your message is "Get lost." If you looked up and smiled pleasantly, your message would be "OK, let's."

Under the same circumstance, if a friend came into the room, looked at you, and did not sit close by or at least stop to pass the time of day, you would rightly or wrongly decode some message from his or her failure to meet normal expectations in this instance.

Business and industry have only recently become aware of just how important time and space can be in the task of motivating employees raising morale and increasing productivity. Paul Dickson describes some of the efforts being made in these areas.[12] One of the most interesting examples of new thinking concerning space is the Oakbrook, Illinois, office building of McDonald's, the hamburger

12. Paul Dickson, *The Future of the Work Place* (New York: Weybright and Talley, 1975).

empire. In three floors of corporate offices there are virtually no walls. Dickson notes, for example, that switchboard operators, extremely important to any company, are traditionally assigned to lonely out-of-the-way niches. In this instance, however, they were placed on the main floor "in low upholstered bunkers where there could be privacy and quiet while sitting down, and a full view of what is going on—and others to talk with—while standing up."[13] You can imagine how much this visibility meant to the operators.

Dickson also describes new schedules that are appearing in the work place. Among them are flex-time and the variable shift arrangements where unchanging eight-hour work days are no longer used. For example, employees might occasionally work six hours, or nine hours—the choice is left to them so long as they put in the requisite number of hours per week and the work gets done.

These examples show how management can use space and scheduling to communicate new attitudes to employees. You will not start your career as chairman of the board so you will not be able to make such large decisions. You will be able to control to some degree your work space and your schedule. Will you maintain an orderly and neat work area or will it be messy? If it is messy, will it be simply disorderly or will there be a dirty quality to it? You have probably been in a service station that was very orderly. Tools were in precise places and equipment was clean and ready. Weren't you more secure in leaving your car with this station than you were in leaving it in a station where tools were lying randomly on counters and floors and the equipment was dirty?

You will be able to exercise a similar control over your work schedule. You can be prompt or you can be consistently four or five minutes late. You can work to the end of the day or you can begin to clean up early so that you are able to bolt for the door at the moment of quitting time. Which of these behaviors will demonstrate interest and conscientious behavior? The answer is obvious.

Before we leave this discussion of schedule and space, let us identify one more aspect of it. Anthropologist Edward T. Hall has done significant research on *proxemics*, "the use of social and personal space."[14] Hall demonstrates that your message will be affected by how close you are to the receiver. As you perform your career role, particularly if your work is in one of the health or service professions, you will do well to recognize that you will, as a relative stranger, intrude on your clients' intimate space.[15] This will help you understand occasional resistance or tension on the part of that client.

---

13. Copyright © 1975 by Paul Dickson. From the book *The Future of the Work Place*, published by Weybright and Talley, a division of David McKay Co., Inc. Reprinted by permission of the publisher.

14. E. T. Hall, *The Hidden Dimension* (Garden City, New York: Doubleday, 1966), p. 1.

15. See Hall, pp. 108–120, for a discussion of the several categories of space.

Scent Language

Our discussion of scent language or the language of smell will be brief, but it is important for you to know that increasing research is being done in an effort to determine just how much odors have to do with communication.[16] That work has established that the human ability to note and discriminate between odors is extremely sensitive. Manufacturers have, of course, turned selling by smell into a major industry by introducing, among other things, new car smells, musty smells, and fruit smells.

For you in your work, the concern is a much simpler one. Clean bodies and clean clothing are taken for granted. In addition, we have to remember that many people are repelled by excessive and distracting use of heavy-odored perfumes, shaving lotions, colognes, and other so-called "grooming aids." Any kind of smell in your clothing—tobacco smoke, medicines, etc.—also becomes a part of your message. A recent TV commercial makes the exaggerated but still valid point that people shouldn't be able to detect a person's approach before that person is seen.

Try this

One way to highlight the distinction between verbal or word communication is to see what happens when we try to get along with words only as compared with what happens when, in an atmosphere of cooperative interaction, we support the words with gestures.

Sit in a chair with your back to the rest of the class. Now, using words only, describe a pattern of rectangles or squares like that in Fig. 4.1.[17] (For obvious reasons, the pattern you use should be different from the pattern used by any other class member performing this exercise.) Your job is to describe your pat-

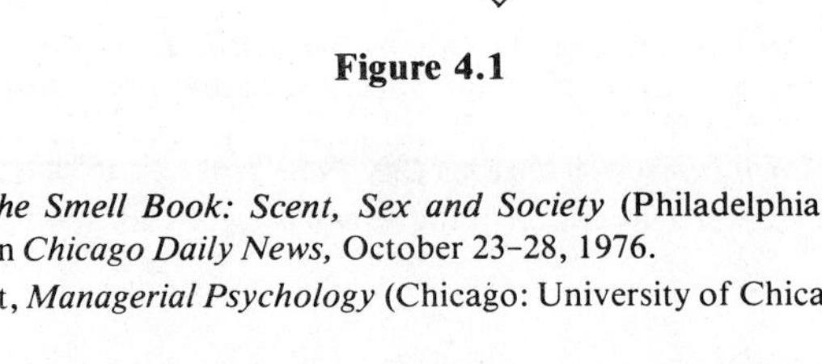

Figure 4.1

16. Ruth Winter, *The Smell Book: Scent, Sex and Society* (Philadelphia: Lippincott, 1976), as described and quoted in *Chicago Daily News,* October 23–28, 1976.

17. Harold J. Leavitt, *Managerial Psychology* (Chicago: University of Chicago Press, 1958), p. 121.

tern, and the job of each member of the class is to try to draw it on one side of a standard-size sheet of paper. You may do nothing but describe in words only. The members of the class may not react in any way–no question, no sighs, no moans, no comments.

When, in the instructor's opinion, you have done what it is possible for you to do with the project above, you stand up, face the class, and describe a second pattern that you've worked out. This time, any member of the class may interrupt at any time to ask any question. You may use gestures but no drawings. Again, your job is to explain the second pattern in such a way that class members can draw it on the second side of their original sheets. There will be a lot of speaking in both directions, speaker to the class and class to speaker, and a lot of listening on both sides. In other words, there will be verbal and nonverbal communication with considerable feedback and helpful interaction between speaker-communicator and listener-communicators.

What do you think?

Would you say that there is much sign language in movies or plays? Can you give any examples? Can a smile or frown change the meaning of a message? Example? Does the way you look or dress affect meaning in a given situation? Example? Does where you sit in a room mean anything? Give an example in which it does. Is it possible to talk with anyone without nonverbal communication? Are phone conversations as satisfactory as direct person-to-person conversation? Give examples of when they are and when they are not. In some situations people communicate by signs alone; can you think of any examples not mentioned in this text?

If a person gets a chance to ask questions, is he or she as likely to make mistakes? Is passing a message along through *speaking only* the same as speech-communication? What are the similarities? Differences? Is it easier to describe a pattern if you can use gestures and other nonverbal signs? Is it a good idea for an employer or foreman to encourage questions when telling an employee what to do? Or does it save time to write out the directions with care and then just give the employee the written directions?

When you walk into a classroom, are you communicating anything? If you get up in the middle of a lecture and walk out, are you "saying anything"? When you expect someone to walk into a room with either good or bad news, do you get all or some of the message before any words are exchanged? Do you extract any message from seeing someone carrying a briefcase? Driving a hot rod? Wearing unusual or extreme styles of dress? Is it possible for someone to be saying one thing and contradicting his or her own message through nonverbal communication? Give an example. Can a member of your family or someone else affect what you do by nonverbal means only? Can he or she tell what your reaction is without your reacting with words?

SUMMARY

Verbal communication consists of word-language and the variations in meaning which speaker-communicators inject in words through *the way* they're said: the ultimate meaning, of course, depends on the interpretation which listener-communicators read into the words and the way they're said.

Nonverbal communication consists of nonword-language which either supports verbal communication through gestures and bodily action or provides nonverbal communication which can be interpreted independently, even though it need not or does not accompany verbal forms. The kinds of nonverbal communication identified in this test: kinesic language (gestures and bodily action), object language, sign language, activity language, schedule-and-space language, and scent language.

One final thought—the scientists and psychologists tell us that word-language or verbal communication reaches us more slowly than nonverbal language. What we *see* and otherwise *sense*, as distinguished from what we *hear*, reaches us first and carries its own message; that message may or may not support what is being said. It may help to think of nonverbal communication as a battery of cannons firing messages subject to the interpretation of the listener; these nonverbal messages fly faster than the words which in the past were considered to be the primary carriers of messages. Over some of the nonverbal signs we have control (gestures, etc.); over others we have little or none (excitement, surprise, our general appearance, etc.). Some nonverbal communication reinforces what we say, some has no effect on it, some detracts from it, and some may even contradict it.

5

Communication: Improving Content and Sharpening Support

EXIT

5
Communication: Improving Content and Sharpening Support

"I worked . . . putting the final touches on the speech—changing a phrase here, a word there, strengthening an idea or a thought. I wanted to say precisely what was in my heart and mind."

Lyndon B. Johnson in *The Vantage Point*

Informal conversations and discussions are one thing and, as you well know, the special communication skills required of you in your career are something else. Some situations require little or no preparation and others call for a considerable amount of advance effort. It is that kind of effort that the late President Johnson is talking about in the quotation above. He's saying what most of us realize, namely that we must prepare carefully if we want to be sure of saying exactly what is in our hearts and minds.

In other words, the care with which you engage in communication as a part of your career has a direct bearing on your "on-the-job" success. It also has a direct impact on the lives of those with whom you are carrying on that communication. If you are a real estate salesperson and you sell a home, the interpersonal communication leading to purchase of that home is a very important experience in the life of the purchaser. The messages of a law enforcement officer may save a life. The medical receptionist's ability to communicate has much to do with whether or not an emergency call is properly handled.

In short, we often underestimate the importance of our communicative efforts. Our communication may have little effect on national affairs, but all of us exert influence on those we meet in our work and everyday lives. If those effects are to be the effects we desire, we need to give our messages careful attention and sometimes thorough preparation as well.

On situations calling for complete preparation, Lee Bowman, speech-consultant to corporations, puts it bluntly: "Poor preparation is insulting to your listeners, so don't risk it."[1]

In this chapter, therefore, the emphasis is on the *verbal* components of our messages and what we can do to improve them. We will emphasize the need for careful use of word-language and accurate reasoning. If words are primary carriers of messages, it follows that we have to learn how to use them in ways that will be easily and accurately interpreted by our listeners.

Here's where we're going

The following objectives will help you focus your efforts while you read this chapter. As a result of that reading, you should be able to:

1. Demonstrate that you understand the importance of identifying a precise purpose for your messages by selecting a particular career, identifying a specific situation in which you might find yourself while working in that career, and writing a sentence that would state the precise purpose you might have for communicating in that situation.
2. Show that you are aware of the effect of *context* upon language by finding two words that have a meaning in a particular occupation that would not be familiar to people outside the occupation.
3. Show that you are aware of the kind of *all-or-none statements* that should be avoided by finding an example in your newspaper. The ads and letters to the editor are good places to look.
4. Indicate your awareness of *stereotypes* by listing three qualities generally attributed to three of the following persons: the *average* policeman, librarian, minister, instructor, politician, or person in some other familiar occupation.
5. Display an understanding of the following by finding an example of each in a newspaper or speech.
   a) appropriate self-qualifiers,
   b) a statement of fact which obviously reflects the bias, prejudice, or unique perceptions of the individual who made the statement,
   c) slanting,
   d) specific examples,
   e) direct communicative style.

---

1. Lee Bowman, "Executives as Public Speakers," *Dun's Review,* January 1974, p. 72a.

6. Demonstrate that you are familiar with the following devices or techniques by either finding or developing an example of each:
   a) generalizing,
   b) using comparison or contrast,
   c) employing analogy,
   d) examining cause,
   e) classifying.

IMPROVING THE CONTENT OF YOUR MESSAGES

The best place to begin improving message content is to recognize that you are able to exercise control over the verbal content of your messages. You have choices available to you. You *don't have* to use profanity; you *don't have* to use big words; you *don't have* to use long sentences; nor do you have to avoid profanity or use short words or short sentences. Rather, you are able to choose which of these and other verbal options will be most likely to allow you to communicate successfully. You should also recognize that much of the responsibility for the success or failure of your messages is yours. The total responsibility is shared by all the participants in a communication situation but, to the extent that you are the source of messages, you must accept a major portion of that responsibility . . . because *you* want to communicate something.

During the 1976 Christmas season, the Latino community of Chicago suffered a series of tragic fires in which a number of children died. One of the apparent reasons for these tragedies was the inability of firefighters to communicate warnings and directions in Spanish, the only language many of the area residents could understand. People were quick to shift the responsibility to those who had not yet learned to speak English. Much to the Fire Department's credit, the Department immediately initiated a language-training program aimed at solving the problem. The Department recognized that its purpose was to save lives, not to force people to learn to speak English, and that this purpose would be better accomplished if its members were able to speak in words the listeners would understand.

The second important step in improving your messages is to recognize the importance of knowing *exactly why* you are trying to communicate. What is the precise purpose of your message?

Try this

Each of the following sentences asks you to try to determine one of the purposes a person might have for communicating in a particular occupational situation. See if you can complete the sentences:

1. A dental hygienist explains the proper manner of brushing teeth to a six-year-old child. As a result of that message, the hygienist wants the child to ______________________________.
2. A police officer gives a speeding motorist a stern lecture about the dangers of going too fast in a school speed zone. As a result of that message, the officer wants the motorist to ______________________________.
3. A secretary asks an executive a series of questions about the dictation the executive has given. As a result of the message, the secretary wants the executive to ______________________________.

Try this

What happens in the above situations if:

1. the hygienist uses very technical terms?
2. the police officer uses profanity?
3. the secretary is afraid to use direct terms in asking the questions?

Is it likely that the purpose of the messages will be satisfied?

Those two exercises should demonstrate to you that a failure to define your purpose and to select your words with care may result in miscommunication, that is, the idea that the other person receives may not be at all like the idea you want him or her to receive.

Try this

Identify a career or occupational area that you are interested in and identify five communicative purposes that you would have in that career.

In my occupational role of ______________________________,
I want others, as a result of my communication efforts, to:

1.
2.
3.
4.
5.

Note that in each example you *want* the listener to respond to you. Once you've decided precisely why you want to communicate and what you want to happen as a result of that communication, you can see how important it is to shift your concern to the *other* person. Think back to chapter 4. There we emphasized the fact that meanings are not in words but in the minds of those using the words.

If the meaning you have for a word is *in you*, it follows that the meaning a listener has for a word is *in him or her*. In an attempt to communicate with a listener, it becomes tremendously important for the speaker to put his or her message into language that the listener will understand. The word "fuzz" may mean one thing to you and your friends and something entirely different to an elderly lady or a child. When you talk to one or the other, you need to *choose* language that will make sense to that person. You adapt your language to him or her. This section in the chapter reviews some "rules of thumb" to follow in improving your message content with the idea of getting your ideas across to listeners more readily.

Use Words in a Context Your Listener Understands.

How many meanings does the word "fine" have for you? A dictionary will list a number of different meanings, but the *meaning in a given instance depends on the other words used with "fine."* This meaning depends on what we call *context*, and, when you use a word, you hope that context will help your listener get the meaning intended. It is only through context that anyone can decide what "fine" means in these sentences.

The judge gave him a fine of twenty dollars for speeding.

That's a mighty fine pig.

This comb is too fine for my hair.

The thread is exceptionally fine.

The weather is fine for swimming today.

He's a fine man.

On the other hand, many people have learned the meaning of some words in a particular context only. If your "meaning" is the result of learning the word in one context, you will be puzzled by someone else's use of the word in another. When the dental assistant speaks of *caries*, it means decay. If the patient in the chair is a bookkeeper, that patient may not understand why the assistant is discussing the transfer of numbers. If the greenskeeper joins the chef in the clubhouse and talks about trouble with *molds*, the chef may respond with "understanding" because of his or her own difficulty with *molds* of another kind. We should be alert to the fact that the kind of work a person does may dictate his or her interpretation of the meaning of a particular word.

Since context, or the other words used with a word, helps a listener understand the meaning of that word, it also follows that if you take a word or series of words out of context, the listener is going to find it harder to know what is meant. For example, you've seen a movie ad carrying compliments about the movie from reviewers or newspapers. You don't have the complete reviews in front of you and, for all you know, a sentence appearing in the ad may be the only thing complimentary in an original attack on the picture. In other words, if you personally decide to quote a statement from somebody, you owe it to the listener to make sure that the statement shows the real view of the person quoted. And sometimes even context isn't much help. The captain of a tramp steamer reported to have entered this note in the daily record: "The first mate was drunk today." When it was the mate's turn to take over on the captain's day off, he entered this note: "The captain was not drunk today." A listener would have to know more than the context to extract the "truth" from the second statement.

We arrive at two conclusions. (1) The words used with a word help the listener understand a speaker's intended meaning. Another way of saying the same thing: If the words the listener hears are familiar ones used with other familiar words in familiar ways, the listener won't have to ask you, "What do you mean?" (2) You take unfair advantage of the listener if you "lift" a few words which seem to say one thing from a longer series of words which actually say something else.

What do you think?

Can you decide what the word "chisel" means without seeing or hearing it in a sentence? How about "mean"? Does a dictionary give you the meaning of a word? If a word is not in the dictionary, does that mean it doesn't exist? How does a word get into a dictionary? When did you last say, "What do you mean?" Why? Even when someone is quoting a *word-for-word statement* from a speech, can the listener be sure that the original speaker did not give a word a different twist through his or her tone or expression?

Avoid All-or-None Statements.

"Everytime he leaves the room, he forgets to turn out the light." "He never gives a dime to any charity." "She's always ready to believe anything." The foregoing statements are generally untrue, and both the speaker and the listener know it. It doesn't take a genius to see that such blanket statements are seldom right. Therefore, it is a good idea to get used to thinking in terms that the listener will accept as accurate. For example, instead of using "all-or-none" expressions, we should be using terms like *normally, some, a few, almost, quite, occasionally,* and so on. We should be careful not to overwork words like *everybody* (as in "Everybody knows . . . " or "Everybody's doing it"), *nobody, all, always, never, first, last, every,* and *constantly*.

What do you think?

Can you give an example of your recently using an "all-or-none" expression? Would some other way of saying just about the same thing have been better? Do you think that talking about "all-or-none" statements may result in your using them less often? In what ways could your being careful in this respect have any effect on your future? Do you have much confidence in statements from people who *habitually* use all-or-none expressions? Can you think of other all-or-none expressions not mentioned above?

Be Careful About Classifying People.

Just as you want to be careful about putting an *all* before people, it is wise to be slow to put people in any one class or stereotype (Greek for *standard pattern*). The next law enforcement officer you meet may not fit into your idea of the typical officer, and your listener's idea of law enforcement officer may be still different. The individual Indian may not fit your stereotype of Indians; the same is true for individual blacks, whites, politicians, salespersons, landlords, and so on. What we regard as true of a group may not be true of specific individuals in it and may not even be true of the group.

Not only is classifying people a bad practice generally, but it often leads to mistakes in approaching the listener and *his or her* stereotypes. In a listener's background as well as in his or her current thinking, there are going to be certain words that are filled with feeling. For example, your listener may be violently anti-Communist, and when seeing or hearing the word "Communist" attached to anybody, may need no further argument. We'll never know how many good reputations have been blasted away by too free a use of such name-calling terms. Other listeners react in much the same way to their stereotypes of *capitalist, liberal, Democrat, Republican, Socialist, Chicano, Yankee, Southerner, black, hippy, activist;* the list is endless. One point to remember is that we can be name-calling *without being aware of it*; what's only a name to you may be a "red flag" to your listener. Like the meanings of words, the meanings of stereotype classifications are *in us and in listeners*; they are not in the terms or in the people we classify.

The lesson in this caution is one that the good salesperson learns quickly. Not all people who wear overalls are lower middle class, and people who have rough, discolored hands may be much better prospects than those who are wearing tailored clothing, shiny shoes, and fancy colognes and perfumes. More than one auto salesperson has lost a large commission because of a decision to ignore the modest looking fellow in the corner who "couldn't possibly afford this car." We know a plumber who makes service calls in a new, black Cadillac. Remember: Customer 1 is not customer 2! Client 1 is not client 2! Employer 1 is not employer 2!

In your career role, you need to remember that you will have to deal with the other person's tendency to stereotype. This listener may see all police officers as sadists, all auto salespersons as dishonest, all teachers as individuals who couldn't do and so teach, all lawyers as tricky, all barbers as gabby. The listener may place you in a group, but you can't dismiss that attitude because you want to communicate, to accomplish some definite purpose.

What do you think?

Is it possible for two people to be using exactly the same term and for only one of them to be name-calling? What has feeling or emotion to do with such name-calling or labeling? Do you think you have ever been guilty of name-calling without knowing it? How did you find out that the listener was unexpectedly aroused or offended by your using a particular label for somebody or something? Are you inclined to fit people into broad classes or groups? What are the dangers to you in doing so? What are the dangers to your ability to communicate with others?

Use Appropriate Self-Qualifiers.

A self-qualifier is a word or words showing that the writer or speaker knows he or she can be wrong. Listeners don't like "know-it-alls." You can avoid being one and be more accurate at the same time if you stop short of being too sure that you're right. It is good sense to get into the habit of using expressions like:

It seems to me
In my opinion
From my point of view
Although others think differently
The facts seem to show
Apparently
I have the impression that
I now believe
There is some reason to believe
Evidence suggests
Maybe we can conclude
Available information seems to indicate

Self-qualifying can, of course, be overdone. Whenever possible, it is better to introduce the specific conditions surrounding the content of the message. Instead of a landscaper's saying "In my opinion," he or she could limit the statement by introducing backing for it; for example, "A five year study at the University's Department of Agriculture has established the fact that. . . ." Although listener's don't like "know-it-alls," they do want to be satisfied that you have a thorough knowledge of your job. If every action you take or suggest is preceded by "in my opinion," your listener may consider you an egotist or may become concerned about your level of competence. Use self-qualifiers to indicate limits but not to compensate for a failure to acquire the necessary information about your occupation.

What do you think?

Is it a sign of weakness to admit that you could be wrong? If you are not sure about a conclusion you reach, how can you expect listeners to be sure? Ben Franklin said the way to convince somebody is to state your case and then shake your head and say, "That's the way it seems to me but, of course, I could be mistaken." What do you think of that approach? Is it hard to change your mind after you have told everybody what your opinion is on some subject? Why? Would it be easier if you were less positive in the first place? Is there some advantage in planting "escape hatch" expressions in our language patterns? Do such expressions help us be accurate, or do they show that we're not sure of anything?

Distinguish Between Facts and Statements of Fact.

You often hear the comment, "That's a fact, and you can't escape it." What it really is is a statement of fact, a comment describing someone's perceptions of an event or thing. Those perceptions are subject to the same human limitations that all the rest of us have. Facts exist independent of those who perceive and report them. Statements of fact are personal. As you know, five witnesses to an accident may give five different versions of what happened. These people are not dishonest; they just see things from different points near the scene, and their different backgrounds cause them to notice different things. A mechanic may see cars being damaged, a nurse may see people being hurt, a policeman may see traffic violations, an insurance man may see who's responsible, a merchant may see trouble and loss of business, and so on. It is not surprising that people often disagree about facts because their perceptions of fact become fact for them. It is important, then, to find out if your listener's perception of fact is the same as yours on a particular question. If it is not and if you cannot reach agreement on the facts, communicating is going to be difficult.

What do you think?

Do facts ever change? How? Is there such a thing as a fact that everyone agrees on and that cannot change? (Name one and defend your choice.) If you see someone wearing a blue sweater, can you be sure it's blue? It was once considered a fact that the atom was the smallest particle of matter which could not be split. What happened to change that "fact"? Does the source—the person who says something is a fact—have any bearing on our accepting what he or she says is a fact? Do you readily accept what some say about any "happening"? And reject what some others say? As a child, did you accept as a fact something which you now reject? If it was a fact then, why isn't it now? In other words, is a fact a fact only when you say it is?

Try Not to "Tilt the Board."

People "tilt the board" when they want to get a higher score. Some people tilt an argument toward a higher score by reporting only the facts supporting that argument. They choose to cover up any opposing facts or arguments. Of course, any writers or speakers are free to say what they want to say in the way they want to say it. Nevertheless, those who have respect for themselves and their listeners will make an honest attempt to get at the truth and present it fairly without tilting. Tilting is easy. It can be done by covering up some of the evidence, as pointed out above. It can also be done by throwing in assorted adjectives and other descriptive words. For example, one newspaper may say, "The arresting officer took the suspect to the squad car." Another may say, "The cop seemed to take pleasure in manhandling the suspect and roughly shoved him along to the squad car."

In your career you will benefit from strong, long-term, positive relationships. This is particularly true in service and sales occupations. If you enter one of them, you will want to establish relationships that result in people returning to you as well as telling others about you. One of the best recommendations grows out of a reputation for truth, consistency, and integrity. Clearly, tilting is not the way to build this reputation.

What do you think?

When someone "forgets" to say that the house he or she is trying to sell has a leaky basement, is that person "tilting"? Does a used-car salesman trying to sell you a car usually tell you *everything* about that car? Why do two newspapers or two networks sometimes differ in their stories about the same event? Will a newspaper supporting Republicans cover a Democratic rally in the same way as a paper supporting Democrats? Or will the rally end up at the bottom of page 13? Is this "tilting"? Would it be bad for someone running for public office to admit that his or her opponent had a good quality or two? Have you ever heard someone say something which did *not* support his or her case? Would doing so damage that case? Why? Why not?

Insert Examples.

Listeners enjoy stories, illustrations, specific instances, and down-to-earth examples of all kinds. If you say, "It's no fun to have a flat tire on a gravel road in the middle of a rainy night," the listener practically asks you to follow with "For example, one night. . . ." "Working in a gas station isn't as easy as it looks" should be followed by "For instance. . . ." Examples and "for instances" help listeners understand what you're talking about, and they add some human interest at the same time. It is an especially good idea to use such "short stories" to explain general statements. Examples may also take the form of figures or of quotations you want to call to listener attention. In fact, there is really no substitute for a timely example related directly to listener interest in the subject at hand.

What do you think?

What is your reaction to speakers who freely use "for instance" and "as an example"? Can you remember a speaker's giving you an example that helped you understand an idea that wasn't too clear when he or she first mentioned it? Do figures or statistics make good examples? Do you sometimes get bored listening to stacks of figures and percentages? Do you like an occasional quotation in a talk? Would you say that the good speaker, like the good quarterback, "varies his calls" by using different kinds of examples? How do you explain the general liking listeners have for examples?

Be as Direct as Possible.

When you're talking with someone, you use a good many pronouns (I, you, we, etc.). In speaking with two or more people, using the same pronouns in the same general patterns will help you "reach" the larger audience. Further, remember that big words do not make a speaker nor do they hold a listener. Use the words that will do the job. And use active word combinations like "The hunter shot the deer." Avoid *passive* combinations such as "The deer was shot by the hunter." Try to use *exact* words: "Chevrolet sedan" is better than "car" because it helps the listener get the picture. For the same reason, "red rose" is better than "flower," "ranch home" is better than "house," and "hurried" or "tramped" is better than "walked." And what is true of words is true of sentences; make them short and as simple as possible. Make an effort to use words and expressions that will *help the listener "see" exactly what you "see"* in talking about a thing, a person, or an idea.

Lee Bowman offers an interesting observation on directness: "The really effective speakers are the people who have learned that public speaking is little more than private conversation—amplified."[2] We haven't really begun to talk about "public speaking,"[3] but Bowman's advice in this context—as well as in others—means that you should avoid stilted and artificial communication and that you should always "be yourself."

2. Bowman, 71.
3. "Communicating Publicly" is discussed in Chapter 10 of this text.

What do you think?

Do you know someone who tells a story so well or describes something so exactly that you can ''see'' the action or ''see'' the thing described? Is a part of the secret that person's *action* language? The use of words like *you, we, us, I,* and *me* helps a speaker be direct. Why do you think such words can make a speaker more at home, more relaxed and natural? And make the listener more at home, etc.?

SHARPENING THE SUPPORT IN YOUR MESSAGES

Familiar words and familiar language patterns will help the listener understand what you are trying to say. If, in addition, that listener is able to determine that your patterns of thinking are sound, he or she will be more willing to accept the things you are saying.

There are those who say that human beings don't reason, they only feel. They point to history and the emergence of demagogues. They refer to Hitler and contend that no group of rational persons could have allowed such an individual to rise to power. And, indeed, if we look around, we are able to find large numbers of speakers who say very little that stands the tests of reason, but who are, nevertheless, enormously powerful. In short, there are speakers who rely almost totally on prejudices and emotion and not on reason.

Perhaps our criticism of those speakers should also be directed at listeners who are unwilling or unable to examine the speaker's words and their own responses to those words. For the moment, however, our emphasis will be on the fact that you have a responsibility to go beyond emotions—to provide your listener with a warrant, a reason for accepting your position.

However, let's suppose that you're the sales manager for a pump company. You want the company to drop its own brand-name product and to adopt a plan to sell the pump only through companies like Sears or Montgomery Ward. You will have to do some ''arguing'' to get the company to make the change. Some pride (feeling, emotion) will be involved, and you will have to direct it into different channels, such as higher profits and bigger dividends. Mostly, you will have to *reason* with those who have the decision power. Since reason does play a part in *some* communication situations and since listeners sometimes want *some* proof, it makes sense to review a few standard rules for ''logical thinking.''

Generalizing

You will often generalize in your messages. As you carry out the duties of a particular occupation, you will be gathering information. At certain points in the process of gathering this information, you will recognize patterns of consistency. If you eat at the company cafeteria every day during your first week on the job, and you are very impressed by the quality of the food, you may be ready by Friday to generalize—"This cafeteria really provides good food." You have generalized. You have arrived at a general idea as a result of having discovered and examined separate pieces of information.

If you are given some information or if you are able to collect some information on a given subject, you may be able to make some general statements based on that information. Clearly, you must be careful that the general statement you arrive at is really justified by the information you have in hand. In other words, one or two pieces of information do not "make a case." If, on the first day you eat in that company cafeteria, the food is not to your liking, you should not immediately conclude that the cafeteria prepares terrible food. A second caution is one that far too many people ignore once they have a job. They cease to learn. You will do well to do just the opposite. Make a continuing effort to learn about your work, to acquire as much information about your career as possible. This will have twin benefits. It will increase your competency in the immediate position and prepare you for new challenges as they arise.

What do you think?

What is generalization? Can you give an example of a generalization arrived at without enough information to back it up? If you presented a generalization in a talk and then followed it up with the information that led you to it, would you still be reasoning from information or would you be generalizing?

Using Comparison and Contrast

In comparison, you look at ways in which things are like each other; in contrast, you identify differences. If you are organizing a supermarket crew in preparation for rearranging fixtures and stock, one of the easiest ways to explain the changes would be to describe the things that would remain the same, and then focus on those things that would be changed. A dietician might teach good nutrition by comparing "typical" approaches to nutritious meals or by contrasting examples of good meals and poor meals. A dental hygienist might compare photos of the mouths of individuals who had not taken care of their teeth, and then contrast them to pictures of those who had good dental habits.

What do you think?

Do you use comparison and contrast to make decisions? When you're buying clothing? Deciding what movie to go to? What candidate to vote for? Where to live? Would you say that comparison is just another way to put information together in order to arrive at a conclusion?

Employing Analogy

In talking about generalizing, we said it involves collecting pieces of information about something and using those pieces to generalize. Reasoning from comparison and contrast also involves collecting information, but the information is usually collected with the idea of making it possible for you to make a choice among two or more things. Things analogous to each other are similar to each other. To illustrate, let's assume that you know a great deal about item A but considerably less about item B. If you discover that item B is like item A in several respects, then by analogy you may predict or conclude that B may also be similar to A in other respects—those respects that you know about A but not about B. In other words, you predict the unknown qualities of a particular person or thing by first establishing that the unknown item or person is in many respects similar to an item or person that you know a great deal about and then predicting that the pattern of similarity will also exist in unknown areas. If the members of a medical team encounter a mystery disease, they may try to identify areas in which it is similar to a disease with which they are familiar and, in this manner, prepare for problems that may well occur.

In the course of your work, you will find analogy helpful because it allows you to draw upon the familiar to explain the mysterious or unfamiliar.

What do you think?

Reasoning from information, reasoning from comparison and contrast, and reasoning from analogy make it possible for us to draw conclusions. All three are based on piling up information and then handling it in different ways. What are these different ways? Have you ever used analogy? What do you think would be a disadvantage in using analogy?

Examining Cause

In your work environment you will frequently encounter a need to determine *cause.* When something goes wrong—when a problem emerges—successful solutions depend upon your being able to identify the cause of the problem and then deal with that cause. It is very difficult, if not impossible, to establish absolute causality, that is, to be certain that you have identified the real and only cause of a problem. Despite the fact that determining cause may be extremely difficult, it provides an important speaking pattern. If the dental hygienist is able to establish that the cause of an individual's dental problem is poor nutritional habits, the hygienist can demonstrate the effect that will occur if the habits are not changed. Following a cause to its ultimate effect can be a powerful speaking approach. On the other hand, once the hygienist discovers the cause—in this case, poor nutritional habits—he or she can teach the patient new and better habits, once again demonstrating the effect that will result from a certain pattern of behavior.

The reverse of this pattern is often more difficult. When the members of a family lose their lives in a Christmas-season fire, the city fire inspectors try to pin down the cause of the fire. They may decide that "The wiring in this new home was faulty," or "Somebody set the fire," or "There were exposed wires on the Christmas tree," or "A cigarette dropped in a sofa," or any one of a number of other causes. Let's say they decide the cause was "exposed wires on the tree." Can they be *sure* that the parents did not turn out the tree lights? Could news of some kind have made them forget to turn out the lights? Did the children wake up early to turn them on again? Was a surge in neighborhood electric power more than the circuit could take? If the tree lights and wiring system were UL (Underwriter's Laboratories) certified, maybe the cause was careless inspection on the assembly line? Or perhaps carelessness by a worker worrying about a sick wife?

You may wonder why the inspectors are so persistent when the task appears so frustrating. The answer is an important one. In the case of the Christmas fire, if the cause were a manufacturing fault, the determination of that cause might prevent needless loss of life and property.

Reasoning from cause takes a variety of forms, but in every case you need to exercise caution. It is critical that you be as careful as possible in the process of identifying cause and that you keep open the possibility that some other factor may be the real cause.

In summary, we find three forms of reasoning from cause: one form is *effect-to-cause;* you observe that "We have a situation here" and the cause "must have been this." In other words, you look at an effect or result (fire) and make as good a guess as you can about a primary cause (faulty wiring). Another form is called *cause-to-effect;* You tell your listeners that "We have a situation here" and "If we don't do something about it, the result will be this." For example, a city fire inspector looks at the piles of newspapers in your basement (cause) and predicts that a fire (effect) will happen. To say it another way, looking at what you think is a cause makes it possible for you to predict what you think the effect is going to be. Politicians do a lot of "viewing with alarm." They are often arguing from cause to effect: "If you keep so-and-so in office, the result will be higher taxes." A third way to work with cause is to reason from *effect-to-effect* or, if you like, result-to-result. We can agree that two effects or results often come from a particular cause. In a given instance, you can see one of the effects in front of you and you ask your audience to accept the idea that the other effect must also exist. For example, bananas in a grocery window may be almost black in color. You are looking at the result or effect of decay (cause), and anyone would conclude that, if you went inside the grocery, you would also be able to smell that decay. You are reasoning from one effect (bad color) to cause (decay) to another effect (bad smell). For another example, you can reason that if students graduating from your school with about the same background get good jobs, maybe you and those graduating with you will also get good jobs. You ask the audience to look at *one effect* of a possible cause and take *another possible effect* for granted.

Reasoning from cause will be extremely important to you in your career. As your level of responsibility increases, more and more of your work and more and more of your communicative activity will involve solving problems. As you work to answer the questions "why?" and "how?", you will be looking for causes. One of the most critical factors in developing effective messages will be your ability to answer these questions by identifying the probable or possible causes while remaining alert to the possibility that still other things may actually be the real causes.

What do you think?

What is meant by the statement that "cause cannot be proved"? Is it possible to find *one* and only one cause for anything that has happened, is happening, or will happen? Other than the examples of reasoning from cause which are given above, can you give an example of cause-to-effect reasoning? Effect-to-cause? Effect-to-effect? When you see someone hurrying down the hall after the beginning of a class period, are you looking at an effect? At a cause? Possibly both?

Classifying

If you can place somebody or something in a group or class that your listener considers good (or bad or somewhere in between), you are classifying.

If, for example, you are able to display a professional credential that is familiar to a potential client, you will be able to classify yourself and enhance the value of your service. This is why so many professions and careers employ licenses and initials: P.E. (professional engineer), C.P.S. (certified professional secretary), C.L.U. (chartered life underwriter), C.P.A. (certified public accountant), A.I.D. (American Institute of Design). The legitimate use of one of these sets of initials allows the client to reason in the following manner:

> To qualify for the C.L.U. designation, a life insurance counselor must have a broad knowledge of insurance and must have demonstrated that knowledge by passing a rigorous set of exams.
>
> Elizabeth Schute is a C.L.U.
>
> Elizabeth Schute has a broad knowledge of insurance. If I am going to purchase life insurance, I want to purchase it from someone who knows what life insurance is all about.
>
> Elizabeth Schute, C.L.U., clearly knows what life insurance is all about.
>
> I will buy life insurance from Elizabeth Schute.

What do you think?

Would it make sense to say that *classifying* is just about the opposite of *reasoning from information* or generalizing? In which of the two do you collect information and then come to some general statement or conclusion about it? In which do you start with a general statement or conclusion about a group or class and then try to put somebody or something into that class?

SUMMARY

Since the way you put your messages together has much to do with how well you communicate, this chapter began with suggestions for improving message content by (1) using words in a context your listeners understand, by (2) avoiding all-or-none statements, by (3) being careful about classifying people, by (4) using appropriate self-qualifiers, by (5) distinguishing between facts and statements of fact, by (6) not "tilting the board," by (7) inserting examples, and by (8) being as direct as possible.

Very much a part of messages is the way we string ideas together in a way that listeners will accept as "common sense." To help you further sharpen the support in your messages, five devices were reviewed: (1) generalizing, (2) using comparison and contrast, (3) employing analogy, (4) examining cause, and (5) classifying.

6
A Look at the Listener

6
A Look at the Listener

"If I could be you and you could be
me for just one hour,
If we could find a way to get
inside each other's mind
I believe you'd be surprised to
see that you'd been blind."

Joe South in "Walk a Mile in My Shoes"[1]

The songwriter's advice is significant because it emphasizes the importance of being able to assume the role of your listener—to try to think and feel as the listener does. In the first chapter of this book, we presented an overly simplified model of the communication process. In succeeding chapters, we have identified and explained some of the factors that affect the process, factors which make the act of communicating very complex. We have frequently demonstrated just how important the listener is to the process and have highlighted some of the things that you need to take into account if your communicative efforts are to be successful.

In this chapter, we want to give you some additional insights into why persons listen and respond as they do. We want to help you find ways to "get inside each others mind(s)" and show you how doing so will make you a better communicator.

---

1. From the song "Walk a Mile in My Shoes," Copyright © by Lowery Music Company, Inc., Atlanta, Georgia. International copyright secured. All rights reserved. Used by permission.

Here's where we're going

As a result of studying this chapter, you should be able to:

1. Display an awareness of one's basic needs by preparing a brief explanation of each and by describing how someone could appeal to each of those needs.
2. Demonstrate your ability to detect a writer's use of basic-need appeals by finding an editorial or a letter to the editor which is based on a specific need or want of the reader-receiver.
3. Show how emotions affect behavior by describing a situation in which your own emotional condition led you to respond in a manner that surprised you.
4. Select a particular occupation and explain how a negative attitude toward that occupation might lead to *selective perception.*
5. Show an understanding of mind-set by identifying a situation in which you discovered that you behaved in a certain way because of your own *mind-set.*
6. Demonstrate the relationship between attitude and perception by describing your class, first from the point of view of one who has a negative attitude toward the instructor, subject, and room, and then from the point of view of one who has a positive attitude toward the instructor, subject, and room.
7. Identify a situation in which you felt it was appropriate for you to use "evaluative listening" and explain how you employed any one of the eight categories of that kind of listening.
8. Explain the effect of group influence by identifying an occupation which you would not enter because of the attitudes of your friends; explain which of the types of influence was at work.

A primary objective of the preceding chapter (Chapter 5) was emphasis on one of the most important steps in successful communication: determining *why* you want to communicate with a particular individual in a particular situation. You want to "own" your messages in the sense that you want them to serve *your* purpose. The reason behind this desire on your part is obvious in career communication, but it is just as important in all of your communicative relationships. A second point of emphasis was that, once your purpose is clear and the communication begun, you want your receiver-listener to respond to you in some positive way—to think something or do something. Under these circumstances, it is easy to see that your listener becomes the critical focus of your communication. You have to determine "where that listener is coming from" and what that listener thinks and feels in order to develop your message effectively.

THE LISTENER'S EMOTIONS

We may be tempted to overlook the role of emotions in behavior. We sometimes forget that people love, hate, become frustrated, feel insecure, experience guilt, are calm or are indignant. But we don't forget for long. You know that you've been angry. You know that you've been afraid. You know that you have felt secure, and if you think for a moment, you can reconstruct work situations in which you experienced a variety of emotional responses.

Try this

Select one of the following situations and try to recall *how you felt.*

You were getting ready for a job interview.

You were going into a dentist's office.

You were being praised for doing a good job.

You were requesting a loan.

You were making a major purchase.

If you are able to remember your feeling(s) in one or more of these situations, you may also be able to determine just how that feeling affected your actions. For some people, the trip to the dentist's office generates such a high level of fear that they find a reason to cancel the trip. And more than one person has put off a physical examination for the seemingly irrational "reason" that he/she felt ill and was almost certain that the doctor would find something wrong. In short, people's emotional states have a great deal to do with how they will behave and how they will communicate.

Even if we recognize the existence of emotional behavior and also agree that an individual can shift abruptly from one emotional state to another, we need to understand why emotional behavior occurs and how a knowledge of it can be applied to communication.

THE LISTENER'S NEEDS AND DESIRES

In Chapter 2, you were urged to arrive at a clear sense of your "self"—to determine what you can do and can't do as well as what you want to do and don't want to do. Awareness of "self" is important because the most of our behavior is an effort to satisfy the "self." We do the things we do because there is a pay-off for us. We see, or at least sense, that our actions will somehow protect or benefit us. As we learn more about ourselves, we are better able to understand why we respond in the way we do. Likewise, as we learn more about others, we can better understand how they respond and, more importantly, how they are likely to respond if certain conditions are changed.

As you know from your own experience, every human being has certain needs which must be satisfied, and those needs must generally be satisfied in a certain order. Psychologist Abraham H. Maslow identified a Hierarchy of Needs, listing the types of human needs in the order of their importance. His theory was that until each broader, more basic need is met, the less basic needs above it will be more or less ignored–or at least the pursuit of them will be delayed. Maslow's Hierarchy of Needs is clearly shown in graphic form in Fig. 6.1.[2] As you see from the diagram, the first and fundamental need is satisfaction of "body requirements." Further, an individual who is starving, dying of thirst, or being deprived of air will probably combine fear and anger, and his or her responses to any message will be measured in terms of the question: "Will this message help me live?" In an extreme example, one who is starving will not respond positively to the sales message of a hairstylist or someone selling cars.

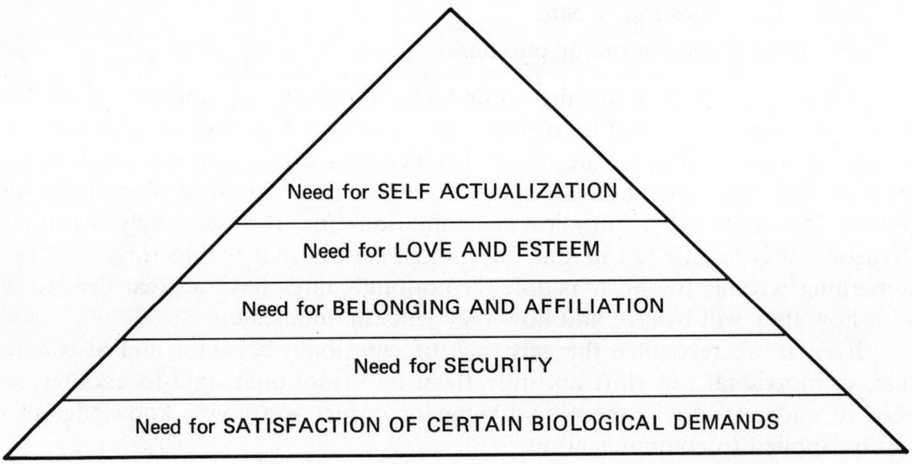

Figure 6.1

2. Data of Hierarchy of Needs from *Motivation and Personality,* 2nd Edition, by Abraham H. Maslow (pp. 35–58). Copyright © 1970 by Abraham H. Maslow. Reprinted by permission of Harper & Row, Publishers, Inc.

Like other psychologists, Maslow observes that the individual's concern about security does not really emerge until the biological needs are satisfied. Once those basic biological needs are satisfied, then security becomes the next dominant need. We should note that security is a term having different meanings for different people. It may mean security of person, economic security, or job security. We put dead-bolt locks on our doors when we are convinced that such locks might save our lives. We invest our money when we are "sure" that the investment will pay us well. To help us hold our jobs, we argue for grievance systems and complex firing procedures. And then, when we have achieved relative security, we move up to the next step and begin to seek out friends and search for groups to join. When that level of need has been satisfied, we try to expand those relationships to include reputation, affection, and love. Even then we aren't through. When those first four needs are satisfied, we may experience "a new discontent and restlessness . . . unless [we are] doing what [we] individually are fitted for."[3]

These needs are the sources of our emotional responses. When there is a threat to the progress we have made in satisfying a need, we try to counteract that threat. When someone promises to satisfy one of our needs, we respond favorably to that someone.

Let's look at these needs from a career perspective. If a secretary finds that the boss is becoming quick-tempered, the secretary may be dealing with an executive who is reacting to threats to his or her self-esteem or financial security. And if the executive becomes extremely agitated when the secretary asks questions to clarify instructions, the executive may be displaying fear or anger that the person in the lower position knows more or is a better communicator than the executive.

If a dietician visits a hospitalized patient and outlines a new diet, the patient may reject the diet (and the dietician) because a quick acceptance of the advice is an admission that earlier eating habits were bad. On the other hand, if the patient's life has been threatened by a serious heart attack, the desire to live may be greater than the need to save face. In the latter case, the dietician may be immediately successful.

Try this

In each of the following occupations, it would be possible for the worker to either threaten or satisfy certain of the listener's needs. Read each case and see if you can determine what would happen if the worker responded in the described manner.

3. Ibid, p. 46.

1. Accompanied by a young and attractive female companion, a middle-aged man driving a flashy sportscar pulls into a gas station with a minor mechanical problem. The attendant, a handsome young male, quickly diagnoses the problem, laughs in amusement at the driver's helplessness, and then makes the necessary minor adjustment.

   How would the driver react? Is there a potential threat to any of his basic needs? Could the threat have been avoided? Would it make a difference if the attendant were 60 years old with a mechanic's certification? What if the attendant had been a young female?

2. A dental hygienist is preparing to demonstrate the importance of good dental hygiene. The hygienist selects an individual from the listening group in order to demonstrate how plaque (bacteria) can collect on the teeth by using a red solution that will stick to the plaque. When the individual comes forward, the hygienist immediately notes that there is an unusually heavy collection of plaque.

   Should the hygienist proceed? Is there a potential threat to the "patient's" basic needs? Is there a way for the hygienist to deal with the situation?

3. An auto salesperson is preparing to ask an interested prospect about her income level and the sort of financing arrangements that will be necessary. There are several other potential customers close by.

   Should the salesperson seek more privacy? Is there a potential threat to the customer's needs? What may happen if the salesperson pursues this discussion in the crowded showroom area?

The point of the above activities and questions is that it is important to determine what needs the listener brings to the career situation, what kinds of threats are inherent in it, how the worker can minimize those threats, and how the worker can employ an understanding of basic needs to build a positive experience for the listener.

Advertisers are, of course, masters at this process of adjusting the message to basic needs. According to them, all products help satisfy our needs—the toothpaste that will make you sexier, the automobile that will raise your status, the deodorant that will help you make friends. Other advertisers suggest that the failure to use their products will result in your friends avoiding you or in your having a lack of success and a lesser chance of reaching your ultimate goals.

Nevertheless, it is true that success in a career depends in part upon one's ability to recognize needs and respond to them. In effect, workers and employers alike should be skillful in predicting, preparing for, and shaping responses.

Try this

1. You are a dietician and one of your patients is very reluctant to accept the diet you are advising. How might you appeal to the patient's needs in order to ensure that the patient will accept your advice?
2. You are a secretary who knows that your boss is very sensitive about his or her inability to spell correctly. How might you deal with this problem?
3. You are a contractor who knows that your client is extremely concerned about costs, but you believe that the added expense of smoke and heat detectors should be included in the home you are building for him or her. How might you introduce basic needs to justify the inclusion of the detectors?

In summary, you are going to have to identify needs, and determine just how your product or service can contribute positively to meeting the needs of a potential client or customer. You have to be prepared to show your listeners "what's in it" for them.

What do you think?

Is it a boost to your view of yourself to have good food, attractive clothing, and a clean place to sleep? Do you find yourself reacting more positively to others when you have these things? If you don't have them, do you find yourself depressed and difficult to deal with? How do you react when someone treats you pleasantly and makes you feel that they value your presence? If a salesperson pays an honest compliment to your appearance, do you find that your reaction to that salesperson warms? If someone shows you how you can improve your view of yourself, has that person found a key to getting a particular response from you? Do you agree that listeners want to know what's in it for them? Is there a lesson here? If a man wants to buy a boat but doesn't have the money or any way to get the money, can he still be induced to buy? Should he be induced to buy?

THE LISTENER'S ATTITUDES

Have you ever been told that you have a good attitude? or that the reason something was a failure was because of the negative attitudes of those involved? If you have heard these or similar expressions, you've encountered another of those qualities that has great significance to a communicator but something that most people refer to in only very vague terms. There is an overlap between attitudes and emotions and many people use the word *feeling* to define both of them. We would like to consider *attitude* separately because it becomes such an important factor in career communication. Attitudes are our predisposed responses to people, ideas, and things that we encounter. Since many occupations and careers are clearly described and highly visible, it is inevitable that most people will have attitudes toward them.

Try this

Each of the following individuals is a member of an occupational group. Do you have an attitude toward each of them? How would that attitude affect your communication with each?

Police officer
Chiropractor
Life insurance agent
Teacher
Garbage collector

Most persons do have an attitude toward these occupational groups. (This attitude is separate from one's attitude toward an individual functioning in an occupation.) If we were to record the attitudes of the other students in this class, we would no doubt discover that some people have a very positive attitude toward certain occupations and others have very negative attitudes toward those same occupations. Two aspects of attitude should be considered.[4]

Direction

The first aspect is that of direction. Is the listener in a positive or negative mood? Go back for just a moment to the list of occupational groups. How many of them stimulated a positive response in you and how many a negative response? Now, consider an interesting potential conflict. If you decide to become a police officer, that is some evidence that you have a positive attitude toward police officers, but many of your most important communication encounters will be with individuals who have a highly negative attitude toward law enforcement personnel. As an individual entering a career, it will be important for you to discover just what sort of attitude most people have toward that occupation. This will allow you to distinguish between criticism directed at the occupation and criticism of you as a person. You will need to assess the attitude of the individual with whom you are communicating and compensate for it if it is highly negative. It is obvious that, if you encounter a listener who has a highly negative attitude toward law enforcement officers, you will need to be substantially more cautious and more prepared to deal with

4. The discussion of attitudes draws upon James McCroskey, *Introduction to Rhetorical Communicaiton* (2nd ed.). (Englewood Cliffs, N.J.: Prentice-Hall, 1972), pp. 40–41.

that someone as one who is likely to be a hostile communicator. In other words, if you know (or can reasonably anticipate) the direction, positive or negative, of a listener's attitude, you are in a very good position to deal with it.

Intensity

The relative strength of an attitude may be described as its intensity. If a person holds a positive or negative attitude toward something, that fact is no gaurantee that his or her reaction will always be the same. You know yourself that if you hear a derogatory rumor about an acquaintance you like, you may accept it. If you hear that same rumor about a very close friend, you may reject it. In each case, the friendly attitude you have is on a different level of intensity. As a result, your response may be quite different, and so it is with your listeners. On some subjects they feel very strongly; on others, they are less sure of their positions, and more easily led to change them.

If we return to our police-officer example, we may find that an indiviudal may have a very negative attitude toward city police, but that negative attitude may not be at the same level of intensity in relation to state police.

What bearing does this discussion of attitude have on your communication? First, it will help you remember that a listener may have a positive attitude toward the individual but a negative attitude toward the occupation of that individual. Secondly, an understanding of the varying intensity of attitudes will help you deal with them in others and in yourself. You need to recognize that the listener will react not only to you, but to the job and the setting in which the communication occurs—as well as to the issue that you are addressing during the encounter. We may not like nurses in a hospital setting because they remind us of pain. However, if the nurse is a good friend and is coming to tell us that all has gone well in an operation, our attitude is different.

Try this

Focus on a career in which you are interested. Is it possible that you will be the focus of negative attitudes from others because you are pursuing that career. What can you do to eliminate, modify, or counteract those attitudes?

PERCEPTION AND THE LISTENER'S PERSONAL SCREEN

Let's now consider *how* a listener arrives at his or her particular views and attitudes. In earlier chapters, we emphasized the importance of recognizing that each of us is different, and we introduced the terms *perception, selective perception,* and *mind-set* in partial explanation of those differences.

Perception

As we've previously defined it, *perception is the process of making sense out of what we have learned through the other senses.* You have processed the things you've seen, heard, felt, smelled, and tasted in order that they might work for you. For example, you learned early in life that touching a hot stove could be a painful experience. When you see a stove at the present time, you are careful in approaching it. As a result of past sensory experience, you have *perceived* that it's a good idea to be careful around stoves.

Selective Perception

As we have already learned, *selective perception is the conditioning of each of us toward noticing certain things and ignoring others.* Since no one person in this world has the same sensory experiences as any other person, each of us is going to have his or her own set of perceptions or ideas drawn from those experiences. Why is it that people often do not see things from the same point of view? The answer is that each of us looks at things through *our* senses (different from those of any other person) and fits the incoming impressions into our past experiences (different from those of any other person). In short, we employ our personal screens. In other words, your total past life and experiences have much to do with your present selection or selective perception of things you pay attention to. Two people sitting side-by-side in the front seat of a moving car do not see, hear, or smell the same things. And a driver of one car going down the street does not see, hear, or smell the same things as the driver of a second car. You and your date, sitting side-by-side at a football game, may not see or hear the same things. Let's say that you know the game very well and are watching the fine points of play in the line, etc. Your date knows very little about the game, and is interested in the ball carrier only or in the general scene, large crowd, bands, etc. You may come away and say, "The game was a bust." Your date may say, "The game was fun." As a fence salesman goes down a country road, he or she'll probably see fences, a horseman will see horses, a building contractor will see houses, and an artist will see landscapes, all because of selective perception.

These explanations of selective perception point to the differences in physical abilities to perceive and opportunities to perceive. Consider now how much your emotions, attitudes and needs have to do with selective perception. If you dislike smokers intensely and are quite concerned about the possibility that their smoking is threatening your health, you may reach the point at which your initial concern about a new acquaintance will be whether or not that person smokes. If he or she does, you may find yourself screening out (ignoring) other, more positive qualities entirely.

The health professions have been very much concerned about the continuing (and in the case of young persons, increasing) tendency of Americans to smoke. Many smokers screen out various arguments against smoking and instead perceive the habit to be relaxing. The American Cancer Society has recognized the problem and has altered its campaign against smoking. The society's campaign no longer confines itself to our need for security. Rather than focusing on this need level, public service announcements presently emphasize the effect you may be having on others: If you smoke, will you be irritating your associates and friends? Will your children smoke in imitation? Don't you love them enough to quit?

Fear also severely limits the scope of our perception. If we are afraid to talk with someone, we can make ourselves "not see" the person. Likewise, if we feel guilty about something, we may react to other events in an unusual manner because of that guilt. When we see people whispering, we "hear" whispering about us. We begin to notice "No Hunting," "No Smoking," and "Shoplifters Will Be Prosecuted" signs. If we see a traffic officer, our eyes will check the speedometer and we'll be careful to stay within speed limits. If there is no officer in sight and the road seems clear, we may relax, let the speed move up, and even ignore a few traffic signs.

Try this

Examine a photograph of some individual. Note five things that stand out most to you. Ask a friend of the same sex to do the same thing. Compare your answers. Did you note the same five items? Try the same experiment with a friend of the opposite sex. Are the results the same?

Mind-Set

Mind-set is a state of readiness to receive and take note of certain experiences and avoid others. As we go along through life, not a day passes without our receiving myriad impressions through the senses, but, as already indicated, it is our past life and experiences which set apart the impressions to which we pay special attention. This process of selecting the sensory impressions we choose to organize often sets the stage for repetition of those selective perceptions. We can't perceive (perception) everything around us, so we come to select those stimuli (selective perception) that for some reason are of special interest to us. Successive selections build up in us states of mind (mind-sets) which make us especially susceptible to repeated selections of the same kind. For example, if you now prefer country music, your past experiences and selective perceptions have had much to do with your liking such music; your present mind-set is such that, given a choice, you'll go to a country music affair in preference to one featuring another type. We see, then, that mind-set grows out of selective perception, and our tendencies to perceive selectively are reinforced by mind-set.

This is particularly true in the case of *negative mind-set.* If an individual has a succession of painful or embarassing reactions to a particular stimulus, that individual will, in all likelihood, develop a negative mind-set. He or she will reject the stimulus or shut out its existence. The conscientious insurance counselor is likely to encounter large numbers of individuals who have developed a negative mind-set because of an excessively persistent or high-pressure salesperson.

What does all this talk about *perception* and *selective perception* and *mind-set* have to do with the listener? It emphasizes once again that what makes sense to the speaker may make little or no sense to the listener. It reminds us that we will find it easier to listen and to communicate if we adopt the habit of looking at *every* person as the very complex result of circumstance of background plus perceptions plus selective perception plus mind-sets. It is clear that we need to learn as much as we can about the listener in order to enhance our chance of communicating effectively.

What do you think?

What do we mean when we say that perception is the process of making sense out of experience? Is it sometimes possible for those who know you well to predict what you will do or say in a particular situation? How are they able to do that? Can your past experience be applied to your walking down a hall with friends? Or would you expect your walking down the hall to be pretty much like other times you walked down the hall? Would you say that you generally have your mind set on "a little good-natured fun" during such walks? Did you get that way through *perception*? To what extent does *selective perception* operate in these situations? Do you see and hear *everything* on the way to the next class? Or do you screen out bulletin boards, passing students and teachers, general hall noise, conversations, etc? In other words, has *perception* in general led you to feel that walks down the hall are pleasant? And has *selective perception* led you to pay special attention to those parts of the experience that are especially pleasant? And would your *mind-set* be a state of pleasant anticipation and readiness to repeat all such experiences?

THE LISTENER AND GROUP INFLUENCE

Another factor concerning listening and the listener comprises the attitudes, behavior, and reactions of *those around the listener,* the groups of which the listener is a part. Group membership can affect listening and speaking in at least three ways. You owe it to yourself to be aware of these forces and to take them into account as you try to be efficient and fair in your communicating and listening.

Perceived Group Consensus

Group-held views are characteristic of clubs, organizations, and institutions of all kinds. For example, members of the American Legion tend to have one concept of patriotism, and members of Common Cause, a citizens' better-government lobbying group, tend to have a different one. Members of a particular religion often share the same view on, say, capital punishment or abortion. Some people vote Republican all the time, and others vote the Democratic ticket all the time; some share the belief that the political system is corrupt and don't vote at all. If you belong to an organization taking the position that Communists are evil, you won't be much interested in hearing that they are no more evil than their counterparts in the "free countries." So it is that any view you perceive to be held by a group to which you belong is one you are likely to defend uncritically and without examining alternatives. It becomes a part of you, and it is practically impossible for anyone to talk you out of it.

Perceived Group Pressure

The approval or disapproval that you anticipate from others has much to do with many of the actions you take. If you're sitting in a theatre when the management decides to take up a collection for needy actors, you may resent your being a member of that captive audience, but you may also feel obliged to make a contribution because most of the people around you are doing so. If you and five friends are accosted by a candidate for some office, you will find it more difficult to disagree with the candidate if your friends are clearly in agreement with him or her. And when everyone stands up to applaud someone you don't particularly like, what do you do?

In other words, *the opinions and views you express in a given situation are often shaped or modified by your awareness of the presence of others* whose collective attitude is known to you or assumed by you.

Perceived Group Leadership

If you are the leader in an organized or unorganized group, you don't have to worry about the influence group leadership may have in determining your behavior in that particular group. However, those of us who may be leaders of one group are usually followers in a dozen others. The theory of group leadership is that followers look to a leader or leaders before they make a decision. You frequently see this principle in action. For example, the person selling kitchenware door-to-door calls first on a housewife he or she perceives as a possible center of neighborhood influence; then tells every other housewife in that area that "Mrs. Jones bought some of these items, and you know she is a very careful buyer." A salesman of farm fencing tries first to sell to the leading farmer in the county; if he buys, selling to others becomes easier. A number of young people, all of them friends, are approached by someone asking them to accept a product or an idea; typically, the group hangs back until one or two of the leaders make their decision, and then the others "follow the leader."

THE LISTENER AND EVALUATIVE LISTENING

You will recall that the topic of listening was first introduced in connection with a diagram of "communication basics" in Chapter 1. It was pointed out that through *active listening* you give a speaker encouragement, come to understand and share his or her feelings about a subject, and almost always learn something. The emphasis in that chapter was on what you could do to help a speaker and gain some personal benefit at the same time.

The discussion below is not a retreat from the helpful, appreciative, and self-improvement approach in Chapter 1. Nevertheless, there are times when you feel the need for evaluating a speaker and what he or she has to say. You should also be aware that your listener—whether client, patient, or customer—may be evaluating *you* and what you have to say.

If, in evaluating or being evaluated, you understand every listener's basic needs and have some idea of the attitudes and biases in your own personal screen, you are in a position to ask yourself these clusters of questions based on your perceptions, selective or otherwise. They will help you in "presenting a case" as well as in providing a hearing to anyone presenting one to you:[5]

1. *Perceived friendship:* How friendly is she? Is she genuinely interested in me?
2. *Perceived common ground:* What do we have in common? Are we members of the same political party? Graduates of the same school? Have we had some of the same experiences in an area of interest?
3. *Perceived authority:* Does he seem to know what he's talking about? Does he have enough training and experience to be an expert in this area?
4. *Perceived credibility?* Can she be trusted? Does she have a reputation for honesty? Is there reason to believe her simply because *she* is making these statements? Do others have a high regard for her "ethical appeal"?
5. *Perceived intent:* Why is he talking in this way? What is his purpose? Is he just presenting information for my consideration? Is he trying to win support for himself? Is he trying to pressure me? What are his real motives?

---

5. The questions in this section are based on headings on pp. 43–48 in *The Psychology of Speakers' Audiences* by Paul D. Holtzman. Copyright © 1970 by Scott, Foresman and Company. Reprinted by permission of the publisher.

6. *Perceived skill:* Assuming that her purpose is one I accept as valid, does she have the skill to put her message across? Does she understand listener needs and desires? And the need to build up a listener's self-concept? Does she seem organized? Does she have any support for her views or position? Does she seem aware of such elementary attention-getters as movement (gestures, etc.), vocal variety, visual aids, and references to the familiar as well as to the novel? In other words, does she handle the speaking requirements of the situation in a way that I can respect?
7. *Perceived language-expectancy:* Are his speech-patterns those I would expect? Or is he trying to palm himself off as an educated man when he isn't? Or as an uneducated man when he is? Is he posing? Assuming a character not his own? Does his speech fit *this* setting and *this* occasion? Or are some of his remarks crude or otherwise out of order?
8. *Perceived sponsorship:* Is someone or some organization listed as sponsoring this speaker? How sure can I be that she is actually sponsored? If so, to what extent should I be influenced for or against the speaker by my attitude toward that sponsor or sponsoring organization? To what extent is the speaker a free agent? Does she really believe what she's saying or is she spouting "the party line"?

Keep in mind that neither you nor any other listener is likely to raise all these questions. However, if you can keep some of them in mind when you are sharing a message, you will find it easier to perform in a manner that will create positive responses.

What do you think?

In the list of categories for evaluative listening, why does *perceived* appear as the first word in each heading? Is it possible that, in reference to a particular speaker, someone else's answers to the questions under a heading might be different from yours? How do you explain the differences? Is knowing that we are susceptible to group influence any defense against it? Does it make sense to you to speak of "listening" to the different kinds of group influence? Is it possible for group influence to prevent a very good speaker from succeeding? Or for group influence to make a success out of a speaker's inferior performance? Can you think of any instances in which group influence rather than the speaker determined the outcome of a communication event?

SUMMARY

This chapter begins with a discussion of the listener's emotions and, secondly, moves on to his or her underlying needs and desires.

The third section of the chapter describes the effects of attitude upon listening.

The fourth part of the chapter is a review in more detail of concepts of perception[6] as they relate to the listener's personal screen.[7] That screen, like listener needs and desires, affects the way you or any other listener "looks at" a speaker.

A fifth topic is "the listener and group influence." The last section, on "the listener and evaluative listening," is a listener's checklist based on the preceding sections in the chapter.

6. Cf. Chapter 2.
7. Cf. Chapter 3.

7

Getting a Job—Data Sheet and Interview

7

Getting a Job—Data Sheet and Interview

"He or she who gets hired is not necessarily the one who can do that job best but the one who knows the most about how to get hired."

Richard Bolles in *What Color is Your Parachute*[1]

The advice is blunt but crucial. Bolles emphasizes something that has been a part of all our earlier chapters. It isn't enough to possess the technical skills required in a career. These skills are necessary for successful performance in a career—but you can't perform successfully in a career until you have found a way to enter it—that is, to get a job. In this chapter we are going to consider two of the steps in the job hunt: preparation of the data sheet and the employment interview. Both of these steps demand effective communication, and both of them are vitally important to you.

Here's where we're going

If you examine this chapter carefully, you should be able to:

1. Prepare a data sheet that reflects your education, background, and experience.

1. Richard Nelson Bolles, *What Color is Your Parachute*? (Berkeley, Calif.: Ten Speed Press, 1977), p. 152. Bolles offers an excellent systematic treatment of the job hunt. The book is particularly appropriate for one who is changing a career.

2. Write a letter of application for a real or hypothetical position similar to one that you are now or will be interested in when you complete your studies.
3. Effectively participate in a simulated employment interview.
4. Judge the effectiveness of an interview that you observe.
5. List at least five pieces of advice for an individual preparing a data sheet.
6. List at least five interview suggestions for an applicant.
7. Explain how at least five of the communication principles offered in earlier chapters might help you in an interview situation.

In the early chapters of this book, we examined the bases of communication and the components of the process of communication. We have tried to support that examination with a variety of examples so that you might gain a clearer sense of how communication relates to you and your career. Now, so that you will be better able to make practical application, we turn to an examination of specific communication situations which you are likely to encounter in your career. There is no more practical application than to the task of finding and getting a job.

PREPARING A DATA SHEET

In looking for a job, don't start reading classified ads, making your first phone call, or mailing your first letter of application until you have prepared a data sheet or outline of your background and education. You may be mailing this outline as a part of your request for an interview. It will also make it easier to fill out the on-the-spot job applications that you encounter because you will have already made a careful inventory of yourself. And it will help you prepare for the interviews themselves.

As you begin working on your data sheet, you will see how some of the earlier advice about knowing yourself and your objectives now becomes very practical advice.

The data that you list fall into three general categories: personal, educational, and experience. In addition, you will want to construct a list of possible references—people who will be able and willing to furnish meaningful recommendations on your behalf.

As you begin to fill in these categories, keep in mind the question "What makes me unique?"[2] What has happened to you that makes you a special person?

---

2. Francis Weeks, "Data Sheets and Resumes," reprinted in *American Business Communication Association Bulletin,* December 1975, pp. 13–14. This entire issue of the *Bulletin* is committed to employment, job search, resumes, and application letters.

Try this

Complete the following preliminary data sheet as carefully as you can.

Your name
Present address
Permanent address (if different from present address)
Present telephone number
Permanent telephone number (if different from present number)
Date of birth
Marital status

(There is nothing unusual in the items above. In fact, questions about age and marital status will often be irrelevant and sometimes illegal. There are certain jobs for which they *are* relevant questions. You must, for example, be a certain age before you can become a sworn officer. Do take special care with the simple matter of phone numbers and addresses. Many jobs are filled by the individual who happens to be at the right place at the right time. If the employer has to search for you, rest secure that it will be a brief search.)

Education

Schools attended

(Have any of these schools presented you with unusual opportunities?)

Honors earned

(Do some of these honors reflect special skills that are not obvious in the name of the honor?)

Grade point average

(No matter what your average may be, do you have especially high grades in certain areas related to your job interests?)

Major and minor fields

(Do your fields of study complement one another? Have the combinations resulted in certain unique skills?)

Activities

(What have you done outside of the classroom that adds to your uniqueness or special ability?)

Experience

Prior work

(Be sure to explain gaps. If you haven't worked for a period of time, explain why. If you are searching for your first full-time job, have your previous part-time positions provided you with skills and/or opportunities that are not obvious in the job titles?)

Experience-Related Activities

(Don't forget that some of your community activities may have helped you gain certain skills that will be helpful in your work.)

References

(List persons from whom you are willing to ask permission to include their names. You do this not only because it is courteous but, equally important, because you find out in advance whether or not they are willing to recommend you.

In addition to listing an individual's name, enter a brief sentence which summarizes the particular qualities or abilities he or she might be able to comment on.)

Occupational objective

(State in some detail your occupational objective. You will want to have that objective firmly in mind before you go back and select from this preliminary draft of the data sheet those things which you will want to include on your final version.)

You've now completed your basic data sheet. But, before you begin the process of selecting materials for the finished data sheet, sit down with a close friend or one of your parents or your husband or wife, and share the data with them. Let them double check you. This will help you remember everything—and, if at some point, they should be unable to restrain a laugh, you may want to reexamine that particular listing.

THE FINAL DATA SHEET

What's the difference between your first data sheet and the final version? Not a whole lot, but if you've prepared a very thorough and complete preliminary listing, you can now engage in an evaluative process to decide which of the materials on that first data sheet will best *sell* you. The first data sheet is a record of everything you and others can list or remember about you; the second version is *selective*—it describes, discusses, and explains why you are exceptionally well qualified for a particular job.

There are many formats that you might follow, and before we present a sample, it is important that you recognize that no one format is the best format nor is any format a guarantee of a job. If there are any absolutes with respect to data-sheet writing, they are:

1. Be careful and neat.
2. Be concise. (Try not to exceed one page. Don't exceed two!)
3. Be aware that, until you meet the interviewer, the *you* that he or she knows is the *you* revealed by your data sheet and cover letter.

The following format is one form that could serve you well.

Name:
Present address:
Permanent address:
Present phone number:
Permanent phone number:
Date of birth:
Marital status:

Space for photo if you have one available and if you believe it is to your advantage to attach it.

(Other headings may be relevant. For example, you may want to include additional biographical material such as date and place of birth, height, weight, military status, number of children, etc. If you do, limit yourself to those materials which are factual.

The matter of photos is a tricky one. If it is possible to remove the photo, some personnel officers will do so before forwarding the application to those who do the hiring. Personnel officers do not deny, however, that the photo may have some effect on the hiring decision.)

Occupational goal

(Prepare one or two carefully worded sentences in which you present both your immediate and your long-term career objectives.)

Education

(List your educational experiences beginning with your most recent and working back to your high school days. If you are currently enrolled in a program, list that program first and include the date of expected completion.)

Work experience

(Follow the same pattern, listing your most recent experience first. If you have only a limited number of experiences, you may want to describe one or more in some greater detail.)

Activities and honors

(Do not be reluctant to note honors that you have received.)

References

(Select two or three of the references you recorded on the preliminary list and include their full names, titles and addresses.)

Example of a Final Data-Sheet

John Baker
240 Crescent Street
Toledo, Ohio 43604
Phone: 216-762-8250

Photo
if desired

Occupational Goal

I would like to become an assistant to a marine biologist. I am also prepared to work in quality control for seafood processing, in water-associated pollution-control programs, or in water-conservation programs. I am willing to relocate as necessary.

Education

Toledo Community College, Toledo, Ohio. I am currently enrolled in the two-year associate degree program in marine technology. I anticipate graduation in June 1978.

Central High School, Akron, Ohio, 1977.

Work Experience:

Summer 1977: I worked as student assistant to a University of Cincinnati faculty team studying the problem of pollution in Lake Erie. I worked closely with Professor Edwin Young, a marine biologist on that team.

1974–1976: I have been a lifeguard and assistant pool manager at the Akron YMCA.

Activities and Honors

I am now serving on a student-faculty committee charged with the responsibility for reviewing courses in the program and suggesting changes. The position is an elective one.

My grades have qualified me for the Dean's list for two successive semesters, and I have received a nomination to Phi Theta Kappa, the national community college honors fraternity.

References

Professor Edwin Young
Department of Biological Sciences
University of Cincinnati
Cincinnati, Ohio 45201

Professor James Snider
Department of Marine Technology
Toledo Community College
Toledo, Ohio 43602

Now, compare your final data sheet with the earlier and longer version. Make certain that the final form presents the most effective picture of your abilities and unique qualities. Type it or have it typed on good bond typing paper. Unless you type well, it is worth paying an able typist to type it for you; it will look professional, it will demonstrate that you are really serious in your search for a position, and it will minimize the possibility of embarrassing errors.

When you are satisfied with your master copy, you can have a duplicating service prepare multiple copies which have the appearance of originals. Do not have too many copies made. If you do, you will end up with either a lifetime supply of scratch paper or an out-of-date sheet that you continue to mail because you don't want to waste the copies you have on hand. Incidentally, stay away from ditto machines, and throw away any bad copies from any source. Remember, you want the person who receives the material to know that the job is important to you.

Occasionally, discussions of data-sheets or résumés seem to focus on the ridiculous. In a 1977 United Press release, reporter LeRoy Pope recounted some of the stories of executive placement specialist, Robert Half.[3] According to Half, data-sheet blunders include the Omaha accountant's observation that he could " . . . type, shear sheep, and pitch hay [and] . . . like[d] groundhog hunting and ballroom dancing," and a California applicant who noted that she had "received the Gregg Typting [sic] award." Another questionable item was offered by a Chicago jobhunter who indicated that his career objective was to make money and that "if there were two jobs available, one as a corporate treasurer and the other shoveling manure, I'd shovel manure if it paid better."

Half summarized his advice by saying that "a properly written résumé can open many doors. A carelessly written résumé can be fatal."

THE COVER LETTER

If you are able to deliver your data sheet in person, fine. Keep in mind, however, that leaving it with a receptionist, no matter how pleasant that receptionist may be, is not delivering in person. If you want to mail it, or if you must leave it with a receptionist, prepare a cover letter. The cover letter is important because it establishes that you have taken the time to identify and relate to the company to which you have directed the letter. The following format is an example of general form. It *should be adapted* to meet the needs of the particular situation. In other words, prepare an original and individual letter for each position for which you apply.

3. LeRoy Pope, "Accountant Claims Ability to Type, Shear Sheep," UPI, *Elgin Daily Courier News,* April 4, 1977, p. 9.

January 00, 0000

Mr. C. M. Pepperdine, Personnel Manager
Acme Life Insurance Company
Danville, Illinois 61832

Dear Mr. Pepperdine:

The recent article in the *Danville Daily Courier* describing Acme's plan to increase the use of computers was exciting. I was especially interested in it, because I believe that my background would allow me to make a contribution to the development of those plans. Accordingly, I would like to be considered an applicant for a position in your computer department.

The attached data sheet will give you specific details on my background and education. I will be happy to supply further information at your request.

If you feel that an interview would be helpful, I could make the trip to Danville at almost any time.

Sincerely yours,

Frank Thompson
110 Bridge Street
Champaign, Illinois 61820

The letter should be short and to the point. In the first paragraph, *explain how you happen to be writing* to Mr. Pepperdine or to anyone else. If you're answering an ad, open with "This letter is being written in answer to your ad of [date] in *The Daily Badger.*" In the second paragraph, *refer to the attached data sheet* and *offer to supply additional information.* In the third paragraph, *offer to travel for an interview*; many companies will pay out-of-town expenses for such travel. If no travel is involved, the offer to meet for an interview is still in order.

Show a first draft of the letter to one or two others who may be able to suggest some helpful changes. Then type it or have it typed in final form for mailing.

Try this

Using the preliminary data sheet as a source, prepare a final version of it. Then visit your placement office or read the classified ads to find a position that interests you. Once you've identified such a position, prepare a cover letter that you would be willing to send.

What do you think?

Why bother with a data sheet? Why not just walk in on an interviewer and tell him or her the same things? Since it is illegal to *require* a picture or photo with an application, what possible advantages might you gain by including one? It's hard to say everything you want on one or two pages; why is it wise to limit the length? Some experts say that the names of references should not be given until they are requested. Which do you think is better practice—to type references at the bottom of the data sheet or to leave them off? What advantage do typed papers have over handwritten ones?

THE APPLICANT'S PART IN THE INTERVIEW

Let's assume that your application letter and data sheet have been effective and that a job interview has been arranged for you. What can you do to get ready for it?

First, the fact that you have already prepared a careful and thorough data sheet means that you've taken an important first step. You know yourself and your capabilities.

Second, if you're not sure what an interview is, it can be defined as a prearranged conversation in which two people, at least one of whom has a definite purpose in mind, discuss a specific topic or topics. In the job-application interview, a job applicant tries to convince the employer that she or he is the person for the job, or the employer tries to entice the job applicant to take the job, or neither person has made up his or her mind, and both are simply looking for information and exploring the possibility of making a deal.

Remember, the employer has a vested interest in the interview, too. Employers can't afford to make many hiring errors, so the interview is as important to the interviewer as it is to you. The interviewer wants to find out if the particular prospect (in this case, you) is a strong candidate for the position.

Before the Interview[4]

Get the facts straight—you will want to know and write down the *exact* name of the man you will be talking with and how to pronounce it (a company receptionist or secretary can tell you), and the *exact* time and place of the interview. And plan your arrival about 15 minutes in advance of the time scheduled for the interview—excuses about heavy traffic, a flat tire, mistake about the time, etc., won't get you the job.

4. Much of the discussion here and immediately following is adapted from *Making the Most of your Job Interview* (New York: New York Life Insurance Company).

Find out as much as you can about the company, agency, or institution offering the job. Sometimes folders, pamphlets, and annual reports are available. Any reference librarian in a college or public library can refer you to a number of directories and catalogs providing such information. Having it at hand will prevent your getting "caught short" if the interviewer decides to check out the extent of your information.

If you are knowledgeable about the particular company, it is another demonstration that you care. (We knew a young man who emerged from an interview in a state of excitement and with one piece of advice: "Don't forget that you spell Xerox with an X, not a Z." Needless to say, he had not demonstrated a great deal of knowledge about or care for the company.)

Although the person doing the interviewing will be asking most of the questions, you will want to *prepare in advance* a short list of basic questions you want to ask him or her. For example:

1. What exactly will I be expected to do? Do you have training program?
2. Can a person learn and grow on this job? Is there a chance for later promotion?
3. Can you tell me something about this community and living conditions in the area?
4. What is the beginning pay? Is there a schedule for increases in pay? (Questions about wages, pay, salary, fringe benefits, etc., should be asked *near the end* of an interview. This subject—and the others above—is usually covered by the interviewer in the course of the meeting; if it is not, don't hesitate to bring it up.)

Other questions from you should be related to your goals and how working for a company will help you attain them.

Some people defend the right of students to be different in their dress and in the way they conduct themselves. Total independence is great if you can afford to take the time to find an employer who feels the same way. Otherwise, it's best to play it safe in the interview and wear whatever would be acceptable for work in an office. After you get the job, you'll have time enough to adjust to the work dress and habits of those working with you.

So what do you do when you show up for the interview? You take your cues from the person doing the interviewing. If you can pronounce the individual's name, use it in your greeting. If there is an indication of uncertainty about your name or about its pronunciation, don't be afraid to introduce yourself. Be prepared to shake a hand that is offered. Sit down when the interviewer does.

Now that you're comfortably (or uncomfortably) seated, let's take a short "time out" while we review the speech-communication process in relation to the interview situation. For one thing, an interview is face-to-face interaction of the most direct kind; what you say and do will directly influence the interviewer, and what he or she says and does will directly influence you. You want a job and the interviewer is the individual with the power to give you that job.

There are clear purposes on the part of both the interviewer and the interviewee. As a result of your communicative efforts, you want the interviewer to give you the job. As a result of the interviewer's communicative efforts, he or she wants you to demonstrate that you either are or are not the person for the job.

Words and signs will be winging their way back and forth and passing each other en route. The interviewer will make a certain impression on you; she or he will appear to be friendly or cold, or sympathetic, or hurried, or relaxed, etc. In other words, your message-receiving will begin immediately and continue constantly throughout the session. In fact, your message-receiving will have begun when you saw the outside of the building. If it's new and modern, you may have thought "prosperous and progressive." If it's old and dirty, "old-fashioned and barely making ends meet." In any interview situation, you keep getting messages from the time you enter the building until you leave it, although the most important period of the message-sending-and-receiving will normally be the interview itself.

And what about interfering "noise"? A call from the interviewer's wife in the middle of your conversation? Clattering typewriters? Sun through a window directly in your eyes? Strange habit of the interviewer—maybe he or she smiles constantly for no apparent reason?

The interviewer's "personal screen" is another problem. It's just as well not to take any stands on subjects which are not connected with the job or with your future. Questions about politics can be met with answers like "I try to vote for the best person" or "I haven't yet made up my mind." We're not suggesting that it's always good practice to sidestep such questions, but in an interview they serve no useful purpose except, possibly, to test your reaction.

And while you're thinking of the interviewer's personal screen, you will want to be careful about your own. As previously pointed out in this chapter and others, we select the things that we pay attention to, and our selections aren't always the best. If the interviewer looks like your uncle George, avoid transferring your dislike of uncle George to the interviewer. If the interviewer's race is different from yours, that doesn't mean that he or she fits into your stereotype or standard pattern for that race. See to it that you don't saddle the interviewer with a set of ideas that he or she may not have. The photo of the Republican governor on the wall doesn't mean that the interviewer is Republican or even conservative. The ashtray full of cigarette butts doesn't mean he or she smokes. *Assume nothing* and you'll avoid "putting your foot in your mouth."

Your goal, then, is to find out as much as possible about the job in order to be in a position to decide whether you want to take it if it's offered. The interviewer's goal is to find out everything possible about you and your job objectives in order to decide whether the job should be offered to you. Elements of persuasion will creep in, especially if you decide at some time before or during the proceedings that you really want the job. Likewise, the interviewer may also decide at some point that you are the person he or she wants. Throughout the interview, of course, you will be trying to make a good impression, and the interviewer will normally be doing the same. Within that framework, you have an interest in being friendly. An interviewer is a human being, and his or her normal response to "friendly signs" will be "friendly signs."

When we began the "time out" above, you and the interviewer were both seated and ready to begin talking about employment. Just as you were getting initial impressions when you approached the building, when you met one or two people in outer offices, and when you were shown into the interviewer's office, so the interviewer may have already formed some impressions of you from letters you wrote, from the outline of your background and education, from any references he or she contacted and, possibly, from your voice over the phone. In any event, it is common for an interviewer to begin the conversation with some "small talk" about the weather, sports, the morning headlines, etc. This is supposed to put you at ease and ordinarily does accomplish that purpose. It is also worth repeating the fact that the interviewer may be anxious too. This initial segment may serve to relax both parties.

In the working period which follows, the interviewer gets down to business with questions and statements. You're expected to answer the questions directly and honestly and react to statements if reaction seems to be called for. Except for your being careful to get answers to the questions you have prepared, the responsibility for carrying on and managing the meeting will be the interviewer's.

Before the interview comes to a close, you will often be given instructions as to what additional steps you should take. Follow them exactly. On the other hand, the interviewer may promise to contact you or make certain decisions by specific dates. If this is the case, wait for the interviewer's action. If you don't hear by the specified date, it is proper for you to write or call in an effort to determine what is happening. Do allow a week to pass before you initiate the contact in order to provide for a problem with the mails or busy phone lines.

Finally, a good rule-of-thumb throughout any such interview is to *be yourself* but avoid talking about *your* personal problems, need of money, etc. The employer is primarily interested in one thing at this point: what you can do for the company. You have to demonstrate positively that you know what the job requires and that you fill those requirements. In short, you must vigorously sell yourself.

THE INTERVIEWER'S PART IN THE INTERVIEW

In the normal course of events, it is entirely possible that you will at some time find yourself interviewing applicants for a job with an organization you have joined. Although some details about the job may be unknown to you and although it may not be your role to do the actual hiring, you still have the responsibility to represent your company and to determine as best you can the fitness of a job candidate. To help you understand what an interviewer should be doing, as well as to help you in that job if you take it on at a later date, we move now to a discussion of the interviewer's part in the job interview.

First, on the assumption that the applicant is entitled to a thorough and accurate job description, the conscientious interviewer takes full responsibility for giving him or her complete information about the job. Reading a job description in a newspaper ad or hearing about it in some other way does not give an applicant the full story. Consequently, many interviewers use a check sheet to be sure that, at some specific time in the interview or during the course of it, they cover four basic areas describing a job. The topics below are typical of those appearing on a job-description check sheet.

1. *Specific duties* and job title (if any).
2. *General working conditions:* name of supervisor (if other than interviewer) and number of co-workers in department or area; any unusual physical requirements; any unusual conditions of heat, cold, etc.; travel requirements, etc.; working hours, pay, fringe benefits, etc.
3. *Chances for advancement,* including job security, company reputation for fair treatment of employees, etc.
4. *Information on the community* (if applicant is from another part of the country): availability of housing, location of schools, cost of living, churches, amusement facilities, shopping centers, etc.

Second, the good interviewer approaches every interview with a determination to *listen actively*. Although the interviewer may have been over the same route time and again with job applicant after job applicant, he or she understands the need to listen attentively. Throughout the interview, this attitude helps the job applicant talk freely. The applicant receives encouragment through such phrases as "That's very interesting," "Tell me more about that," "I see," "You feel that this job would be one you could handle?" The interviewer smiles and nods encouragement as the applicant answers questions.

The interviewer acts like a human and understanding person trying to help someone make an important decision.

Third, the interviewer begins the real business of the interview after the applicant is at ease as a result of talking about general topics having little or nothing to do with the available job. The interviewer may begin by taking some time to fill in details about the job, or lead off with questions on the subjects the applicant knows very well: What courses have you taken? Which did you like best? Which least? How do you feel about your educational preparation for a job? When do you expect to (or when did you) graduate?

In continuing the questioning, the interviewer often uses as a guide the outline of background and education provided by the applicant. In any case, these are questions meant to keep the applicant talking about his or her background, education and work experience. Then the interviewer may move to other questions like these:

Why do you want to work for *this* organization?

What do you know about the organization?

Do you know anyone now working for the organization?

Do you find it easy or not so easy to get along with people (if getting along with people is important in this job)?

What activities, social or sports, appeal to you?

What do you do to relax?

Do you belong to any organizations?

Have you held any offices in any organizations?

Did you work any part of your way through school?

How did that kind of pressure affect your grades?

How did it affect your activities in general?

What kind of job would you like to be holding 10 years from now?

In this questioning, the interviewer normally makes a special effort to use language that the person interviewed will readily understand. The interviewer not only notes the verbal answers but also tunes in to the signs or nonverbal answers giving clues to the feelings of the applicant. If the applicant is a nervous type, the good interviewer will spend more than the usual amount of time "in the social period" and will not begin the actual interview until he or she sees that the applicant is ready for direct questions.

As for the form of the questions or statements, most of them are of the open-ended type—they give the applicant an opening for talk. For example, "Tell me how you decided to study law enforcement." "How do you feel about the courses you have completed?" "In what ways do you think they have helped you?'' ''Why do you prefer a sales job to other kinds?'' Questions which can be answered by ''Yes'' or ''No'' are sometimes necessary but are used sparingly. A leading question is ordinarily defined as one which suggests an answer—that type of question, too, should be avoided. For example, ''You do feel that an employee should contribute toward a pension fund, don't you?''

What do you think?

Since the interviewer can tell you just about everything you need to know about his or her company or organization, why take the time to look up that kind of information in advance? Why make a point of getting the right pronunciation of the interviewer's name? If you make a mistake in it, the interviewer won't hold it against you, will he or she? What should you say if the interviewer asks ''What kind of job did you have in mind?'' Should you say, ''I'll do anything''? If you've been fired at some time in the past, what should you say to this question: ''Have you ever been fired?'' Lie or explain what happened? The interview situation is sometimes described as ''a close-up of the communication process.'' What do you think that means? In what ways does the interview give you a close look at the process?

JOB APPLICATION INTERVIEW

The following is an example of an interview between the representative of a highway construction and paving company and a student in the last semester of a two-year associate-degree program in civil engineering technology.

Read through it carefully and then discuss it with your classmates. How effective is this interview? What would you do differently as the applicant or as the interviewer?

Interviewer: [to student coming through his office door at the time set for the interview]: Jerry Jones?

Applicant: Yes, Mr. Graham.

Interviewer: Please sit down. Do you smoke [offering cigarette]?

Applicant: No, thanks.

Interviewer: Still storming outside? Looked like a blizzard when I came in.

Applicant: It's not so bad. Some snow on the ground and it's still windy, but the worst seems to be over.

Interviewer: I'm glad to hear that. I want to drive to one of our plants tomorrow.

Jerry, your being here means that you want to know more about the sales jobs we have open. I've been checking the outline of your background that you sent to me, and, for a starter, would you tell me a little more about your preparation for this kind of work?

Applicant: Of course. As I understand it, Mr. Graham, you are looking for people with enough background in civil engineering to talk about street and highway paving with local, county, and state engineers.

Interviewer: That's right, Jerry. We operate asphalt emulsion plants over a five-state area, and we need good company representatives to maintain contact with street and highway engineers and to talk with them about the advantages of doing business with our organization. How can you help us do that?

Applicant: First of all, my technical background should be just about what you want. In my freshman year, I took courses in elementary and route surveying. Both of those courses are directly related to road building and paving. Then, I also studied building materials and methods; there was a heavy emphasis on aggregates and gravels of all sorts, plus the methods used in constructing road bases. A course in English composition and another in speech-communication were also helpful. There was a lot of business-letter writing in the English course, and the communication course helped me understand people. Both courses would be useful to anybody interested in selling products and services like yours.

Interviewer: That all sounds good. What are you doing in your second year?

Applicant: In the first semester, we studied subdivision surveying; your company does some subçontracting for the pavement of subdivision streets, so that course should be helpful to one of your representatives. We also worked on problems of hydraulics and drainage, material strengths, and contract specifications. I not only know something about those subjects, but I know how paving contracts ought to be worded.

Interviewer: And how about this semester?

Applicant: Right now, we're working on testing of materials and estimating the quantities required for different paving contracts. Accurate bids are a must in your business, and my course work has given me some beginning experience in that area.

Interviewer: I agree. Have you studied anything else as a part of the civil engineering program?

Applicant: Yes, I have. Our program includes a good grounding in basic mathematics, physics, and social science.

Interviewer: How about drafting? We have to lay out drawings and blueprints for much of the work we do. Could you handle any of that?

Applicant: With some help and direction, I could. I forgot to mention that we had a course in construction drafting in the first semester of my freshman year.

Interviewer: Fine, Jerry. You seem to have the kind of academic background that we need. What about any other activities, such as sports, club memberships, and the like?

Applicant: Well, to tell the truth, I haven't had time for anything but the course load I've been carrying. Clubs and extracurricular activities are valuable, I know, but keeping myself in school has been more important to me. On Friday nights and weekends, I work as a clerk in the local Sears store. That work—20 hours a week—pays most of my living expenses. As you can see, there's not much spare time in a schedule like that.

Interviewer: You're right. Of course, out-of-class activities are only one measure of a person's ability to meet and get along with people. If you've been clerking regularly at Sears, I'd say that you have done well on two counts, earning your way and meeting people as well. Hasn't school work during the week and clerking on weekends been pretty tough?

Applicant: Not really. My class work is very interesting, and, as far as the work at Sears is concerned, I really enjoy selling.

Interviewer: I can see that, but there are many other good jobs in civil engineering. Have you ever considered taking a job with a highway department or a city street department?

Applicant: I've thought about that. Still, it seems to me that a sales job is more interesting than a desk job in some agency of government. Besides, I like the idea of getting paid according to the amount of effort I put in.

Interviewer: Did you know that we pay straight salaries and no commission?

Applicant: Yes, I do. But I also know from talking to other people in civil engineering that the managers of your plants usually come up through the sales representatives' ranks. And a couple of your salesmen told me that their salaries are tied fairly closely to their annual sales. In other words, your best salesmen make the most money—and that's a kind of commission.

Interviewer: You have me there, and you're exactly right. You also seem to have done some "homework" on our company, and that's always a good sign in a prospect for a sales appointment. By the way, how would you feel about being moved from assignment to one plant to assignment to another?

Applicant: That wouldn't be a problem, Mr. Graham. I wouldn't mind being moved around, especially in the first two or three years. That would be a good way to gain different kinds of experience. Later on, especially if I got married, I think I'd prefer a home base that wouldn't be subject to change.

Interviewer: I can certainly understand that, Jerry. In fact, you've just summarized company policy. We like to have a new man pick up everything he can during a so-called training period of two or three years. Then we assign him more or less permanently to the plant where he seems to fit in best.

Applicant: I'd like that.

Interviewer: We seem to "see eye to eye" on almost everything so far. Do you have any questions you'd like to ask me?

Applicant: Well, we touched on salary but you didn't mention what it would be for a new man. Can you give me some idea of what it would be?

Interviewer: Yes, I can. If you go to work for us, you'll be paid $900 per month for a start. After six months, the pay goes to $1100. At the end of a year, the minimum is a flat $14,000. After that it's up to you. Salaries are reviewed every six months with the possibility of a raise at the time of each review. If a man is doing a good job for us, he usually gets a raise at least once a year.

Applicant: That seems to be a good pay scale for someone like myself.

Interviewer: It's not bad, but you understand, of course, that some of the people we hire don't work out, and we have to let them go.

Applicant: I would expect that. That answers all my questions. I'm definitely interested in going to work for you. What do I do next?

Interviewer: Nothing for the time being. You won't be out of school for another three months. In the meantime, I'll make my report on you and discuss your application in comparison with the others we get. I can tell you now that I'll recommend that you be hired.

Applicant: That leaves me a little "up in the air." What should I do if some other company offers me a job before I hear from you?

Interviewer: Call me if that happens. There won't be any great delay on our part. You'll hear from us one way or the other before the end of the month—that's only a little over two weeks from now.

Applicant: I can certainly wait that long. Thanks very much, Mr. Graham.

Interviewer: Not at all, Jerry. I guess that does if for now. [Rises and shakes hands with applicant.] So long.

Applicant: Thanks again, Mr. Graham. Nice talking with you.

What do you think?

Jerry Jones asked some questions about pay near the end of the interview. Why not ask such questions at the beginning? After all, if the pay isn't good, what is the point in further conversation? Did Jerry seem to say just about what he should say? Did he talk too much? Too little? If an interviewer doesn't bring up the subject of "outside activities," is it wise at some point to ask, "Would you like to know something about my outside activities?" Is it a good idea to pretend that others are begging for your services and that you're not really too sure you're interested? Or is it better to "play it straight"? What are some of the nonverbal cues or signs that an applicant should be watchful for in an interview? If the interviewer frequently looks at his watch, does that mean he wants the interview to go on as long as possible? Should you sit on the edge of your chair so the interviewer will know you are *really* interested?

GAINING INTERVIEW EXPERIENCE

There is no substitute for actual experience, but it is possible to set up planned class situations which provide practice for both "employers" and "job applicants."

First, one or two local businessmen, personnel officers, or other officials are often willing to attend a class to demonstrate interview patterns and to talk about them before or after a demonstration interview. One of the students is, of course, the job applicant in one of these demonstrations. Well in advance of the interview, the interviewer-to-be should be asked to fill out an *Employer Interview Form* and give or mail it to the student who will be "applying for the job." The student also fills out an *Applicant Interview Form* and gives or mails it to the "employing interviewer" who will be talking with him or her about the job.

On the day of the class interview, the "interviewer" may have the *Applicant Interview Form* in hand as a partial guide for a line of questioning. The student being interviewed should be familiar with the details of the "job opening." He or she should have no need for keeping that document in hand during the interview.

If people from the business or academic areas are not available, student volunteers can easily serve as "employers."

Following these demonstration interviews (and after any others in which students take part), a *Job-Application Interview-Rating Scale* can be used to provide some feedback to those taking part in a specific interview. The forms below—or modifications of them—can be readily dittoed or mimeographed for the purposes described above. The forms will serve the dual purpose of helping you evaluate the interviews and reinforcing some of the behaviors that will make you a better interviewee.

If, for the purpose of a demonstration interview, you are going to be "a job applicant" fill out the Applicant Interview Form for the information of the "employer."

If you are going to be an "employer," fill out the Employer Interview Form for the information of the "job applicant."

APPLICANT INTERVIEW FORM

____

Last name First name Middle initial

Major: ____________________ **Minor:** ____________________

Anticipated date of graduation: ____________________
Present address: ____________________
Home address: ____________________
Present phone: ____________________ Home phone: ____________________

Personal Data: Height: ________ Weight: ________ Marital status: ________
Date of birth: ____________ Place of birth: ____________________
Physical limitations: ____________________
Hobbies or outside interests: ____________________
Activities? ____________________

____

Belong to any organizations—educational, professional, or other? ____________

____

Earned ________% of total expenses while attending college.
Grade average: ________
Locations preferred: ____________________
Kinds of work preferred: ____________________

Work Experience:

Organization and address	Kind of work	Full- or part-time	Dates employed From To

Military service record, if any: ____________________
References (one faculty and one professional—give names and addresses):
1. ____________________
____
2. ____________________
____

Date available for employment: ____________________

(To be given to the person interviewing you.)

EMPLOYER INTERVIEW FORM

Name and address of the employing company or organization:

Name of the interviewer for the company or organization:

Official position of the interviewer:

Write a short description of the (imaginary) job which you "have available" and list the personal qualities that an applicant for it should have.

Specific Job Description **Required Personal Qualities**

(This completed form should be handed to the instructor. He or she will turn it over to the student who is to interview you "in the effort to get the job." The "job applicant" will then return it to the instructor after the interview is finished.)

INTERVIEW RATING-SCALE

(Name of *interviewer*) ______________________________

After interview, place an X under one heading on each line.	Poor	Fair	Average	Good	Very good
Made "interviewee" feel at ease					
Asked worthwhile questions					
Seemed to "listen actively"					
Made sensible statements					
Brought interview to good close					
Overall skill in communicating					

Write *one* helpful suggestion below:

- -

(Fold and tear along this line.)

(Name of person *being interviewed*) ______________________________

After interview, place an X under one heading on each line.	Poor	Fair	Average	Good	Very good
Handled self well at beginning					
Gave direct answers					
Asked good questions					
Was generally tactful					
Handled self well at close					
Over-all skill in communicating					

Write *one* helpful suggestion below:

(This form may be used for almost any kind of interview.)

SUMMARY

This chapter began with suggestions on preparing a preliminary data sheet. The chapter then demonstrated how you can use that first effort as a base for writing a final and polished data sheet. A model cover letter showed how you might approach a potential employer.

A second section dealt with the need to (1) prepare in advance for an interview and (2) be a good communicator during it. The interview, in other words, is an opportunity to put into practice almost everything you know about interacting with another person in communication.

The third section asked you to take part in an interview. Suggestions were made on how to act as an applicant and on how to act as an employer. The assumption is that you will get a chance to use both kinds of interview skills in your student and poststudent life.

The chapter closed with a model interview, an *Applicant Interview Form,* an *Employer Interview Form,* and an *Interview Rating-Scale.*

8

Communicating with Another in the Occupational Setting: Occupational Interviews

8

Communicating with Another in the Occupational Setting: Occupational Interviews

"[Organizations] involve interdependence. Interdependence calls for coordination. And coordination requires communication."

William V. Haney in *Communication and Organizational Behavior*[1]

If you are successful in the employment interview, if you get the job, you become a member of an organization. It may be a small one or it may be enormous. Whatever the size of the organization, your effectiveness in it will depend in large part upon your ability to communicate. Your own growth as an individual also depends on that same ability and on your doing what you can to develop it at work and elsewhere.

In Chapter 7, we put the materials of the earlier chapters to work in a specific situation. We intend to make the same kinds of practical applications in this and the following chapters. We will identify specific communication situations which occur in most careers, and we will present plans and patterns to help you perform effectively in them.

---

1. William V. Haney, *Communication and Organizational Behavior* (Homewood, Ill.: Richard D. Irwin, 1973), p. 11.

Here's where we're going

The contents of this chapter should enable you to:

1. Select an occupation and show how an individual in that occupation might be placed in each of the five interview situations described in the chapter.
2. Prepare to participate in any of these types of interviews.
3. Understand the purpose of and plan an information-seeking form appropriate to your career interests.
4. Prepare an information-giving plan that would allow you to function more effectively in a selected occupation.
5. List a set of five qualities that will contribute to positive communication relationships in interviews occurring in occupational settings.
6. List five qualities that will almost surely result in negative communicative relationships in occupational interviews.
7. Explain the unique demands of a counseling interview, and list and explain the components of a counseling interview.

In Chapter 1, we spoke of social communication. When you enter a job, there will be certain social demands. There will be coffee breaks with random conversation, and there will be casual exchanges of pleasantries. It is important to realize that these moments affect your work. If you sit in a corner during those breaks and refuse to communicate with a group of happy and extroverted co-workers, their perceptions of you will be affected. If you are aggressive and overbearing in your relationships with your co-workers, quite a different set of perceptions will emerge.

On a new job, getting along with co-workers is mostly a matter of being friendly and considerate. Workers already on the scene may be wary and uncertain about you as a newcomer. They are curious: How well will this person fit in here? Will she work *with* us or will she be trying to make herself look good at our expense? Will he try to take over one of *our* jobs? The challenge once again is a challenge to your ability to communicate. You have to show co-workers that you are in no way threatening their job security, and at the same time, you have to avoid letting any co-worker become your unofficial "boss." You'll be sending verbal and nonverbal messages, some of them intentional and some of them unintentional. Your co-workers will be attaching their own meanings to the messages. If they see you as "no threat" and "cooperative," you will soon be an accepted member of the work force.

Our focus in this chapter, however, is not on social communication but rather on those specific communication situations which emerge in an occupational setting. In this chapter that focus will be limited to one-to-another relationships—the kinds of relationships that exist when the salesperson meets a customer, the hygienist meets a patient, the law enforcement officer meets a distraught parent, the employee relates to a supervisor, a supervisor communicates with a subordinate.

There is a common quality in all of these relationships. They are more than simple conversations. They have a purpose—a purpose that is predetermined, typically serious, and occasionally critical. Building on our Chapter 7 definition of an interview, let us agree that each of these relationships is "a process of [two-party] communication with a predetermined and serious purpose designed to interchange behavior and usually [involving] the asking and answering of questions."[2] This definition underscores the fact that occupational relationships do have purpose. Indeed, the earlier advice to make careful decisions concerning your communicative purpose is especially important. Just *why* are you communicating with the other individual? In addition, the definition emphasizes that the interview does not occur in isolation—that what has gone before and what comes after will affect the interview. If a customer has been treated badly in an auto dealership, that negative experience may place the customer on guard. On a later occasion, it may be harder for the salesperson to talk with that customer to determine the customer's wants and needs.

The successful interview will also result in a sharing of information and feelings. It will be an interchange that will allow both parties to achieve objectives. Finally, the interview reflects the typical work behavior of asking and answering questions.

All of this points to the fact that an awareness of interviewing techniques will not only contribute to your ability to get a job, but also to your ability to keep that job and perform effectively on it.

SOME GENERAL PRINCIPLES OF INTERVIEWING

Although in the preceding chapter we focused attention on the employment interview, many of the principles presented there apply equally well to the kinds of interviews you will participate in during the performance of your occupational duties. For example, our earlier caution that you prepare careful-

2. Charles J. Stewart and William B. Cash, *Interviewing: Principles and Practices* (Dubuque, Iowa: Wm. C. Brown, 1974), p. 4.

ly remains urgent. Likewise, the recommendation that you carefully determine the purpose for which you are engaging in an interview is basic. As for format, the various types of occupational interviews will reflect the same components found in the employment interview; there will be an opening, body, and closing—or there will be some confusion and frustration on the part of the participants.

If you are an employee and you want to talk with your supervisor, both of you will do some planning. You may even go so far as to practice or rehearse what you intend to say. For example, you may want more time to get a project finished. You decide to talk with your supervisor about it. Problem: What reasons can I give for the delay? My view of myself and my problem tells me I have good reasons to ask for more time. Which of those reasons will make sense to this "supervisor"? What kind of person is the supervisor? Easygoing and sympathetic? A letter-of-the-law type—get it done on time or else? Will the supervisor listen to me as an individual? Or should I try to enlist others to ask for a general extension of time? How should I raise the issue? How should I present it? Should I treat the whole business lightly as if I don't really care one way or the other? How is the supervisor likely to react? What exactly shall I say to make the best impression? If the supervisor gets angry, what do I do?

The supervisor will be asking the same questions about you. In other words, each of two persons taking part in an interview has self-perceptions and perceptions of the other person. These perceptions affect the communication which takes place; as outlined in Chapter 6, our perceptions or ways of looking at people and things give rise to mind-sets or *tendencies to act* in certain ways. You may see a particular supervisor as a "square," and that same supervisor may see you as a "know-nothing beginner." Each of you adjusts general approach and language. You figure out what you're going to say and how you're going to say it after you come to some conclusions about the listener. Even before an interview gets under way, therefore, you make assumptions about the other person, and you conduct yourself accordingly; the other person makes assumptions about you and proceeds accordingly. Since we *know* that our perceptions have these effects on us, it's important that we avoid making snap judgments of any kind about what another person is like, about what his or her viewpoints and attitudes are, about how he or she will react to certain statements or questions.

Instead of the snap judgments, then, the important thing in an interview is to get in the habit of "feeling with" the other person. An employee needs to remember that a supervisor generally *wants* the employee to succeed; an employee's failures only complicate the supervisor's job. The supervisor has to be aware that the employee is a human being with problems. The supervisor has to be careful not to talk too much; the supervisor's job often depends on his or her ability to listen in an attentive and sympathetic way. Unfortunately, as studies show, the average supervisor talks up to 85 percent of the time in this sort of an interview.

Although no one wants to make the mistake of talking too much, either as supervisor or employee, there is a need for *verbal encouragement* in any interview. Watch any two people in active conversation and you will agree that there are many opportunities for "the listener" to interject short but honest reactions, such as "I believe you." "That seems to make sense," and "What happened next?" You're also aware that *nonverbal encouragement* in the form of active listening is equally important. Listening to a person helps the person to go on; it shows respect. We're not suggesting that you pretend interest in their views; we're suggesting that, if you are interested, you can and should indicate that you are.

In addition to offering verbal and nonverbal encouragement to the other person in an interview, you can often see to it that you have a *comfortable physical setting*, one that will help the conversation along. The supervisor may be able to come out from behind a desk and sit with the employee at a table or in some other less formal situation in the room. An employee won't have too much to say about where the interview is to take place, but if something about the setting makes you really uncomfortable (for example, the sun is in your eyes, the room is too hot, too cold, etc.), it makes sense to call such a handicap to the attention of the supervisor. People work better, think better, and react to one another better when the physical conditions are right. Suffering in silence will get you nowhere.

One of the things that becomes clear in this description is that you may shift back and forth between the roles of interviewer and interviewee. This will be true in a variety of occupational settings. If you are a salesperson, for example, you will be both asking and "fielding" questions in your effort to determine what the customer needs.

The following pages cover five types of occupational interviews which you will almost certainly encounter during your work experience: (1) the training interview, (2) the informational interview, (3) the corrective on-the-carpet interview, (4) the corrective-probing interview, and (5) the performance-appraisal interview. In addition, we will close the chapter with an examination of a type of occupational interviewing that has reached professional status, the counseling interview.

In the *training interview*, the supervisor explains to the employee what that employee is to do in the performance of the particular job; in other words, the interview is a training session. In the *informational interview*, someone is seeking and/or transmitting information. In either type of *corrective interview*, the supervisor is faced with the need to convince the employee that he or she should change some aspect of his or her behavior in order to perform acceptably or more effectively in the occupational setting. In the *performance-appraisal interview*, the employee is offered an assessment of his or her performance on the job. In the *counseling interview*, the counselor encourages an individual to help himself by changing his attitude(s) and solving his own problem(s).

Unless you already have some practical experience in your chosen field, your first job status is likely to be that of an employee working under the direction of someone else. This may cause you to wonder why our focus is so often on the supervisor, a position that you won't be holding immediately. The reasons are that: (1) as a trained person, you will probably move to the level of supervisor relatively quickly; (2) it is the supervisor who normally takes the lead in employee-supervisor interviews; (3) your knowing what a supervisor is doing—or trying to do—in an interview will give you valuable assistance in your handling of the employee side of that kind of interaction; and (4) even in nonsupervisory positions the responsibility for initiating communication will rest on your shoulders and make you a "supervisor" of sorts. The nurse and dental hygienist, for example, become supervisors of their patients' behaviors. You will note, too, that the chapter shifts focus from supervisor to employee frequently enough to be helpful to you during your initial "employee period."

THE TRAINING INTERVIEW

General Approach

When you put in your appearance to begin work on a job, the supervisor will often have your original job application in hand together with a report of your job-application interview. Those documents and any others in your file—recommendations, credit transcripts, etc.—will contain considerable information about you and what you can do. Nevertheless, the supervisor will first talk with you about any experience you may have had which is directly applicable to the job. In other words, an effort will be made to determine exactly how much guidance and training you're going to need. When that preliminary conversation is finished, the supervisor will generally know at what point to begin your training. *That portion of the interview will reveal whether you know nothing about your new duties, whether you know something about them, or whether you have enough experience to get along without any instruction at all.*

When you finish your course work, you *may* be ready to step right into the job. However, it is still possible that you would know nothing about some special phase of your new duties; for example, you could be an expert in marine propulsion technology and find yourself needing a "postgraduate" training session in protecting metal fittings from electrolysis. Assuming, then, that you know little or nothing about the details of the job you've accepted and assuming further that, like many jobs, this one involves physical activity, a good supervisor would normally go through these steps:[3]

1. The supervisor would show you what to do and, at the same time, tell you what to do, how to do it, and why it is done in a certain way.
2. Then the two of you would repeat the routine a second time, and you would tell the supervisor what to do, how to do it, and why.
3. Finally, the supervisor would allow you to take over completely and both explain and show what to do, how to do it, and why.

In this sort of interview, the interviewer should be facing the same direction as the interviewee and should be assuming the same basic position as the interviewee. In this manner, the interviewee is able to view a right hand doing what his or her right hand will eventually be doing, etc. It will be easier for you (that is, the interviewee or trainee) to move in and take over.

This process is obviously best in those situations in which the supervisor can show the employee how to do something. Not all three steps will be necessary if you have had specialized training nor does the process work in the giving of routine assignments or special instructions. If you and your co-workers are supposed to plan a move to another room in the building, there is no practical way for the supervisor to demonstrate what each person is to do. If, however, that supervisor wants you to prepare a special report, you should be given a detailed explanation as to exactly what information is to be included, how the information should be prepared and presented, and why it is needed. In situations like these, the supervisor must give detailed instructions and allow time for employee feedback.

As an employee, you should be taking an active part in the proceedings, especially in the second and third phases of the training routine outlined above. If you have any questions to ask at *any* stage, you will want to ask them as they occur to you rather than take a chance on forgetting them. If you have any suggestions to make, make them. The supportive supervisor will be glad to get them, and you won't want to work very long for the other kind. Properly approached by both parties, the training interview is a cooperative venture, so, instead of playing the role of the silent sponge, feel free to say or ask anything that you feel will make the interview a successful attack on the training problem.

Before we move on to an exercise, consider how many applications this training interview might have. This is the pattern that the grill chief uses in a fast-food restaurant in order to break in a new cook. It is the format an industrial arts

3. Adapted from Martin T. Broadwell, *The Supervisor and On-the-Job Training* (Reading, Mass.: Addison-Wesley, 1969), pp. 101–109.

teacher employs when explaining a project to a student. It is the approach a hygienist uses when teaching a young patient brushing techniques.

In all of these situations, both parties have a purpose. One of them wants to teach, and, at least ideally, the other wants to learn. As a result of the training interview both members of that interview want the interviewee to *know how to do something.* If you find yourself in a situation where you want someone to know how to do something, you will find the training interview an effective approach. If you discover that you want to learn how to do something, you may want to guide the knowledgeable person into the role of trainer.

Try this

Team up with another student, select one of the following situations (or a similar one), and prepare a training interview. You will need to plan (1) the description of a problem, (2) instructions to the supervisor, and (3) instructions to the employee. The problem can be anything from showing a laboratory assistant how to check a person's blood pressure to . . .

1. Showing an apprentice baker how to make different kinds of pastries.
2. Showing a factory employee how to operate a drill press.
3. Showing a clerical worker how to fill out a variety of forms.
4. Showing a sales clerk how to handle complaints about faulty merchandise.
5. Showing a supermarket employee how to keep a running record of stock.
6. Showing an aircraft "service station" employee how to direct parking, tie-down, fill tanks, check oil, etc.
7. Showing a worker in marine technology how to collect and record water samples.
8. Showing a farm worker how to mix feed according to formula.
9. Showing a fireman-trainee how to administer oxygen to smoke victims.
10. Showing an electrician how to service traffic lights.
11. Showing a traffic-officer-trainee how to handle a difficult traffic control assignment.
12. Showing a chemist's assistant how to conduct a certain test.
13. Or taking your own career goal into consideration, what special instruction could you possibly expect on a first job?
14. Or taking your own career goal into consideration, what special instruction could you, as a supervisor, expect to give to a new employee?

In working with other students to prepare model interviewing problems (below), the first step of choosing and describing a real or imaginary problem is seldom difficult. The second and third steps of working up instructions to two people are not as easy. However, you can use the checklist below to decide what background and characteristics you want the employee in the case to have. Once "the facts" about the employee have been determined, it is easier to write about him or her in "instructions to the supervisor." It is also easier—because you now "know" the employee better—to write the "instructions to the employee."

1. Employee's name, real or imaginary?
2. Employee's title or job assignment?
3. Length of time in present job?
4. Apparent goal or goals at present time—security? acceptance by co-workers? recognition of worth? chance to get ahead?
5. Relations with co-workers?
6. Typical reaction to problems—attempt to solve them? withdrawal? shifting blame to somebody or something else? "taking it out" on somebody or something else? quitting?
7. Attitude toward present job assignment? General level of performance?
8. Attitude toward present supervisor?
9. Specific incident, occasion, or situation calling for an interview?
10. *Relevant* (to the incident, etc.) information about off-the-job interests, problems, home life, etc.?
11. General information which can be used at the beginning of the interview (1) to establish a good relationship or rapport with the employee and (2) to provide an early opening for bringing up the purpose of the meeting.

The following model is offered in order to give you a clearer sense of how to develop the points of your training interview.

Model of a training problem

Description. Many graduates of programs in marine or aviation technology are specialists in engine service and maintenance. They take jobs with governmental agencies, airlines, or private companies requiring service and maintenance personnel. In those jobs, they must know how to tune engines, inspect fuel systems, align engine and prop shafts, adjust controls, etc. They must be able to find out why an engine is not functioning properly and to correct that malfunction. They must know how to perform any standard service or maintenance task and properly record it in a service or maintenance log.

For this particular exercise, any two or three students can team up to choose a training problem arising out of their own experiences in the classroom or lab. Anything they find especially difficult could serve as a problem which could conceivably require a supervisor to give special training to a new employee. The specific problem chosen should be described in a question, sentence, or paragraph. For example: "When choosing fittings and fastening underwater hardware, how do you guard against electrolytic corrosion?" If a new employee could not answer that question to the satisfaction of the supervisor, a training session would obviously be in order.

Instructions to the Supervisor. You have determined through conversation with a new employee that he or she is a competent marine mechanic in practically all phases except that of fighting electrolytic corrosion. You decide to go into a training session with him or her for the purpose of (1) discussing galvanic corrosion in general, (2) providing an understanding of the galvanic series of metals in sea water, and (3) outlining protective measures for a zinc-anode system. All of this work can be done in your office with the help of whatever printed materials, diagrams, and other visual aids you consider necessary; specific applications can be pointed out in the shop at a later date.

Instructions to the Employee. From a preliminary talk with your supervisor, you've learned that he or she considers your qualifications to be good in every department except that of methods for protecting against electrolytic corrosion. In your work on marine engines, that subject was mentioned but more or less passed over as not being directly related to engine problems. To get ready for a training session with the supervisor, you do some "boning up" on the subject. However, the details are somewhat confusing, and you are depending on the supervisor to give you step-by-step information on exactly what to do, how to do it, and why.

What to Look for in a Training Interview[4]

Some training sessions are practical on-the-spot at-the-work-station demonstrations. Others necessarily take place in an office or some other convenient place, so that the "watch-how-I-do-this" step is impractical. No matter how the training is conducted, these questions should be asked about any training pattern.

4. "What-to-look-for" questions follow each kind of interview in this chapter. In addition to providing a base for evaluation of practice interviews, they are also useful as discussion questions for the type of interview under consideration.

1. Is the need for a training session apparent? Does the employee get a chance to tell the supervisor what he or she already knows about the job? About any experience he or she has had in a similar situation? If the supervisor doesn't give the employee an opening for providing such information, does the employee take the initiative and try to make such an opening? In other words, is the interview one which covers a demonstrated deficiency in the employee's past training and/or experience? Or is it training for training's sake, with the supervisor blundering forward and the employee submitting meekly to unnecessary training?

2. Do both employee and supervisor take responsibility for a thorough training session? If the employee has no relevant training or experience, does the supervisor follow through on the three-phase series recommended in this text: doing *and* instructing, doing *as* instructed, and having the employee handle the doing and instructing? Does the employee concentrate on all three phases? Or does the employee seem to assume that the first phase is all that is needed? And show boredom with the other two?

3. Does the employee show an interest in knowing *why* something should be done? Or *why* it should be done in a certain way? Or does the employee give the impression of only superficial interest in *what* should be done? Does the supervisor make any effort to explain *why* something is being done or is only the *what* emphasized?

4. Do supervisor and employee listen to each other? Does either one talk past the other into a vacuum? Does the supervisor give the employee a chance to break in with questions and comments? Does the employee feel free to ask questions? Does the employee feel free to ask for additional explanation? When the session is over, is there a feeling that real communication took place and that the employee is now competent to take over the duty that was being explained?

5. Does the supervisor provide for follow-up with comments such as: "If you have any problems, check with me again"? Or "If any questions come up, drop around and we'll go over them"?

THE INFORMATIONAL INTERVIEW

As we have just seen, a training interview calls for the efficient transfer of specialized information on the procedures required for handling a particular job. To that extent, it is a kind of "informational interview." However, we use that term in this text to cover the more general situations which one may encounter with some regularity in his or her occupation.

As you well know, many occupations are dependent upon an individual's ability to gain information from others. An insurance investigator's stock in trade is skill in asking proper questions. A doctor's success is in part dependent upon the ability to question. A veterinarian faces an even trickier interviewing situation. The veterinarian cannot interview the patient; rather, he or she must depend upon careful questioning of the owner. A clothing salesperson must diplomatically determine a customer's size. On the other side of the coin, the whole purpose behind a nurse-patient interview may be to provide information the patient needs for basic self-treatment or rapid recovery. In still a third one-to-one situation, there may be close to a balance in the exchange of information. For example, a newly hired baseball pitcher describes his initial meeting with the first-string catcher: "He asked me questions about how I work the mound, and I asked him questions about his behind-the-plate action. Each of us traded information that would help us work well together."

In brief, most occupations require at least some skill in informational interviewing. In one situation, the emphasis may be on gaining information; in another, it may be on giving it; in a third, the give-and-take balance may be about equal. Whatever the circumstances, it will pay you to become aware of the varied requirements of informational interviews.

General Approach

The opening of the informational interview serves the same functions as in the employment interview (Chapter 7). It gains the interviewee's attention and also tries to relax the interviewee to ensure that communication will be comfortable and free.

Once you have initiated the interview, you move on in an effort to give and/or acquire specific information. In certain occupations, this segment of the interview may be highly structured. Sometimes there are certain critical questions which must be asked and sometimes, as suggested in the paragraph above, a novice or new worker "needs" anxiety-reducing questions before necessary information can be obtained.

If you've been to a modern hospital, for example, you may have noticed some changes. For one thing, some hospitals now have an admission team consisting of a number of interviewers, one of whom sits down with each incoming patient in a kind of information-seeking-*and*-giving interview. If you're one of the incoming patients, you're asked a number of general questions—name, address, marital status, name of next of kin, name of health and accident insurance company, religious preference, and so on. The interviewing room is pleasant and so is the interviewer, the whole idea being to make the situation as easy and nonthreatening as possible. After you've answered all or most of the questions, the interviewer proceeds to an information session and tells you about such things as general hospital routine, policies about visiting hours, how a TV and/or radio can be rented, how to arrange for a phone, and what to do if you're not satisfied with some phase of your care, including the food service. At the close of the interview, you may be asked if *you* have any suggestions for nursing care. Then you're escorted to your room by this new friend, and if you're in the hospital for any length of time, the individual may drop in occasionally to check on your reactions to "the service." In other words, you're no longer a prisoner of the system with absolutely nothing to say about anything.

Once you're officially admitted as a patient, it is entirely possible that a nurse from your "nursing care team" will visit you to seek information about your understanding of whatever it is that's wrong with you. For example, if you are in the hospital for a diabetic condition, the nurse may ask a series of questions on how you give yourself insulin for diabetes, or what your practice is in taking pills for the same condition, or what is your history of diabetic upsets, or how you handle your diet. Throughout the questioning, if he or she is well trained, the nurse will be sympathetic, reassuring, helpful, and will do as much as possible to build up your confidence during the interview.

Typical Information-Seeking Form

The form below is typical only in that, like other information-seeking forms, it lists the questions to be asked and provides spaces for the answers. This particular form could be used only in hospitals or clinics; it was developed in the Nurses Training Department of Purdue University. It is currently used by personnel in St. Elizabeth Hospital Medical Center, Lafayette, Indiana. In practice, two nurses may call on the patient; one does the actual interviewing and the other acts as recorder by writing down the answers and noting added comments by the interviewer. The recorder may also write comments on the form. The form and any comments on it may serve as a base for a later nursing care conference.

ST. ELIZABETH HOSPITAL MEDICAL CENTER
Lafayette, Indiana

Oral Hypoglycemic Regimen

Patient's name ______________________
Interview date ______________________
Interviewed by ______________________

Doctor's Orders:

Date of Order ______________________ Ordered by: ______________________

Comments

1. What is the name of the pills you take for your diabetes?

____

Comments

How many pills do you take, and what time do you take them?

Takes _____ pills at _____ o'clock

_____ _____

_____ _____

2. Do you always do it exactly this way?

Yes No*

*Variations ______________________________

____

Do you always remember to take them?

Yes No*

*Frequency of doses skipped _______________

____

3. Is this the only medicine you ever take for your diabetes? Yes No*

*Other medicines and frequency _____________

____

4. Please show me the pills you have on hand.

Kind and strength _________________________

____

Pills are in a tightly covered container.

Yes No

5. What would you do if you were too sick to eat or take your pills?

____

____

6. Do you take any other medicines for any reason?

Yes* No

*Takes regularly _________________________

____

____

*Takes occasionally _______________________

____

____

Typical Information-Giving Plan

If the nurse seeking information on a patient's ability to handle self-treatment discovers that the patient is doing everything she or he has been directed to do, there is no need for an information-giving interview unless the doctor has changed his or her directives and prescriptions. In that case, the interview can serve the very useful purpose of ensuring that the patient thoroughly and completely understands what changes have been decided. However, let us assume that, as a result of the information-seeking interview outlined above, it was discovered that the patient had become very careless and apathetic about the pill routine. The job of reeducation would then have to be undertaken.

In working out the plan for the interview, the nurse responsible for it would use the results of the information-seeking interview as a base. If there were four main areas in that particular interview and the patient's answers had shown that he or she was not too well informed in three of them, the plan for information-giving would obviously stress those three weak areas. The other could be simply reviewed in passing. Assuming that our particular patient was weak in all six areas noted on the information-seeking form in question, the nurse would follow the plan below with plenty of time allowed to encourage and answer any questions the patient might choose to ask.

ST. ELIZABETH HOSPITAL MEDICAL CENTER

Lafayette, Indiana

What the Patient Should Know about Oral Hypoglycemic Drugs

The statements below are numbered to correspond with each question on the assessment guide.

The Patient Should Know:

1. The doctor's order regarding the oral hypoglycemic drug, including the name, number of pills to take, and the time(s) to take them.
2. That he should follow the doctor's instructions exactly, neither varying nor skipping a dose without the consent of his doctor.
3. That there are a number of different oral hypoglycemic drugs and that the kind prescribed was selected as being suited to his diabetic status; that the drugs are not interchangeable, so he must always use the kind prescribed for him.
4. That he should check the labels carefully to be sure he is taking the right medicine and that it matches what the doctor has prescribed. That the pills

should be kept in a tightly covered container so that they will not absorb moisture.

5. That if he is unable to eat or to take his pills, he should CALL HIS DOCTOR at once.

   That at times of special stress or illness, a person taking oral drugs may need to be given insulin.

6. That certain other drugs may change the action of oral hypoglycemic agents; that he should seek advice from his physician prior to taking other drugs.

Other than following the form which is normally available as a guide for the information-seeking interview, the interviewer uses essentially the same questioning patterns, probes, and skills discussed in the preceding chapter. Although the question-answer form is structured in different ways to serve different purposes, it is not absolutely necessary to hold rigidly to it or to any other form. For example, if the person being interviewed volunteers some information that fits in elsewhere on the form, it can be recorded without saying something like "We'll come to that later," a remark calculated to turn anyone off. As in all interviews, the person from whom you're trying to get information should be encouraged to talk. It is possible for the interviewer to say very little and still remain in control of the situation by making open-ended comments and stepping in just often enough "to keep the interview on track."

In the information-giving interview, there is a natural tendency and a natural opening for the information-giver to talk too much. The interviewer looks at the information to be given and too often plunges in to give it practically nonstop. Here again, the listener must be given a chance to listen; the information should be given in a series of small doses, each followed by a series of *planned* questions aimed at finding out whether or not the message is getting through. *Let the person being interviewed talk* and encourage him or her to ask questions. In many instances, after you have provided some basic information, the interviewee will do a better job of restating it than you could possibly do.

Patients will be able to understand the reasons for a precise (and sometimes mechanical-sounding) set of questions. Customers in an appliance store will be far less comfortable when a salesperson confronts them with a set of obviously prepared questions. Accordingly, the salesperson will want to work toward a less-structured set of questions. However, with rare exceptions, a structured interview is typical in an occupational setting. While a salesperson, or a hygienist, or a police officer might elicit some important information by allowing an individual to talk randomly, the investment of time and energy would almost certainly exceed the amount of information revealed.

Questioning Technique

Assuming that you have a particular kind of occupational setting in mind, you are in a position to build a list of general questions to control and guide the interview. As you prepare your questions, it will be helpful for you to keep in mind the different kinds of questions you may ask. You may ask *open* questions or *closed* questions. An open question allows the interviewee to talk at length and places the burden of identifying relevant information on the interviewer. When a dental hygienist says to a young patient, "What kinds of things do you like to eat?" the hygienist is asking an open question. As you prepare for an interview, you will want to recognize that *open* questions have certain advantages. For example, since they do not specify the response they are nonthreatening. For that reason, open questions are especially helpful at the beginning of an interview. On the other hand, they are close to being unstructured in that they take up considerable time and may not yield necessary information.

A *closed* question is one that severely limits the answer. When an interviewer converses with a blood donor, the interviewer may say, "Please answer the following questions with a yes or no." The interviewer then proceeds to determine if, among other things, the donor has given blood in recent months, has served in Vietnam, has had ears pierced, has been tattooed, has had surgery within the past six months. These are important questions and furnish the basis for initial acceptance or rejection of a donor. There are, however, certain disadvantages to closed questions because of the limited information they reveal. If, for example, the hygienist asks a child if he or she has candy every day, and the child answers *no*, the hygienist may miss the fact that the child eats caramel corn three times a week but doesn't think of it as "candy." Nevertheless, in most occupational interviews in which you are seeking information, you will find it useful to ask a number of closed questions. Perhaps the best early suggestion is that you plan to use a combination of open and closed questions and, as your skill and confidence grow, you may want to increase the number of open questions.

If, as an interviewer, you follow our earlier advice to be an active and helpful listener, you will recognize that some of the answers to your questions may raise more questions than they answer. Accordingly, you may resort to the follow-up question—you *probe* to solicit additional information:

"Why do you say that?"

"Really—could you explain that further?"

"Let me see if I understood you correctly when you said. . . . "

Remember, the purpose of the informational interview is to elicit or pass on information. If you don't get that information or don't succeed in transmitting it, the interview has no value.[5]

Try this

Join a friend who is planning on making a substantial purchase. Act as an observer while the salesperson and your friend communicate. Do not intrude. Rather, watch them and take note of the kinds of questions asked and the procedure followed.

1. What sort of opening did the salesperson employ in order to initiate the interview?
2. Did the salesperson seem to have structured the interview or did there seem to be a total absence of structure?
3. Did your friend get necessary questions answered?
4. Did your friend bring adequate structure to the interview?
5. Was the interview brought to satisfactory close?
6. How could both parties have made the experience a more profitable one?

What to Look for in an Informational Interview

In addition to the questions included in the preceding exercise, you will want to look for these elements.

1. Do the participants have a clear sense of the information they are seeking? Is there a tendency to get off the track—to deal with irrelevant material? When the interviewer digresses, does it appear to be with purpose? Is the interviewer, for example, trying to make the interviewee more comfortable?
2. Does the interviewer include a variety of types of questions or does the interviewer structure the interview so strictly that opportunities for securing additional information are lost? Does the interviewer follow up on a question until the interviewee offers the necessary information?
3. Has the interviewer taken steps to make the situation as comfortable as possible? Does the interviewer employ a private tone of voice when dealing with sensitive issues?

5. For a more detailed discussion of questioning strategies, see the Stewart and Cash text mentioned earlier in this chapter.

4. Does the interviewer give the respondent reason to answer completely and honestly? Are basic courtesies extended? Does the interviewer listen actively? Does the interviewer display *real* interest in the other individual?

THE CORRECTIVE INTERVIEW

General Approach

Frequently, an informational interview precedes the corrective interview. A supervisor, for example, may become aware of some sort of problem that is affecting production or sales or general morale. Effective informational interviewing will furnish the supervisor with an awareness of possible causes of the problem and allow that supervisor to plan a corrective interview to eliminate or lessen those causes.

In the corrective interview, the supervisor talks with an employee in an effort to bring about a correction of some deficiency in the employee's on-the-job performance. The deficiency may stem from any one of a number of causes. For example, the employee may have inadvertently slipped into some careless habit, such as more or less regularly submitting a weekly report two or three days late. Perhaps a worker is having trouble with some particular phase of the job because of a lack of training for it; the supervisor has to track down the difficulty and make provision for some additional training. On-the-job performance can be affected by many factors, some of them intentional on the part of the worker and some of them unintentional. When an employee takes money from the till, the act is presumably intentional; when the employee fails to get the job done because of deteriorating health, the failure is unintentional. Job performance can be affected by personality conflicts, romantic interest in a co-worker, racial or religious prejudice, family problems, resentment at being passed over for a promotion, inability to make decisions, and so on. Any drop in an employee's efficiency or any failure of the employee to live up to performance expectations is cause for a supervisor to consider a corrective interview with that employee.

In an effort to avoid employee problems like those above or to solve them when they do occur, a competent supervisor tries to be "employee-need conscious." You will recall a listing of "Listener Needs and Desires" early in Chapter 6; for our purposes here, such goals can be combined and summarized as *security, acceptance by the group, recognition of accomplishment,* and *opportunity for personal growth*. An employee's successes or failures in attaining those goals have much to do, as you know, with the employee's self-concept. If one or more of these goals is blocked or if the employee thinks it is blocked, the employee's frustrations are often reflected in one or more of these behaviors: (1) trying to solve the problem; (2) withdrawal symptoms—

daydreaming, concentration on hobbies, etc.; (3) blaming poor performance on someone or something else—bad supervision, health, etc., (4) "taking it out" on the company or on anyone else, including himself or herself; or (5) quitting the job. Many supervisors make a point of working out questions to cover at least the four goals mentioned above in order to pin down the frustrations leading to any undesirable behavior an employee may show. The same goals can be used, of course, in pointing out to the employee how the goals can be reached through the job or how those goals are already being reached.

Faced with below-standard work by an employee, the supervisor must first decide whether the employee's difficulty is an "on-the-carpet" problem or a "probing" problem. If the employee has broken or is breaking work rules, the problem is in the "on-the-carpet" category. If the employee's work is below standard for no clearly discernible reason, the problem is undefined and *the supervisor has to probe for it.*

Handling a Corrective-on-the-Carpet Problem

A problem of this type may be as minor as an employee's coming in late three mornings in succession. You don't want this late arrival to devlop into a habit, so you decide to talk with the employee about it. On the other hand, the problem may be serious; for example, one employee informs you that a co-worker is stealing from the company. If there is any hard evidence to that effect, you have no choice but to confront the employee with the evidence and make a decision on what to do about it.

If the man or woman exists who has not at some time been involved with a supervisor in a corrective interview, that person is not human. Even with good intentions and exceptional effort, everyone fails at one time or another to meet expectations. When the day comes that you are an employee about to meet with a supervisor in a corrective interview, it's in your best interests to adopt a "wait and see" attitude. Since you haven't already been fired, you can assume that the problem is one that the supervisor feels can be solved. If you know what the problem is, spend little or no time planning a defense; think instead about what you can do to solve the difficulty. You will expect the supervisor to be honest and objective; the supervisor will expect the same of you. Of one thing you can be certain: wailing, weeping, or gnashing of teeth will avail you nothing. In fact, neither of you can afford to be emotional, but you have more to lose in an argument than the supervisor. The best approach for both of you is a calm examination of the facts and an equally calm discussion of what can be done about them.

The supervisor should keep the conversation centered on the job and how it is affected by the broken rule or by some other offense. In other words, *this is not the way to begin* one of these interviews: "When are you going to get some sense into your head?" Neither should there be any suspicious cross-examining. As suggested above, the atmosphere should be one of "let's find out what actually happened; then, maybe we can find some solution to the problem." (Humor is generally out of place because it may give the employee the idea that the supervisor is just going through the motions so that he can report doing something about the situation. Likewise, humor may minimize the importance of a serious situation.) The interview should close with (1) the supervisor's summary of the facts and (2) the supervisor's summary of the solution or solutions decided upon. Finally, if the supervisor has had any real regard for the feelings of the employee, the interview can and should end on a cooperative note.

As we move through this discussion of the types of interviewing, you will find it profitable to review earlier chapters and note how the materials presented can be applied to real occupational settings. Take, for example, what has been said earlier and in this chapter about the listener's "needs and desires." As a result of that emphasis, if the supervisor creates a highly threatening situation for the corrective interview, we know that the employee will react to the threat to security. It is impossible to predict precisely how the employee will respond, but we are able to anticipate possible reactions. We know that one response to a threat to security is *fear*, fear that one may lose a job. We know that distress and nervousness may accompany fear, so we are able to determine that a highly threatening interview may result in a frightened employee who may eventually be very embarrassed by his or her behavior, and who may in the long run become very bitter.

On the other hand, we are also aware that sometimes the response to a threat to our security is *anger*, and we know that angry people often do things that they later regret. If the situation is so threatening that the employee quits and walks out, little has been accomplished. Even worse, the angered employee may react to the corrective interview with strained silence and even destructive behavior. Peter Drucker, noted management consultant, cautions that a dictatorial supervisor may create an employee capable of sabotage. He speaks of this employee as a "loser" and warns that " . . . losers always learn one thing, and [they learn] that to perfection: resistance against being driven. They may not be able to achieve, but they know how to sabotage."[6]

Here, too, we see the need for the good listening habits described in earlier chapters. Is the supervisor really listening or has the pressure of the situation led that supervisor to forget the possibility of conflicting perceptions or equally distracting pressures on the employee? Has the employee made an effort to *feel* with the supervisor and to understand that the corrective interview is not a personal attack but a response to specific job behaviors?

---

6. Peter F. Drucker, *Management: Tasks, Responsibilities, Practices* (New York: Harper & Row, 1974), p. 240.

And what about nonverbal elements of the situation? Has the supervisor worked to remove contradictory nonverbal elements? Is the setting of the interview conducive to success? It is, for example, difficult to carry on an effective corrective interview in a public setting. The supervisor who corrects a worker loudly in front of the worker's peers may solve the immediate problem, but the long-term relationship with the individual worker is almost inevitably weakened.

Try this

Join another member of the class and create a model interview in which you respond to one of the following situations. (A model of a corrective on-the-carpet problem follows the listing.)

On-the-carpet situations

1. An employee is regularly taking half-hour coffee breaks. The maximum time permitted is 20 minutes in the morning and again in the afternoon.
2. A police officer is reported for being out of proper uniform while on duty.
3. A restaurant waitress is accused of pocketing tips left on tables served by another waitress.
4. A supermarket carry-out boy takes more time than seems necessary every time he goes out the door with a customer.
5. The area around a particular machinist's lathe is always littered with razor-sharp shavings. He considers himself indispensable and ignores requests to sweep regularly.
6. In spite of repeated requests that a traffic sign painter check spelling of signs *before* he makes them, he continues to turn out misspelled signs.
7. The driver of a fire truck has twice been warned to stop the practice of driving at high speeds when *returning* from a fire. Last night, on a return run, his truck was involved in a crossing acident. Witnesses say the truck was moving at high speed.
8. Apparently through the carelessness of a farm worker, a valuable horse gets out of his stall and into a feed storage area. He eats himself to death.
9. A 65-foot oceanography-studies boat puts out to sea and soon finds it necessary to turn back because of a lack of fuel. A worker had failed to have the vessel refueled as directed.

10. A plane owner complains to a fixed base operator that the wing tip of his plane has a big dent, obviously the result of a worker's carelessness in shifting planes around the hanger.

11. The pranks of a practical joker are getting on the nerves of other people in the department, particularly the women. Latest episode involved placing a small grass snake in the center drawer of a secretary's desk.

Model of a corrective-on-the-carpet problem

Description. The supervisor of a flight-training program for a major university is faced with the need to call in one of the pilot instructors. A student pilot, Jim Bascom by name, has come forward with a complaint about the way he's treated by Joe D., his pilot instructor.

Instructions to the Supervisor. Each of your pilot instructors works with six students by flying with each one for an hour per day five days a week. Halfway through the current semester, one of the students complains to you that Joe swore at him and used generally abusive language when he (Jim) failed to follow instructions exactly during a recent night flight in the training area. Good pilot instructors are hard to find, and you've never had any complaints about Joe in the past. Nevertheless, if this incident actually took place in the way described by Jim, something must be done about it. Abuse of a student cannot be overlooked or permitted to happen again. You've asked Joe to come in to discuss "a problem in connection with one of his students."

Instructions to the Employee. You like your job, but this six hours per day with six different students is occasionally boring and sometimes downright dangerous. Jim Bascom is the final straw; he really isn't pilot material. No matter how much explaining you do on the ground, he gets up in the air and forgets *everything*. You really let him have it one night recently. He couldn't do anything right. You had to keep yelling at him to watch his airspeed, watch his altitude, watch his heading, watch this and watch that. He'd no sooner get one thing under control than everything else would fall apart. You finally lost your temper and "cussed him out." Now the supervisor wants to see you, and you know it has to be about Bascom.

What to Look for in an On-the-Carpet Interview

1. Does the interview get off to an objective and matter-of-fact start? Is the employee "cool and collected"? Is the supervisor calm and objective?

2. How smoothly does the supervisor move into a discussion of the problem? Does the supervisor give the employee any chance at all to bring up the subject?

3. In discussing the problem, does each participant make an effort to see the problem from the point of view of the other? Does the employee try to understand the supervisor's position? Or does the employee immediately conclude that the supervisor is being unfair. Does the supervisor make a real effort to get at the facts *as the employee sees them*?

4. Does the employee admit making a mistake? And possibly promise that the situation will not happen again? Does the supervisor keep attention centered on "the mistake" rather than on "blame" for it? And if a penalty of any kind is decided upon by the supervisor, does it seem fair in relation to the offense?

5. Is the interview brought to a satisfactory close? Does the employee now know *exactly* what behavior is expected in the future? Is the employee encouraged to ask questions about his or her understanding of what that behavior should be? Does the employee seem to accept the idea that there must be a change? Do supervisor and employee part on reasonably good terms?

Handling a Corrective-Probing Problem

The "on-the-carpet" problem above ordinarily involves a clear-cut infraction or series of infractions of work rules or accepted ethical standards. Other problems are not so easily pinned down. The supervisor may see that the work of an individual is not going well, but the reasons *why* may be harder to come by, especially since the employee may not know what is wrong. (In fact, the employee may not even be aware that there is a problem.) The supervisor therefore finds it necessary to probe for the problem by using questioning and other relevant interviewing techniques.

In this situation, it may be helpful for the supervisor to try to work out the answers to these "goal questions" in advance.

1. *How secure does this employee feel in the job*? How does the employee feel about me? About the company?

2. If the employee *accepted by the other* workers? How well do they get along?

3. *Does the job carry with it any sense of accomplishment*? Does the employee take any real interest in the quality of work?

4. Does the employee see the job as having a future? As a dead end? What job-related frustrations exist? What gets the employee down?

5. *Any problems off the job?* Any family difficulties? Any off-the-job static about the line of work? About working for this company? What are the employee's worries? What is the state of his or her health?

No matter what system the supervisor uses, the supervisor should make a discreet but conscientious effort to locate the source or sources of the employee's difficulties. As for the interview itself, the supervisor's approach should be sympathetic and objective at the same time. After opening pleasantries, these primary questions often serve as bases for associated clusters of questions and comments.

1. "How do you feel things are going on the job?" (The employee may indicate that things are going "pretty well," but tactful pursuit of the subject usually leads to the admission that there is a problem or two.)
2. "In other words, you feel that there is a problem in that . . . ?" (The problem or problems are examined in some detail, so that both participants are in general agreement on scope, gravity, etc.)
3. "Does this situation we've been talking about create any difficulties for you?" Or "Can you put your finger on any of the causes of this situation?" (As diplomatically as possible, the supervisor must be narrowing responsibility for the work deficiency to the employee.)
4. "What do you think we can do to solve this problem?" (Mutual exploration of one or more possible solutions.)
5. "What plan do you think we ought to try?" (Choice of and agreement on a specific course of action.)

What the supervisor knows about the employee and about the general situation should help in the phrasing of additional questions. Nothing will be accomplished, or course, by a comment such as, "How do you expect me to put up with the sloppy work you've been doing?" Nor will the employee have a chance to offer candid answers if asked leading questions which suggest a proper answer—for example, "Don't you agree that . . . ?" or "Aren't you in favor of . . . ?" or "Isn't it true that . . . ?" The supervisor must remember to concentrate on helping the employee to express himself or herself freely and without restraint.

Setting up an atmosphere in which the employee really feels free to talk is an accomplishment. However, moving toward the goal of the interview—that is, to develop a solution to the problem or at least a better understanding of it—can often be achieved only with the aid of the probing and prodding techniques we described in informational interviewing. Here again we see the relationship among the general types of interviewing as well as application of the basic communication principles outlined in the initial chapters. Probes or prods are questions, comments, encouraging grunts, smiles, and any other sounds or signs, verbal or nonverbal, that encourage the employee to talk, help follow up on incomplete or superficial answers, and keep the interview on track. Some common types of probes (or prods):

1. *Probing for additional information*

   In this sense, probing means using "searching" statements or questions to give the person interviewed a chance to provide more information. For example: "Tell me more about that." "You mean that . . . ?" "You're saying that . . . ?" "Do you have anything to add on that point?" "Are there any other reasons for . . . ?" "And you felt that . . . ?" "Then what happened?"

   The simple repetition or echoing of something just said often helps to keep someone talking. This short excerpt from a conversation is an example of the use of echo.

   "I'm not satisfied with this company."
   "How is that?"
   "Well, before I came here, I heard a lot of good things about it."
   [Echo] "*Before* you came here."
   "Yeah . . ."

2. *Probing for additional explanation*

   If the person being interviewed stops short of providing a full explanation where the interviewer feels one is needed, questions can be used to encourage further elaboration. For example: "I don't quite understand what you mean." "Could you give me an example?" "Why did this incident worry you?" "Would you explain that a little further?"

3. *Probing to keep the interview "on track"*

   An interview is arranged with a definite purpose (or purposes) in the mind of one or both of those taking part in it. That purpose is the destination at the end of the "track," and straying too far from it is time-wasting and frustrating. Both people in an interview have a stake in sticking to the subject, and both should assume some responsibility for doing so. Of course, the questioner is in a better position to act as guide through questions and comments like these: "What you say is interesting, but let me ask you this question." "What I was really driving at was this." "Let's go back for a minute to this subject." "Let me ask the question this way." "Are you satisfied that we have the problem pretty well nailed down?" "What do you feel we should do about this situation?"

   Standard summaries and transitions are very useful for making steady progress in an interview: "You've given me a good picture of the problems you're having on this job. Do you have any ideas for solving them?" "In other words, you like some things about working for us, and you have a strong dislike for some other things." "From what you're telling me, I get the idea that you'd really like to stay on here, but you want to be reassigned to a job with more variety. Is that right?" "We've talked about the problem for quite a while. Let's try to find out *why* you're getting hurt so often. Do you have any ideas on that?"

It is possible, of course, to subdivide probes into any number of classifications. However, if you succeed in using them to extract additional information and explanation from an interviewee, and if you are able to keep him or her on track, your probes will help you bring a corrective interview to a satisfactory conclusion. And no matter how skillful the probe, the person interviewed will sometimes dodge a particular question or seem unwilling to answer it. When that happens, it is usually best to move on to another area with other questions. Later on in the interview, possibly when the interviewee is more at ease, the original question can be brought up again with better results.

The interview should be set for a time and place where both persons will be free of interruption from other individuals, from telephone calls, and from routine duties. It is also important that it be arranged in a way that is neither embarrassing nor threatening to the employee. An employee should be given advance notice of the meeting and of the purpose for it, so that there will be time for the employee to think about a response. The employee needs that time to review questions like these:

> If I'm not doing well in some respect, what is my specific shortcoming? What is the cause or causes? Is the situation something I can control, or is it something outside my control? What do I do especially well? Is the supervisor aware of what I'm doing well? Am I "running scared" in fear that I can't hold this job? Does the job give me any personal satisfaction? Does it bore me? Do I have the feeling that there's no future in it? What can I do to improve my work? Or my relations with the others in this department? Should I ask for a different assignment? Or a transfer? Is there something the supervisor can do to help solve the problem? Something the company can do? Has the company met its commitments to me? What specific suggestions should I be prepared to make?

Try this

Select one of the following Corrective-Probing situations and join with someone in the class to act it out. (Again, you will find a model following the listing. This should help you structure your effort.)

Corrective-probing situations

1. Employee *A* complains to the supervisor that "Employee *B* doesn't seem to want to cooperate." The supervisor has begun to suspect that *A* may be trying to dominate *B*, a relatively new employee. The supervisor has

also noticed that the work of *A* is not up to past standards and that *B* doesn't seem to be performing at the level expected. Conflict between the two may very well be affecting their performance. The supervisor decides to talk with *B* in an effort to solve the problem.

2. The supervisor talks with *A* in an effort to solve the problem.
3. A male employee has been doing work of an exceptionally high caliber, when suddenly he goes into a slump affecting his own work and that of others in his production group. He seems to have lost interest in the job. As far as the supervisor knows, the employee is happily married and in good health. The supervisor arranges an interview to try to find out what is wrong and, if possible, to correct it.
4. For some reason, a new employee doesn't seem to be able to bring herself to ask questions of her co-workers or of the supervisor when she is in doubt about how to do something. As a result, she makes costly mistakes. The supervisor decides to try to overcome this reluctance to solve such problems before doing the wrong thing.
5. A fun-loving outgoing employee seems to have lost his zip; in fact, the supervisor notes that he no longer does much talking with co-workers. Instead, he seems to look at the work on his machine without actually seeing it. Some jobs have been ruined while he was standing there "in a daze."
6. An employee is taking more and more time from his job in going to the medical dispensary. He keeps complaining of "stomach trouble," but neither the nurse nor the company doctor can find anything wrong with him. Meanwhile, his work suffers.
7. The supervisor makes a short-cut suggestion to a certain "oldtimer" and is angrily shunted aside with "Don't try to tell me how to do my job!" This veteran's attitude against any changes in her work methods is holding back production of an entire group.

Model of a Corrective-Probing Interview

Description. An employee handling a particularly demanding clerical job disappears from the office once or twice a day over periods as long as a half-hour. The newly appointed supervisor has just discovered that the employee spends the time discussing her work problems with her old supervisor, now holding a higher-level job in another department.

Instructions to the Supervisor. You're new on the job and anxious to make good. The department staff of 10 people seems to be operating efficiently, with the exception of one secretary. She is very efficient when she's on the job, but unfortunately, she "takes off" for a half-hour at a time, and you've discovered that she's taking problems she runs into to her old boss. That boss called you this morning to kid you about the situation. You decide that you have to solve this problem without delay.

Instructions to the Employee. You've been on this secretarial job for the past ten years. You know practically everything there is to know about it, but knotty problems do occur—after all, standard letters don't cover everything. A young supervisor has recently been appointed to succeed the person you had worked for ever since you joined the company. Your former supervisor was always kind and considerate; you felt comfortable with him (or her) and free to ask any number of questions about any special problem. The new supervisor is nice enough, but depends on you to "take care of it," no matter what comes up. You don't like to admit that there is any part of the office routine that you can't handle, so you've fallen into the habit of taking up difficulties with the old supervisor. That person doesn't seem to mind, and your present supervisor hasn't said anything, although he (or she) has asked you to come in on Friday to discuss "possible improvements in office procedures."

What to Look for in a Corrective-Probing Interview

1. Does the supervisor seem to know how to handle the interpersonal problems of the interviewing process? Does the supervisor show any understanding of the varying degrees of an employee's desires for security, acceptance, recognition, and personal growth? And an understanding of the employee's frustrations? Does the supervisor seem to focus on the employee and the employee's problems?

2. Is the atmosphere of the interview one of *constructive interaction?* Does the employee feel free enough and stimulated enough to ask questions like "How about trying something like this?" Or make suggestions like "Let's try this"? Does the supervisor give the employee the chance to recognize *and* state his or her own problem? And to suggest possible solutions? Does the supervisor really listen? Is the general approach nondirective? Or is it primarily "You'll have to shape up—or else"? Does the supervisor know how to use the probing technique to dig out information, get adequate explanations, and keep the interview moving on track? Is the interview brought to a sensible close?

THE PERFORMANCE-APPRAISAL INTERVIEW

To be sure that all employees do get "some attention and encouragement," many companies and other organizations schedule appraisal-of-performance interviews at regular intervals. For example, it is not uncommon for a supervisor to set up this kind of interview one month after a new employee begins work and every six months thereafter. Whether or not company or organization policy calls for these scheduled interviews, any supervisor may use this approach as a means of forestalling trouble and maintaining good contact with *all* employees.

The performance-appraisal interview may be defined as one in which the employee gets an evaluation of his or her work from an employing officer, usually the immediate supervisor. If the interview is scheduled at regular intervals, the employee knows that the interview is coming at a specific time and, as often as not, looks forward to it as an opportunity. Some companies provide evaluation forms designed along the lines of the one below. Prepared in part or in full before the interview takes place, the form makes a convenient base for a point-by-point discussion between the supervisor and the employee.

This type of interview is very much like the information-giving interview described in the next chapter. The performance-appraisal interview is presented here only to call your attention to its existence and to suggest at least one form for the handling of it.

EMPLOYEE EVALUATION FORM

________________________ Continuously employed since ______________
(Employee's name) (Date)

Evaluation for the work period from ______________ to ______________
(Date) (Date)

Relations with others	**Attitude—Application to work**
Exceptionally well accepted	Outstanding in enthusiasm
Works well with others	Very interested and industrious
Has some difficulty working with others	Average in diligence and interest
	Somewhat indifferent
Works very poorly with others	Definitely not interested
Judgment	**Dependability**
Exceptionally mature	Completely dependable
Above average in making decisions	Above average in dependability
Usually makes the right decision	Usually dependable
Often uses poor judgment	Sometimes neglectful or careless
Consistently uses poor judgment	Unreliable

Form adapted from *Cooperative Education* (Washington: American Association of Junior Colleges, 1971), p. 19.

Ability to learn	**Quality of work**
Learns very quickly	Excellent
Learns readily	Very good
Average in learning	Average
Rather slow to learn	Below average
Very slow to learn	Very poor

Punctuality:

Regular Irregular Days absent during period of this report ______

Overall performance:

Outstanding Very good Average Marginal Unsatisfactory

What traits may help or hinder the employee's advancement?

Additional remarks (over, if necessary):

This report has been discussed with employee? Yes No

Rated by: ______________________________

(Immediate supervisor) (Title)

______________________________ Date ______________

(Department)

THE COUNSELING INTERVIEW[7]

Certainly, you will not be thrown into a situation where you will engage in formal counseling interviews until you have gained considerable expertise and experience. Despite this, many people who are not professional counselors often find themselves cast into counseling roles. Many of the occupations that we have mentioned in this text present situations in which an individual may be called upon to give critical advice. Law enforcement officers "counsel." Teachers "counsel." Nurses "counsel." The following counseling interview should give you some insights into the kind of effective approaches that Rogers identified in general terms.

7. The primary source for the development of this section, as well as much of the contemporary counseling technique that is employed today, was Carl R. Rogers, *Counseling and Psychotherapy* (Boston: Houghton Mifflin, 1942), pp. 27–47.

A counseling interview is one in which the counselor tries to help an individual help himself or herself to achieve a constructive change of attitude. Throughout the interview, the primary emphasis is *on the individual as a person* rather than on his or her problem or problems, *on feeling* rather than on reason, on *the immediate present* rather than on past history, and *on the interview itself* "as an opportunity for personal growth." Such an interview is often called therapeutic, from the Greek word for "serving to cure or make well." Therapeutic is an appropriate word in that workers and clinicians in the field of mental health depend on counseling as a primary technique. In other areas, the assumption is that the person or "client" being counseled is not quite well in the sense that he or she is unable to face a particular situation without some expert help. Rogers states his approach this way: "Effective counseling consists of a definitely structured [but] permissive relationship which allows the client to gain an understanding of himself to a degree which enables him to take positive steps in the light of his new orientation."[8] In other words, the help offered is *not* help to solve a problem; the counselor tries to help the client reach a position of self-reliance from which *he or she will feel competent to handle his or her own problem.*

Earlier in the chapter, especially in the section on the corrective-probing interview, some techniques generally acceptable as therapeutic have already been presented. However, this is a good time—before going into step-by-step procedures in counseling—to highlight additional counseling or therapeutic techniques by contrasting them with some which should be avoided.[9]

Desirable Techniques	*Examples*
1. Providing broad openings	Where would you like to begin? Perhaps by talking together, we can find out how you feel about this subject. Is there anything in particular you'd like to talk about?
2. Offering encouragement	(Nodding) Yes, I follow you. Would you care to say any more about that? What kind of work exactly? Could you describe it more fully?

8. Rogers, p. 18.

9. Both lists appear with detailed explanations in Joyce S. Hays and Kenneth H. Larson, *Interacting with Patients* (New York: Macmillian, 1963), pp. 7–38. They appear here in adapted, condensed, and edited form, and are used by permission of the publisher.

Desirable Techniques	*Examples*
3. Seeking clarification	I'm not sure that I follow. Tell me whether my understanding agrees with yours. Are you using this word to convey the idea that . . . ? What would you say is the main point of what you said?
4. Suggesting comparison	Was this something like . . . ? Have you had any other experiences like that? Was this the first time such a thing ever happened to you?
5. Placing events in sequence	What seemed to lead up to . . . ? Was this before or after . . . ? When did this happen?
6. Reflecting and echoing	Client: My brother spends all my money and then has the nerve to ask for more. Counselor: This causes you to feel angry. Client: I can't sleep. I lie awake all night. Counselor: You have trouble sleeping. Client: What do you think I should do? Counselor: What do *you* think you should do? Client: It's a waste of time to talk to you. Counselor: Is it your feeling that no one understands?
7. Expressing doubt	Isn't that a little unusual? That really happened? That's somewhat hard to believe.
8. Waiting silently	(If you wait expectantly from time to time, the "client" will sometimes take the initiative and begin talking again.)

Desirable Techniques	*Examples*
9. Discussing possible plans of action	What could you do to solve this problem? Next time this comes up, what might you do to handle it?
10. Summarizing	Have I got this straight? You've said that . . . . During the past hour, you and I have discussed . . . .

Undesirable Techniques	*Examples*
1. Approving or disapproving	That's good. I'm glad that you . . . . That's bad. I'd rather you wouldn't . . . . I don't want to hear about . . . . Let's not discuss that.
2. Agreeing or disagreeing	That's entirely right. I agree with you. You're wrong on that. I don't believe it. I definitely disagree.
3. Belittling or contradicting	Client: I have nothing to live for. Counselor: Everybody feels that way sometimes. Client: I'm a nobody. Counselor: That's not true. Everybody is somebody.
4. Defending and reassuring	No one here would lie to you. We have your best interests at heart. I wouldn't worry about that. Everything will be all right. Keep your chin up. It's for your own good.
5. Prying and challenging	Now tell me about your relations with your father. Prove that. Tell me your life history and try not to leave anything out.

Undesirable Techniques	*Examples*
6. Demanding an explanation	Why do you think that? Why do you feel that way? Why did you do it?
7. Putting words in client's mouth	What you really mean is . . . . What you're saying is . . . .
8. Advising a course of action	How about doing this? I think you should . . . . Why don't you . . . ?

Steps in counseling[10]

1. Client comes to counselor for help.
2. Counselor defines the helping situation.
3. Counselor recognizes, accepts, and clarifies client's negative feelings.
4. Counselor recognizes, accepts, and clarifies client's positive feelings.
5. Client achieves some insight and self-understanding.
6. Counselor helps clarify possible courses of action.
7. Client initiates positive action.

As Rogers points out,[11] the steps above occur only in that approximate order with no sharply defined beginnings and endings. The counseling or therapeutic interview is, for the client[12] or person interviewed, an experience in personal growth which for different people follows a variety of patterns. All that can be said is that, at some time in the course of one or more counseling sessions, all of the steps above are likely to take place in a professionally guided interview.

In the discussion of the steps below, the illustrative examples are taken from counseling interviews taped by a counselor in his work with a number of inmates in a correctional institution in the Midwest. An understanding of the following terms will be helpful in reading the interview segments.

10. Condensed and rephrased from Rogers, *Counseling,* pp. 31–45. Rogers presents 12 steps.

11. Ibid., p. 30.

12. In counseling interviews, the word *client* simply means the person being counseled; sometimes a fee is involved, but more often it is not, since most counselors are members of agencies providing free counseling services.

a. A prison or reformatory *hole* is ordinarily a maximum security area in a location away from the large block housing units. It provides isolated private cell confinement for a number of reasons, depending on the penology philosophy in a given institution. In the institution with which we are here concerned, an inmate going through the pains of drug withdrawal could request this type of confinement; it was not a punitive measure.

b. A prison or reformatory *Classification Team* normally deals with a quota of inmates and the social workers or caseworkers assigned to them. The Team often consists of a member of the administrative staff who acts as chairman, a correctional lieutenant from the custody department, a correctional counselor, someone from the occupational training division of the institution, and a corrections agent working with parolees outside the institution. The Team makes decisions ranging from the transfer of an inmate from one cell house to another to making a recommendation to a parole board about the timing of the inmate's release. In an institution of any size, there are a number of such Teams, each handling its own specific case load.

1. *Client comes to counselor for help.* In the beginning, at least, the client in a counseling or therapeutic session may be hostile or suspicious. He or she wants help but often has no confidence that any will be forthcoming. It is also characteristic of many a person who comes to a counselor to pass off responsibility for his or her appearance to somebody else. "One of my instructors told me to come to see you." "Coming to see you was the only way I could get my family off my back." "No, it wasn't my idea; if I had my way, I wouldn't be here." When a client takes a position like one of the foregoing, one of the counselor's first tasks is to talk around the subject long enough to bring the client to the conclusion that, whatever pressure the client may be under to put in an appearance, the actual decision to do so was his or her own. The client should come to feel that this is really a decision made on his or her own—and, fundamentally, it is (unless the client was dragged in by the collar, in which case counseling is unlikely to be of any help).

Example—In the segment below as well as in the others in this section, C stands for Counselor, I for Inmate.

C: You wanted to see me about something?

I: Yeah, that's right.

C: Okay, fine. I have some ideas about what it might be.

I: Well—you came in last week and said you'd like to see me five days a week, and just three weeks before that, I told you to give up. I didn't know whether to tell you that again—I had mixed feelings, I don't know. It was something I wasn't expecting. Then, you talked about me rotting up there in the hole, and how it slowly creeps up on you and then pretty soon it hits you, and by then it's too late.

C: What were you confused about?

I: Well, I was confused about—well, I thought that you just wanted me to turn you down again, so you could say, "Well, look, he don't want no help."

C: At that point you decided what?

I: I was mixed up. I didn't know. I had to have time to think.

C: So you were considering both the possibility that my offer of counseling was genuine or not genuine?

I: Yeah. Yeah, that's right.

C: Now, back up to the hole. You said something about our conversation up there. I had told you something to the effect that you could just sit up there and just rot away, hide out, isolate, and on and on.

I: Yeah. Right.

C: And I said that that was kind of a stupid thing for you to do. And you started to run right over me.

I: Yeah. I wasn't even hardly aware there was anybody else in the room. I was trying to figure out where you were coming from. I didn't know. [Pause] I always had this thing about my Classification Team and I felt that—it was the Civil War and you were the South and I was the North. And I had to keep fighting. I could fight you. It was a burden. It just seemed like an endless battle.

C: Here I am a substitute on the Team, and I'm jumping all over you, huh?

I: Yeah. Right.

C: So now you're up there, and you're mulling this over and the next thing that I do is that I route you back into regular cell block population, and you get so angry that you won't talk to me.

I: Yeah.

C: I guess that's where we're at now.

I: Yeah, I woke up last night—I woke up and I started having these muscle spasm attacks from taking drugs the psychiatrist put me on. And it wasn't pleasant. And I've been—I've been on a lot of trips, man, but this one's a lulu. But after I came out of it, my head felt like a—like it was ready to burst, y'know? So like today, this morning I came out and gradually I've been coming down and I'm feeling better. But I was getting to the point where it was either pop again or just come all the way down and see how things would come out.

C: Like how?

I: I just felt like I had a big pressure on me, y'know, just couldn't sleep. Just complete pressure pushing on my head. It was either get out and try to mull things out or live up there.

C: And you decided to—?

I: Well, just talk to somebody, maybe, instead of sitting there and cursing everybody.

C: You're doing this all by yourself, huh?

I: Yeah. I don't have anything to lose.

C: You did a whole lot of considering.

I: Yeah. I had to, y'know?

C: *You* decided it would be a good idea to take me up on my offer.

I: Yeah, because it was getting too much on me. Mentally—and physically, too. It was—I was just wearing down. I just couldn't take it.

---

2. *Counselor defines the helping situation.* Early in any counseling or therapeutic session, the counselor sees to it that the client understands that the counselor does not have all the answers and that the counseling situation is intended only to provide a sympathetic and supportive atmosphere in which the client can talk freely about his or her problems and, possibly, come to some decisions about them. The situation is described in terms like these: "*We* will try to think things through." The counselor makes it clear that he or she will provide the place and the atmosphere, but that the responsibility for coming or not coming to a session is entirely that of the client. The client shows or doesn't show, and if it's the latter, nobody is going to track him or her down.

Example

C: Okay, Steve. The last time we talked you got hung up on the business of how to get started.

I: Yeah—but like I say, man, for me it's really hard, because I think one of my biggest problems is how to confide in somebody, how to go about—I just don't know, y'know, where to start—how to begin.

C: Well, how does this strike you? I think your statement about "I don't know how to begin" is really a statement saying that "I'm not really willing to begin."

I: I think that's a part of it, y'know. Not being able to open myself up to somebody is, I think, is—I want to a certain extent but the other side of me says, "Don't do it."

C: Well, let's do it. Put it upon my head.

[Pause]

I: Okay, how's it work?

C: Well, we both try to zero in on your problems, and I help you dream up some ways to solve them—but, in the end, the choices are all yours with no advice from me. All I do is help you look at and examine all the possibilities—from every angle.

I: Fair enough. I'm still willing to give it a go—if you are.

C: Well, let's do it—but be careful not to expect too much.

I: What's that supposed to mean?

C: Only that you *and* I will try to work out your problems *together*. Some of you guys come in with the idea that you tell us your problem and we give you the answer. It doesn't work that way.

---

3. *Counselor recognizes, accepts, and clarifies client's negative feelings.* A client's problems frequently stem from a list of gripes which he or she has never fully understood and never successfully "vented" to someone *willing to listen actively.* It is crucial to success in counseling that the counselor do everything possible to encourage the client to express his or her feelings about his or her problems and the people in them; whether the client's criticism is directed against others or against himself or herself, nothing should be said or done to block or hinder critical expression in any way. Echoing and reflecting the client's views can be especially effective here: "You feel pretty bitter about this." "You want to correct this fault, but still you don't want to." "You seem to feel pretty guilty about this."[13] At the same time that the client is freely expressing feelings, the counselor can lead the client toward self-recognition of his or her problems and some of the causes of them.

13. Quotations from Rogers, *Counseling,* p. 38.

Example

C: And that's the only problem [not wanting to go to work] you had with drinking "on the outside"?

I: No, sometimes, y'know, I'd get destructive.

C: Could you go into that a little bit?

I: I'd just, you know, man, I suppose I like to fight a lot.

C: You suppose?

I: I—I did like to fight a lot, man, you know—just get with a certain group of people and—uh—

C: And you were drinking?

I: Drinking wine. Yeah.

C: Okay, When you drank, you'd get into a fracas? Is this what you are telling me?

I: Yeah, I mean, right.

C: Okay. Did you—did you find, as you looked back, that you got into more fights when you were drinking than when you were not drinking?

I: Yeah, I'd say so.

C: You'd say do?

I: Yeah, I know I was.

C: You definitely did get into more fights?

I: Yeah.

C: Okay. Now we've learned two things about your drinking. One is that you were drinking until you weren't too efficient on the job the next day or you wouldn't go to work. Secondly, drinking would cause behavior changes in you. It would bring about a—convert you to being more aggressive. You'd begin to fight. [Long pause] Is that all there is to it now?

I: Yeah. You know me.

C: Well, either there is more to it or there isn't. [Pause] Your relationships with other people on your job—were they affected by your drinking?

I: Yeah.

C: How?

I: That I wasn't me, you know? I mean—[Pause] The behavior change was such a hunk to handle I—I'd get too cocky and stuff like that.

C: Cocky?

I: Yeah.

C: Can you use another word to—ah—tell us how it was?

I: Um—[Pause] What *you* call an abrasive attitude, I guess.

C: Did you find the abrasive attitude fun?

I: I used to live with my parents and—when I'd come home, I'd tell 'em off—but good.

C: If you came home and you were sober, how did you get along with your parents?

I: We could—unless I came in drunk.

C: If you came in drunk, there was a fight?

I: It just seemed like we were always—
[Pause]

C: You were always what?

I: They were always getting on me, y'know.

C: So you'd tell them to shove it.

I: I get short tempered—when I'm drunk.

C: Most of us do. But booze will sometimes do that with a temper.

I: To me.

C: Your anger got out a little quicker?

I: I'd do things—whether I was supposed to or not.

C: You were less inhibited.

I: That could be.

---

4. *Counselor recognizes, accepts, and clarifies client's positive feelings.* Assuming that the counselor has been successful in drawing out a client's expression of negative feelings about others and about himself or herself, avenues for the expression of some "positive impulses" begin to open. The counselor's position does not change; in exactly the same way that he or she avoids praising and moralizing when the client expresses negative ideas, the

counselor now does what he or she can to encourage the client to take the first tentative steps toward seeing "an opposite side (or sides) to the coin." In addition to the "bads" he or she has been describing, the client begins to see some "goods."

Example

(The inmate in this instance had spent a considerable amount of interviewing time railing at his young wife, her failures to come to see him, her lack of concern for their child, her going "out on the town" with other men, etc. The transcript segment below begins at a point when the inmate has said everything he could possibly think of against his wife and is now less sure about some of the criticisms he has voiced.)

C: If things are like you say when you get home, are you going after the divorce you've been talking about?

I: Maybe. I don't really want to. I'll talk to her about it and see if *she* wants to.

C: Are you going to talk mostly with her—or with your mother?

I: I'm going to consult with her—probably. [Pause] Mostly her.

C: What about your mother's position in relation to the baby? She's been taking care of it a lot, hasn't she?

I: Yeah, she loves the baby and she cares about the baby a lot.

C: She doesn't want to lose the baby. If you and Dorine got a divorce, and Dorine had custody of the baby, grandma would have no rights at all. You'd have visitation rights but grandma wouldn't.

I: Well, whenever I got him, she could see him.

C: What happens if the divorce papers stipulate that you could visit on Saturday afternoon and that's it?

I: I could still take him over to the house but I hope it won't come to that.

C: Would your mother be willing to settle for that?

I: I don't know. I don't know. It really isn't up to her anyway, y'know. It's up to Dorine and me. I've made some mistakes. She's made some mistakes. Maybe we can make a go of it next time.

C: You're going to talk with her at least and see what happens?

I: Right.

5. *Client achieves some insight and self-understanding.* As the interview proceeds through one or more sessions, the client sooner or later arrives at a better understanding of himself or herself and his or her motives. The client also begins to think about ways to reorganize his or her approach to problems and do a better job of making choices in the future. The counselor helps the client in this process of self-discovery and self-renewal.

Example

C: When you're in a bar, you feel those people are just like you?

I: Yeah. I *know* they're like me.

C: How do you know?

I: They're like me in the sense that they monkey around with burglary, armed robbery, forgery, and stuff like that. I'm comfortable with them so in a sense I guess I'd have to say they are my type of people. When I'm with a higher class of people—say like a businessman, salesman, or something like that—I just totally freeze, because I feel like—I can't describe it—I feel he considers me scrub or trash.

C: All right. So these people are like you because they behave like you.

I: Exactly.

C: Okay. So you go in there and you drink?

I: Right.

C: So this is your identity. This is who you are.

I: That's what I used for identity. It isn't what I *want* for identity. But it's what I used for my identity.

C: That's the way you saw yourself in the past.

I: Yeah. I guess that's the way I still see myself at this time.

C: As what?

I: I guess I see myself as a—scum. That's the best way to say it.

C: Well, what—what's your definition of scum?

I: I've heard constantly, y'know, this guy's been in prison or this guy's been locked up.

C: I'm concerned about how you define or describe yourself as scum, right now.

I: By the feeling that I have in being locked up because—I guess it's—well, we all know there's more good people than bad. By good, I mean they abide by the law. So whenever I get in with different people, I just see myself as a lower type of person, you know. I figure—

C: This is just *right now* though.

I: Right now—

C: How do you see yourself right now—this minute?

I: Right now, this minute, I consider myself more equal. That's because I know people surrounding me work and deal with people like myself—and I know that they can understand the people here—what makes them tick. The people on the outside—they don't know about that—

C: What's that have to do with it?

I: Well, when I'm on the street, the people that are surrounding me are mostly top-notch people, y'know, good citizens, that is to say. I find myself to be under them, a low type of person.

C: Why do you do that?

I: It's something that comes about automatically.

C: Or maybe it's just that you permit it?

I: I have to permit it. It's the truth.

C: Based on what?

I: Living standards of scum.

C: Has it got to do with how you identify yourself?

I: That's what I'm not sure. That's what I'm trying to understand. I'm not sure.

C: Well, I'm not sure you try to understand it.

I: Not too often I don't. I just accept it as it is. I classify it as vile, and accept it as it is.

C: Yeah.

I: At times I'd like to live, I guess, differently, but I never felt strong enough where I could say "Okay, you're not—scum." You're the same way—you're the person you were yesterday.

C: What's your first name?

I: Al.

C: Who are you, Al? [Pause] Or rather, who's Al?

I: Well, Al is Al. He makes his own way of living and makes his own decisions.

C: And what kind of decisions does Al make? And that describes his identity, huh?

[Pause]

I: Yeah, I guess you could say I'm a zero. And that's it. I mean, I never really get into it. I don't see myself as one special thing.

C: You're Al and that's one special guy. You're the only Al you got, and your identity is what you make it. What you live during the course of your day, that's who you are. Now who's Al?

I: I'd have to say that Al is as equal as the next guy in here, y'know.

C: You told us that. Five years, you've been sitting here and you haven't really taken a look at yourself.

I: I've taken lots of looks at myself. That's why I—

C: You glanced in the mirror and went away.

I: I guess that's essentially it. A few times I've tried to go beyond that, but I've always felt that—I think the reason is—

C: Just a little jerk hanging around that mirror, but you make tracks very fast.

I: I think the reason for that is because I didn't want to change—or I just didn't give a damn. Now, I'm starting to care.

---

6. *Counselor helps clarify possible courses of action.* The counselor helps the client identify, examine, and clarify courses of action available to him or her. However, the counselor neither gives advice nor advocates any particular action. If any decisions are made, they are made by the client.

Example

C: What do you say we have a look at some of the changes that you're going to make in your identity, that you feel are going to be good and positive, that will bring about more happiness and bring about enough change that you don't come back here or come back to any kind of a prison.

I: I'd like to say, number one, that a way of looking at it would be that I could force myself to settle down to something—I don't have to be constantly going here, and jumping in the car going there, or going to this building or this job. Set myself in a pattern where I can put in an eight-hour day, so to speak. Then, I could sit down, watch TV, and relax, have dinner and feel content that way. I don't want to feel I have to be constantly on the go, doing something.

C: Have to? Is that the way you felt about it in the past? That you had to be doing something?

I: Precisely. It's a habit that I got into where I—it got to be such a habit that I had to be going constantly.

C: But now you are going to take on some other things, huh? father? husband?

I: I'm not sure within myself that I'm ready for that responsibility—I've got to be sure, you know.

C: Okay. What I'm concerned about is are you going to *have* to do these things like you *had* to be a criminal and you *had* to be a big shot?

I: No. Not at all. I feel that I don't have to change, I feel that I *want* to change. It's what I *want* to do.

C: What seemed to lead up to the change?

I: Nothing I can point to. I've been doing a lot of thinking—and I feel that it's something I want to do. Just ease myself down from all the things that I've been trying to be, y'know. Decide I want me the way I should be.

C: So now what's—what's left?

I: Well, I can tell you right now that thinking about a new identity scares the hell out of me because it's new to me—it's something I've never done. But the way I live now, it scares me worse. Because I know that if I keep on going the way I am, it's only a matter of time till I put a hole through my head or get locked up for the rest of my life. And this is something that I just don't want.

C: Do you know what you just said?

I: I think I understand it. Yeah.

C: You said, "If I keep going the way I'm going, I'm going to end up with a bullet in my head," or something like that. But is this the way you are going right now?

I: Not right at this present time. No.

C: This is something for you to realize. Where are you going right now? Are you going toward the bullet in your head or are you going toward—these other things you talked about?

I: Right now, I'd like to think that I'm going toward the direction—toward the way I want things to be.

---

7. *Client initiates positive action.* The positive action initiated may be scarcely detectable, but it is nevertheless significant. The client may be hesitant to the point of denying that he or she is going to take any action whatever. However, this denial is evidence that the client is thinking about the action, and it is just possible that he or she will actually go ahead now or in the immediate future. With each choice made and with each action taken, the client's self-confidence increases, and the way is paved for further personal growth.

Example

C: Is this what you're saying to me—that you're going to start making your own decisions?

I: Right. I think I made a decision today. I think it was the right one, too. But that was just the beginning. I've got a long way to go. I know that now.

C: That's actually two decisions you told me about. One, you decided to quit the dry rot and start trying to do something for yourself. Second decision was, when you start to get uptight, you're going to talk it over with your caseworker. You've really accomplished something, huh?

I: I think I did. I really did.

C: And now you've found something out?

I: I believe I have.

C: What's that?

I: That life has got a lot more to it than being at the top or thinking you're the top man. Life has got—I'm starting to see life where I want it. Being able to come home from my eight-hour job, and walking into a house—I got a wife and kids there—and I don't have to be something I'm not.

C: Okay. So you're saying you're working right now at making a new identity? A new image for yourself?

I: That's exactly what it is.

C: Does that include your being a homemaker, breadwinner, husband, the father, the taxpayer—all that square stuff?

I: Well, I think I see a lot that's there as fantasy, too. I'm seeing it the way I would really *like* to have it. I'm not saying that's the way I will have it, but I see it the way I would like it.

C: Why fantasy?

I: Because at this stage I just think I can almost reach everything I want. But I'm going to have to get what I can, and settle for it, y'know. Not settle for it, but keep working.

C: Well, that's true of all of us. Right? But this doesn't make you different from the rest of us.

I: But this is something I had never really planned on. Like I used to see myself in only one way, one pattern, the pattern of my life. Now I'm starting to grow, and I see life a lot different, you know? I don't know why, unless it's a stage of maturity and I'm going into it or out of it, whatever. It's just like I completely changed my life-style.

C: You're saying that there's—

I: Let me put it this way. I'm trying to make something of my life now.

Let us remind you that the counseling interview is included not because we think that you will be functioning as a professional counselor, but rather because all of us look for advice and all of us are called upon to give it. If you examine carefully the sample interview and the steps the counselor employs, you will see that the steps are those a good listener and supportive friend might use. Don't play psychiatrist, but do be willing to help—it can be important.

SUMMARY

This chapter emphasizes the fact that the majority of one-to-one relationships in occupational settings contain the essential qualities of interviews. Because of this, one may bring the form and strategies of interviewing to those situations.

After a brief discussion of occupational interviews in general, the focus of the chapter shifted to five broad categories of such interviews: the training interview, the informational interview, two types of corrective interviews, the performance-appraisal interview, and the counseling interview.

Each of the first four categories was discussed under topics including general approach, typical interviewing situations, a model interview, and a set of what-to-look for questions to be used for evaluation of such interviews.

The counseling interview was examined in somewhat greater depth because of its additional complexity. In the case of the counseling interview, the following series of seven steps served as a base for discussion and examples.

1. Client comes to counselor for help.
2. Counselor defines the helping situation.
3. Counselor recognizes, accepts, and clarifies client's negative feelings.
4. Counselor recognizes, accepts, and clarifies client's positive feelings.
5. Client achieves some insight and self-understanding.
6. Counselor helps clarify possible courses of action.
7. Client initiates positive action.

9
Communicating with Others: Groups in an Occupational Setting

9

Communicating with Others: Groups in an Occupational Setting

"The primary goal is . . . relationships between people and groups or between a group and the organization . . . that [result in] more effective problem-solving and greater production effort. . . . "[1]

In Chapter 8, we focused on the one-to-one (two-person) relationships that you are encountering or will encounter in your occupational efforts. We indicated that once you are hired, appointed, or given a job, you become a member of an organization. It is not our intent in this chapter to reduce emphasis on one-to-one relationships, but rather to stress (1) that you are also going to be thrust into groups and (2) that effective functioning in these groups requires an awareness and abilities beyond those required in your interactions with just one individual.

Here's where we're going

A full awareness of the content of this chapter should enable you to:

1. Define the term *group* and demonstrate an understanding of the effect *groups* will have in your occupational efforts by selecting an occupation and showing how individuals in that occupation might function in groups.

1. Robert Blake and Jane S. Mouton, "A 9 , 9 Approach for Increasing Organizational Productivity," *Personal and Organizational Change through Group Methods: The Laboratory Approach.* Edgar H. Schein and Warren G. Bennis, eds., (New York: John Wiley and Sons, 1965), p. 170.

2. Explain why group behavior has become increasingly important in occupational settings.
3. Identify five factors that will work against efficient and effective group activity.
4. Identify five communication behaviors that you might employ to help create positive group action.
5. Prepare the agenda for an effective task group activity.
6. Apply to a group setting three different kinds of communication advice mentioned earlier in this text.
7. Define and explain the function of *norms, goals, roles* and *cohesion*.
8. Establish a set of five criteria for judging the effectiveness of groups.

WHAT IS A GROUP?

Some definitions include the two-person relationship as an example of *group*. We prefer not to because we want to emphasize that the entry of a third, fourth, and fifth person substantially changes the purpose and character of a relationship; therefore, we reserve the term *group* for clusters of three or more persons.

An enormous amount of research has been done on groups, and it appears that each researcher has had a compulsion to create a slightly different definition of the term *group*. We will not do that. Rather, we prefer to cite an existing definition which we feel is very workable in the occupational setting:

> *A group is a collection of individuals who have relations with one another that make them interdependent to some significant degree.*[2]

You will note that this definition could cover any kind of association you have with others of similar interests. For example, just as you engage in a significant amount of communication for social purposes, so do you belong to one or more formal or informal social groups. If you are an Elk or a Moose or a model-railroad enthusiast or a member of the McHenry County Historical Society, you have joined a collection of individuals whose pleasure is affected by or dependent on the other members of the organization.

Groups like those above are extremely important to people but, in this text, we are more concerned with those groups in which your relationships

---

2. Dorwin Cartwright and Alvin Zander (eds.), *Group Dynamics, Research and Theory* (New York: Thomas Y. Crowell, 1968), p. 46.

with the other members will directly contribute to or detract from your on-the-job success and satisfaction.[3] We want to emphasize that you are likely to become a part of an organization, and

> *. . . the fundamental building block of an organization is the team. Any given organizational team is composed of those who work together to discharge that part of the total organization's work for which they share responsibility.*[4]

Try this

In order to gain a clear sense of the impact that groups and teams have on your own life, take an inventory of your own activities. How many groups do you belong to?

1. List any social groups in which you participate.
2. List any "interest" groups to which you belong.
3. Explore your own work experiences, whether they are full-time or part-time. What kinds of work groups do you participate in or have you participated in?
4. For each of the groups that you have identified, write a one-sentence description of the purpose of the group.

If you are like most of us, your inventory has revealed that you participate in a number of groups and, in all likelihood, you have also discovered that you participate in one or more at-work groups even if your work is part-time. Most organizations employ at least some form of "groups," "teams," or "crews" in the work setting. The fast-food industry, for example, uses large numbers of part-time workers. Even here, where turnover is frequent, the "crew" concept is well established. Members of crews begin to identify with other crew members. They begin to assume a common responsibility for tasks and help and reinforce one another.

As each individual's task requires more and more knowledge and sophistication, it becomes more difficult for any one individual to be able single-handedly to take over the larger work task. As, for example, the management of hospitals becomes a more complex task, fewer and fewer hospitals are "run" by doctors. Instead, an administrator is hired. And the ideal administrator creates an environment in which those individuals possessing related types of

3. Some companies do employ socially-oriented groups (e.g., bowling teams) to promote occupational objectives. See "Manager's Memo," *Chicago Daily News* (June 21, 1977), p. 31.

4. Blake and Mouton, pp. 169–183.

expertise are able to group together and make significant contributions to the efficient and humane management of the hospital.

Barring an enormous change in our society, you will undoubtedly have the opportunity, obligation, and experience of functioning in a variety of groups in your work experience. Thus, a primary reason for examining "the group" is that it will have such a strong influence on your occupational behavior. It is probable that this influence will grow in the years to come. In fact, it seems likely that we are going to see significant changes in existing organizational formats in order to accommodate the growing effect of groups. A California management professor contends that society has reached a point where "managerial teams whose members' strong points complement rather than compete with each other"[5] must necessarily replace the concept of the individual manager.

If you acquire the tools that will allow you to examine your own communicative behavior in groups as well as that of others (analysis), and if you become familiar with some of the principles of group behavior that will allow you to determine what will happen in certain situations (prediction), then you will be able to govern your own behavior in groups and help direct the group's effort (control).[6] To put it another way (and as we learned in earlier chapters in this book), we should be trying to interpret the communication behavior of ourselves and others so that we may apply discoveries about such behavior to predict and control the outcomes of our communication efforts.

GROUPS IN OCCUPATIONAL SETTINGS

Our definition of "group" emphasizes the idea of *interdependence*. Each of the members of the group is somehow dependent upon the other members of the group if the individual member's needs are to be satisfied. We have already suggested that the needs we have in our work experiences go beyond those of simple subsistence. We need more than monetary satisfaction out of our work. We need more than economic security. In Chapter 8, we summarized the listener's needs and desires and placed them in four categories: *security, acceptance by the group, recognition of accomplishment* and *opportunity for personal growth*. Note that each of the last three categories requires the existence of and an opportunity to participate in some sort of group for satisfaction. It is easy to see why the President of General Motors cannot com-

5. "Outstanding Managers are Myths from Textbooks," UPI, *Elgin Daily Courier* (July 17, 1977), p. 6.

6. Clovis Shepherd, *Small Groups: Some Sociological Perspectives* (New York: Chandler, 1964), p. 101.

municate directly with each of the individual members of the assembly line in order to commend that member's accomplishments. At least a partial answer to this problem is the creation of social groups—already alluded to earlier in the chapter—in which members of the group are able to reinforce one another's accomplishments; in an organization's sponsoring of recreational groups, it is at least demonstrating some concern and respect for individuals.

A primary reason, then, that groups succeed in occupational settings is that they provide a way in which we as individual workers can satisfy our needs. This becomes particularly true as we are able to move from basic physical and economic requirements to the higher-level needs dependent upon groups for their satisfaction.

A second reason that groups work well is found in the increasing complexity of society. When the task of the individual worker is somewhat complex, only that worker is likely to have a complete understanding of the task. Only through bringing a number of such individuals together and allowing them to become a part of a group can we make ideal use of their separate capabilities. Consider, for example, the fact that violent crimes are no longer restricted to urban areas. The elected sheriff whose background is that of a pharmacist, or farmer, or garage owner, and whose training in criminal investigation is limited to brief seminars, is likely to find himself or herself face-to-face with a multiple murder or a serious bank robbery. Unless this individual is able to allow the other investigative individuals and bodies to contribute special expertise, the crime may remain unsolved. If, on the other hand, the other investigative persons are unwilling to become a part of a group, the same result may occur.

One last reason why groups succeed in occupational settings is that we exist in such a rapidly changing society that many of us have turned to our work to find necessary human relationships. Alvin Toffler suggests that the transient nature of our lives has created a new and booming industry which specializes in providing prepackaged group experiences.[7] Many more of us have been able to employ work groups for purposes of personal satisfaction.

Try this

1. Select a particular occupational category. Examine that occupation through reading, observation, or interview, and list the kinds of specialization that may occur. (The *Occupational Outlook Handbook* is an excellent source for discovery of areas of specialization.)

2. Devise a task or problem that might confront someone in the occupation and put together a group of five persons representing specialties that could be brought to bear collectively in solving the problem.

7. Alvin Toffler, *Future Shock* (New York: Bantam Books, 1970), p. 227.

THE WORKINGS OF A GROUP

We began this chapter with Cartwright and Zander's very broad definition of a *group* and then introduced Blake and Mouton's concept of *team*. In combination, these two definitions give us a pretty good sense of what an occupational group is. The "relations" that members have in the occupational setting are those relations which serve "to discharge" a part of an organization's work, and the "interdependence" is based in the fact that "they share responsibility." Since there is a common responsibility, there is generally some structure to the group—there is a reason for or purpose to its existence. These individuals are responsible for completing a particular task.

Perhaps the easiest way to examine how a group works is to explore your role in one. Let us assume that you have just been hired to work in a fast-food restaurant. The manager introduces you to Mary Jeffries, who is the crew chief, and to four other members of Mary's crew, all of whom have been employees of the restaurant for a year or more. You notice, almost immediately, a large amount of smiling and quiet, pleasant joking. Mary is pleasant, too, and a bit reserved, but you notice how quickly and pleasantly the other crew members carry out the work tasks that Mary assigns them. There is clear, though nonverbal, indication that the members of the crew like and respect one another. One of the qualities you are observing is *cohesion*. In this case, at least when you enter the group, there is a high level of sticking-togetherness. They work easily together; they speak well of one another; they defend one another against those outside the group; they see one another outside of work; they have nicknames and "in" jokes. This cohesion is an important factor in group success. Mary's crew should be, at least on the basis of your observation of it, a successful crew, because the degree of attachment that members have for the group is related to the level of success the group achieves.

On your first day on the job, you notice that the members of Mary's crew, unlike the other workers in the restaurant, wear their hats tipped to the right, and they all have "smiling face" pins on their collars. You also notice that Mary's crew members make a more-than-required effort to be very friendly to customers. You are observing a second aspect of group behavior—*norms* (standards of behavior). These norms reflect the positive kinds of behavior that Mary's group considers proper or ideal. It is quite possible for groups to adopt norms that are much less productive; for example, another of the work teams in the restaurant may move much less rapidly; not so slowly as to be reprimanded by the manager, but slowly enough so that one can see a difference between Mary's crew and the second crew, a difference in group norms.

Let us examine group behavior in a more sophisticated occupational context. This time our group consists of police Lieutenant Zimmerman and those police officers who serve under him on his shift. Even though you are new to this group, you know that, on many occasions, orders and instructions will be presented without having been considered by or developed by the group—police departments almost invariably maintain certain paramilitary chains of command. On the other hand, the effective lieutenant or chief recognizes that the individual officers possess unique skills and knowledge that, if effectively utilized, may make a very positive contribution to the success of the department.

So, Lieutenant Zimmerman calls the members of his command together and poses a task for them. In our hypothetical example, the task is built around current department frustration over the theft of citizen-band radios. Because the organization has assigned a leadership role to the lieutenant, it is likely that he will initially assume the *role* of leader. In this particular case, the lieutenant is hopeful that some other member of the group will assume the role of leader because he knows that group members tend to defer to a leader who has greater power than they do. As the group begins to talk, we notice other roles emerging. Officer Boling is the only female officer on the shift and twice she is asked to keep a record of the meeting. For women in predominantly male groups, the cultural tendency to assign them to the *role* of secretary is real and often frustrating. She resists that assignment and instead emerges as the questioner; as the discussion progresses, she is the critic or "devil's advocate." Officer Carter emerges as a strong resource person and assumes the role of citizen-band expert. The group functions well, and Lieutenant Zimmerman is soon able to relinquish the *role* of leader to Officer Smith who acts to keep the group on target, summarizes material, and tries to keep a balance in the discussion.

As the group moves along in its attack on the problem, it becomes clear that the members are excited about the challenge they face and that they have respect for one another as well as for the group activity. They share a positive *sentiment*, that is, a supportive and affirmative feeling toward what the group does. The group eventually arrives at a plan for action that enlists a network of citizen-band operators. They urge Lieutenant Zimmerman to implement the plan.

The *internal system* of the group, the way the members feel toward one another, has been positive and productive. The *external system*, the manner in which the group relates to its environment (in this case the department atmosphere and organization), is also positive and productive. This *external system* is the product of past experiences. If the group has engaged in similar prior activity and the results of the activity have been ignored by officers of higher status, it is unlikely that even the most sensitive of lieutenants will be able to stimulate this sort of productive group activity. When the external system is negative and unsupportive, the product of the group will generally reflect that negativism and may even lead to confrontation.[8]

8. The discussion of qualities of a group draws from Shepherd and the classic study by George Homans, *The Human Group* (New York: Harcourt, Brace and World, 1950).

Try this

In your earlier inventory effort, you identified groups in which you participate. Select one of those groups, perhaps the one that gives you greatest pleasure, and try to respond to the following items:

1. What factors combine to create *cohesion*? (This question assumes that the group selected—particularly if it is one that gives you pleasure—has a reasonably high level of cohesion. If the level of cohesion is not as high as you feel it ought to be, see if you can identify one or more of the barriers to cohesion.)
2. Can you identify three *norms* held by the group?
3. Become an observer for a brief period and see if you can describe four *roles* that group members assume. Do the roles shift? Are they positive roles in that they contribute to the group's progress?
4. What external agencies must the group relate to and how effective is the *external system*?

YOUR ROLE IN A GROUP

How do you put the preceding information to work? The answer to this question exists, in part at least, in Shepherd's discussion of *analysis*, *prediction*, and *control*. An awareness of the factors that exist in groups will allow you to *analyze* the groups you participate in, *predict* the consequences of certain behaviors, and exercise some *control* over those groups. We do need, however, to reemphasize certain things. First, it is wise for you to remember that group behavior and effectiveness do not depend on you alone. You may be well aware of how groups work, and that it is possible for one person to make a strong personal effort to help a particular group succeed and still see the group's effort result in frustration and failure. The mere fact that more than two people are involved multiplies the possibility of interpersonal problems. And it is perhaps even more important to underline again the fact that the environment must be supportive of group activity.

Even with these reservations, we believe that you can become a more effective member of that "fundamental building block of an organization," the team. These teams have the "basic elements of all groups . . . a power system, group standards, some degree of group unity . . . goals, and most important, relations within an environment containing . . . other groups—above, beside and below them."[9]

9. Blake and Mouton, p. 176.

Let's first reflect on some of the conclusions that you can draw from this chapter and other discussions of group behavior. You may reasonably conclude that effective groups need a period of time during which the group members come to know one another and develop respect for the contributions of the separate members. It is a mistake then to believe that several, relative strangers can be cast together, called a "group," and be expected to produce answers and solutions quickly. You know that there is value in preliminary small talk, in discovering who the members of the group are, what things they hold in common. You know that this is not necessarily wasted time and that, in fact, these moments may be the initial steps in building *cohesion*.

When you enter an established group, you know that the group will have adopted certain *norms*. As a new member of the group, you must observe, identify, and respond to these same *norms*. If you, or any new or old member of a group violate the norms, there will be problems. We have evidence that violation of norms—such as an effort that results in overproduction—can create problems in a group,[10] but we also know that established groups are able to tolerate and even support certain kinds of deviant behavior.[11] In short, if you enter a group and immediately violate or defy, perhaps unknowingly, established norms, there will be group tension. If, however, you become an accepted member of that group, the other members may tolerate some such behavior. Again, the advice is that it takes time to build effective groups and to become a productive member.

As you enter a new group or function in an existing one, you know that each of the members is going to assume certain *roles*. Leaders will emerge and other persons will remain relatively quiet and will function in resource roles and questioning roles. There may be competition for certain roles, and we know that status and power are factors that must be dealt with in group settings. You will remember that Lieutenant Zimmerman was accorded a certain status and level of power because of the organizational hierarchy of the police department. We know that persons of lower status tend to defer, at least initially, to persons of higher status. The members of Zimmerman's command, for example, know that he has access to power that can affect their jobs and so they will move very carefully. If the lieutenant is aware of this tendency, he can work to reduce its effect on the group's behavior. If you hold a status higher than that of others in the group, you need to be aware of the potential effect on its members. If you have a higher level of education, are obviously more wealthy, know certain people, are the owner's son, or simply look important, you may be accorded higher status and more power in the group. If you are insensitive to this, you may be unknowingly reducing the group's effectiveness. Likewise, as a participant, you should be aware of the possibility that you may be responding to status in others and

10. See Homans' "Bank Room Wiring Study," Homans, pp. 48–80.

11. Abstract of Robert A. Dentler and Kai T. Erickson, "The Function of Deviance in Groups," in Shepherd, pp. 78–79.

allowing that perception to limit your participation, your willingness to make contributions.[12]

We should also note that groups are prone to react negatively when the holders of status and power act in a negative or irresponsible manner. The higher the status, the more aggressive and hostile will group members be in their reaction to what they perceive to be irresponsible actions.[13] However, no matter what your status, you cannot afford to view yourself as a group member without identity; you need to become aware of the group's perceptions of you and to employ or compensate for those perceptions in order to be effective in the group. One very simple bit of advice is that the individual with high status and assigned leadership needs to learn to keep quiet and listen, even at the risk of allowing periods of silence, in order to avoid undue influence and to keep the group from depending on that individual for all the answers.

GROUP SIZE

As a member of a group, you should be aware that size has an effect on groups. We established early in this chapter that when we use the term *group*, we are talking about more than two persons. Here we will assert that the ideal group size seems to be from four to seven members.

To the degree that you are able to control the size of a group, you should keep it in this optimum size range. As the group increases in size, fewer and fewer persons emerge as central figures and decision makers. Communication suffers and miscommunication increases. Cartwright and Zander note that the question of productivity has not yet been completely answered, and indicate that there may be occasions when the use of larger groups can yield good results.[14]

In the course of our discussion, we have emphasized that groups have goals or common tasks. This is particularly obvious in occupational settings. In these settings, the specific statement of a goal will often precede the selection of the group. When the groups or teams exist on a continuous basis, they are typically responsive to some larger goal or purpose such as research or product development. The tasks of occupational groups tend to fall into two categories. Some groups come together in order *to share information*. In the case of Lieutenant Zimmerman's group, it is quite possible that the first task or goal of that group might have been to identify all information available concerning the theft of citi-

---

12. See Cartwright and Zander, pp. 215–235, for an introductory discussion of "Power and Influence in Groups."

13. Wiggins, Dill, and Schwartz are among those who have written "On 'Status Liability'." See Cartwright and Zander, pp. 538–546.

14. Cartwright and Zander, pp. 498–499.

zen's band radios. The group would have been sharing information. Other groups have a broader goal, that of *solving problems*.

THE INFORMATION-SHARING GROUP

In this kind of small group, the members cooperate in looking for information and in exchanging the information they find. They are concerned with coming to grips with three guideline questions:

1. *What are the relevant facts?*
2. *What do we make of these facts?*

   How do we interpret them? How do we rank them in terms of their relative importance? What kind of composite picture do they suggest?

3. *What conclusions can we draw from them?*

   Can we come to agreement on a description of the situation based on the facts and on our interpretation of them?

For example, Mary Jeffries' crew could undertake to find out how other departments or agencies like theirs handle employee-training sessions. They could meet once or twice to decide exactly what kinds of information they needed and who should go where to get it. Later, they could meet again to exchange the information collected and to talk about the materials and ideas assembled, the interpretations to be attached to them, and the conclusions to be drawn about them. If they wished to do so, they could present a final "employee-training report" to the other employees in the department.

Essentially the same procedure could be used in a project in which you and other students would work together to answer this question: "What are the facts about local employment practices?" To answer that question, you and the others would separately or in pairs visit local industries and businesses to collect accurate figures and information on occupational opportunities in the community. Here are some questions that could be used.[15]

Do you employ dropouts, high school grads, college grads?

Principal job categories?

How many hired last year in each? Summer or part-time?

Starting salaries?

Nature of work?

15. Adapted with minor editing from Robert Hoppock, *Occupational Information,* 4th ed. (New York: McGraw-Hill, 1976), p. 257.

Qualifications? Age? Sex? Height? Weight? Other physical? Marital status? Tools? License? Aptitudes? Unions? Citizen? Residence? Veteran?

Preparation required? Minimum? Desirable? Time? Content? Approved schools? Preferred high school subjects?

Advancement? Future prospects? Supply and demand?

Hours? Regular? Overtime? Sunday and holiday? Evening?

Steady or seasonal? Effect of depressions? Retirement age? Pensions?

Hazards?

What workers like? Dislike?

Anything else we should have asked?

After the questions above had been adapted to the local scene through discarding some and adding others, you and other group members would fan out to get the answers to them. Then the small group would get together again to make sense out of the collected information and draw some conclusions about employment opportunities.

Another kind of information-sharing, one not requiring a formal survey or search for data, occurs in discussions aimed at the simple exchange of experiences, observations, ideas, and suggestions bearing on a certain subject. Some examples: a nursing-care conference to plan the care of a patient; a police and social workers' conference to exchange information on a family or individual; a meeting of department-store security officers to talk about what they're doing to prevent and detect shoplifting; a group of supermarket managers meeting to share ideas on screening applicants for jobs. In practically every field, it is common for members of a small group to assemble occasionally just to pool information for their own benefit or for the benefit of others.

The advantages of pooling information can be demonstrated through the first example above, the nursing-care planning conference. One of the aims of modern nursing is to preserve the patient's self-respect and self-identity.[16] The nurse learns to "accept the patient the way he is," even if he ignores or flouts instructions. Every individual responds to illness in a different way, and the present-day nurse learns to "allow the patient to respond in his own way without censure." He is no longer "the gall-bladder down the hall"; he is a human being with feelings and fears, and one who has the right to help make decisions relating

---

16. This paragraph is a partial paraphrase from an unpublished paper on conservation principles by Myra F. Levine, R.N., M.S.N. All of the material on "the Cullen case" is based on conversations with Purdue Nursing School staff (see the Acknowledgments at the front of this book) and with Jane Pruett, R.N., and Karen Geyer, R.N., of the nursing staff of St. Elizabeth Hospital, Lafayette, Indiana. A videotape of a team conference led by Karen Geyer was especially helpful.

to his care, just as he had the right to consent to treatment in the first place. (With something of the same emphasis on understanding "what makes people tick," progressive police work now requires that officers know more about communication, especially with young people, and about cooperating with social agencies in the effort to stop crime before it happens.)

Let us examine a model case that is more specific than our earlier examples. In our model case, the patient can be an 80-year-old retired farmer, whom we'll call Mr. Cullen. He has been admitted to the hospital with a heart problem, complicated by a mild diabetic condition. Two days after his admission and while he is undergoing a series of diagnostic tests, he is one of the patients whose care is the subject of the planning conference of the day.

The nursing team taking part in this conference includes the professional nurse responsible for the care of Mr. Cullen (and of other patients) plus these members of the nursing staff: a graduate nurse, two licensed practical nurses, and two nurse's aides. The professional nurse is the team leader; she and all members of the team are in daily contact with Mr. Cullen.

Such a conference is informal and short (usually 15 to 30 minutes). It takes place daily in order to give all the members of the team a chance to exchange information on nursing-care problems. On any one day, no more than two or three patients come up for discussion. Today, it's Mr. Cullen's turn. He's been in the hospital just long enough for individual team members to have absorbed sufficient information about him to make a conference useful.

Mr. Cullen's nursing-care file already includes the following observations, based on his admission interview: He has never been seriously ill in his life, has never before spent a night in a hospital, is somewhat suspicious of hospitals in general, and is concerned about "losing his health."

The team leader opens the conference with "Let's see how we can combine what we know to provide better care for Mr. Cullen." The leader (who also takes notes during the conference) first reviews what is known about Mr. Cullen and then asks for comments and observations on him as a person (rather than as a case). His heart and diabetic problems are not the primary focus of the discussion, although both conditions serve as a base for nursing-care suggestions from the leader and the graduate nurse. The main purpose of the meeting is to encourage questions, comments, and ideas which can be incorporated in an overall plan to help Mr. Cullen adjust to his new problems. Some typical contributions:

"He's extremely shy." "How can we deal with that?" "Ask him how he's feeling when you're in the room?" "That's right; give him an opening to talk, and *pay some special attention to him,* instead of just looking in to be sure he's okay."

"Since his pulse is low and could go lower, should we teach him to take his own pulse?" "We'll certainly do that before he goes home, but right now it might only frighten him."

"He's worried about being short of breath." "We can assure him that his shortness of breath is a temporary problem." "Yes, and that if he turns on his side, he'll have less difficulty breathing."

"What about his diabetic diet? He's complaining about it already." "Well, he's even more worried about his diet after he leaves the hospital." "Where does he have his meals outside?" "He lives close to a daughter and has some meals with her family; otherwise, he says, he shifts for himself or goes to restaurants." "We'll have to be very careful to convince him that the diet is just a matter of choosing the right dishes." "We can also talk with his daughter." "And with all the visiting relatives." "It would also be a good idea to have the hospital dietician come up to the room to ease his mind about the diet." "Good. We'll do that."

"Any other suggestions?" "Each of us should remember that he's fearful. Can we do something about that?" "In talking with him, let's describe other cases like his, in which the patient was able to return to a normal way of life." "He will have to be careful to limit activity and watch his diet." "True, but we can emphasize the good side of the situation." "Such as?" "He won't be bedridden, and he will be able to take care of himself and be almost as independent as he has been all his life." "Yes, that's very important to him; he's afraid of being a burden to somebody."

And so the team conference continues. In this situation, it really consists of a number of conference cells, each concerned with a fact or facts about Mr. Cullen, an interpretation of the importance of that information, and the nursing-care conclusion or suggestion that can be drawn from it. After the group has considered the available information on Mr. Cullen's special concerns and his special needs, and after it has interpreted those factors, the team leader brings the meeting to a close by reviewing the steps everyone on the team will take to provide the best possible care of this patient.

THE PROBLEM-SOLVING GROUP

The primary goal of the information-sharing group is obviously that of sharing information. That process oftentimes provides the base for clarifying problems and for focusing on their solution. However, the task of a problem-solving group is more complex, will require more time and effort, and, in all likelihood, will involve some frustration and considerable interaction. If the group is able to solve the problem satisfactorily, that accomplishment will quite probably compensate for the frustration and reinforce the value of belonging to the group. The questions that the problem-solving group must address are, of course, more detailed.

1. *Is the problem clearly stated?*
2. Given the problem, *what are the related facts?*

a) What is the object, product, person, or thing affected?
What *exactly* is wrong?
b) When did the problem first arise?
c) Where did it arise?
d) How serious is it? What is its size, scope, severity?

3. Given the facts, *can we pinpoint the cause(s)?*
4. Given the cause(s), *what solution will work best?*

In *Solving Managerial Problems,*[17] Laird and Grote provided an excellent example of the small-group approach to solving a problem faced by the supervisory staff of a general hospital: *The nurses' uniforms are dirty.* With their permission, that example is used to illustrate the basic questions to be answered in small-group problem-solving:

1. *Is the problem clearly stated?*
In this hospital instance, our answer must be "yes."
2. Given the problem, *what are the related facts?*
a) What?
All uniforms are dirty. Overall dirtiness, not specific spots.
b) When?
First noticed two weeks ago and continuing since that time.
c) Where?
Floor nurse uniforms are dirtier than those of lab technicians.
d) How serious?
Cotton uniforms worse than nylon.
OK right after cleaning.
Both old and new uniforms affected.
Day and night nurses equally affected.

Perhaps other facts could be uncovered about the dirty uniform situation, but the example above shows an *organized* pattern for getting at the facts related to a problem. When you finish this procedure, the end-product is a complete and thorough description of the problem.

3. Given the facts, *can we pinpoint the cause(s)* of the problem?
Sometimes the fundamental cause of a problem is clear after you have finished step 2 above. For example, the parking situation at your institution may be "not enough spaces for the people who want to park." You can go about trying to solve that problem without much more than facts on the

17. See Dugan Laird and Richard C. Grote, *Solving Managerial Problems* (Reading, Mass.: Addison-Wesley, 1971), p. 45. This set of subquestions and the hospital problem which follows are adapted from Laird and Grote, pp. 44 ff.

severity of the problem. For another example, your pizza parlor business goes into a slump following the opening of a new pizza place across the street. You don't need step 2 or 3 to tell you that the slump in your business is due to the opening of the new establishment close by; you can go immediately to step 4 in the attempt to find a solution to your problem.

More often, the cause(s) will not be so obvious. Consequently, you begin looking for *all the changes* that could possibly have brought about the problem condition. These are the changes listed by Laird and Grote for the hospital example:

a) We started using Ace Cleaners, a new laundry, about two weeks ago.

b) Air pollution has been getting worse lately.

c) All nurses' shifts were changed two weeks ago.

d) Earlier this month, a disinfectant was introduced into the air-conditioning system for the ward and patient rooms.

e) A heating-plant fire two months ago put a lot of smoke into the ventilator system.

With the changes listed, you begin to search for cause(s) through the process of elimination.

a) The hospital uses three other laundries as well as the new one. *All floor* uniforms are dirty. Ace Cleaners—not guilty.

b) Air pollution would affect all uniforms. The lab technician uniforms are not as dirty as the others. Pollution—not guilty.

c) Both day and night nurses are equally affected. Hard to see change in shifts as a cause in any case. Shift change—not guilty.

d) The disinfectant went into the ward and patient rooms where the floor nurses spend most of their time. This is a possible cause.

e) The heating-plant fire occurred two months ago, and the problem didn't show up until two weeks ago. Fire—not guilty.

To make a long story short, further investigation discloses that the disinfectant also affects nylon more than cotton. The disinfectant is therefore pinpointed as the cause of the dirty uniforms.

4. Given the cause(s), *what solution will work best?*
Sometimes the solution is obvious. In the hospital instance, the solution is no further use of that particular disinfectant. *Or is it?* Maybe it's the only disinfectant available for use in the air-conditioning system, and the hospital administration feels that it is necessary as a safeguard for patients and staff. In any event, how should you approach the solution step?

The conventional way to search for solutions is to ask for suggestions and to examine each solution proposed for possible advantages and disadvantages. The objective is to choose a solution or to put one together which is a composite of the best ideas advanced.

Brainstorming is one way to stimulate ideas on the solution to a problem. The basic idea here is to have everyone suggest any and every solution that comes into his head. If you were brainstorming the pizza parlor problem, you could try to come up with novel promotional gimmicks that would attract favorable attention from possible customers. For another example, if a group of students wanted to promote closer relations between school and industry, they could stage a brainstorming session to produce ideas, no matter how wild. An important rule of the game in brainstorming is that *no one criticizes any idea proposed by someone else;* the quickest way to stifle spontaneous suggestions is to permit criticism as ideas are proposed. There is always plenty of time for checking and evaluating the ideas in a later session of the group.

In the hospital situation, you could begin the work of solving the problem by asking the small-group members to come up with other options (in addition to getting rid of the disinfectant). Brainstorming around the table, they might come up with these ideas:

a) Wash the uniforms every day instead of every other day.
b) Explain the situation to everyone and ignore the dirt.
c) Change the color of uniforms so dirt won't show so much.
d) Get uniforms of different materials that won't react.
e) Use disposable paper uniforms.
f) Ask the company manufacturing the disinfectant to experiment with changes in its chemical content.
g) Have the uniforms treated to resist color change.

The best way to handle a brainstorming session is to have everyone act as his or her own secretary in jotting down all options suggested. Each person then has ready reference to what has been suggested, and the growing list of options helps everyone generate new and different ideas.

With or without brainstorming, the final stage in looking for a solution is, of course, *evaluation of the ideas and options suggested* and, again, the elimination of those which, for one reason or another, are considered unacceptable. After one solution or a combination of solutions has been chosen, the small group can go into whatever planning is necessary to put it into effect.

Finally, by way of suggesting other kinds of problems in which employees can be profitably involved, Wesley Wiksell cites two examples of organizations (Humble Oil and U.S. Steel) which improved their safety records by having small groups of employees discussing *safety* and making suggestions on *how it could be achieved.*[18] Additional possibilities:

How can parking regulations be improved?

Should improvements be made in our forms for requisitions, breakdown reports, etc.?

What should be the approach of management to absenteeism?

How can communication between employees and supervisors be improved?

Is there a need for variety in work assignments?

What group health plan should be recommended to the employees?

What should be the physical arrangement of work stations, machines, desks, etc., in the new area?

What color schemes should be chosen for the repainting of the offices?

How should procedures for hiring replacements be handled?

This "involvement" is the critical factor in group activity. We are more interested in decisions we have a part in making than in decisions that are handed down to us. Companies may not be democratic institutions, but to the degree that they are able to encourage real participation in decision making, there should be an increase in employee morale and an attendant increase in efficiency and productivity.

PATTERNS OF INTERPERSONAL INTERACTION IN GROUPS

There is more to worry about in a small-group setting than just exchanging information and solving problems. As you may have noticed, when you move from the interview to small-group discussion, you add interpersonal or "people problems." For example, in a group of three, you are interacting with two different people rather than with one; in a group of five, you are interacting with four others; and in a group of seven, you are interacting with six others. In the first instance, there are three possible directions or lines of communication (in contrast to one in the interview); in the second, there are 10 possible lines; and in the third, there are 21 possible lines! This geometrical increase is illustrated in Fig. 9.1.[19]

18. Wesley A. Wiksell, *Do They Understand You?* (New York: Macmillan, 1960), pp. 162–163.

19. Adapted from Robert D. Breth, *Dynamic Management Communications* (Reading, Mass.: Addison-Wesley, 1969), p. 86.

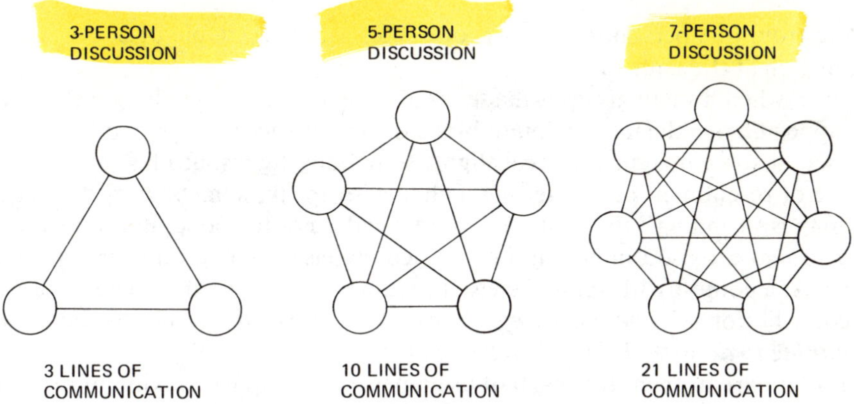

Figure 9.1

In the three-person group, there is a tendency for two to line up together against the third; this tendency often makes each of the three overcautious—nobody likes to be out on the proverbial limb. In a group of seven, according to Bales, there is still a good chance that everyone will say at least something to each other person.[20] When there are more than seven, the communication seems to center on a few active participators, and the type of problems mentioned earlier change.

We also know that the physical construction of a group can have an effect on its behavior and effectiveness. In Fig. 9.1, for example, we see patterns of open access—all members of any one group can interact with all other members of the group. Like the other two groups, the largest of the three will have high morale, but it will take longer to complete a designated task, and the possibility of error will be higher.[21] However, as the cohesion and experience of the circle group grows, leadership will emerge and the group's speed will increase. The advice to be drawn from these observations is again that for groups to be effective in an occupational setting, supervisors, superiors, and managers must have patience and be willing to take some temporary risks.

In the interview, then, only two people are involved and communication is quite direct. In the small group, several people are involved and, as indicated in Fig. 9.1, communication becomes somewhat fragmented—your attention keeps

---

20. See Robert F. Bales, "In Conference," *Harvard Business Review,* March–April 1954, pp. 44–50. Copyright © 1954 by the President and Fellows of Harvard College; all rights reserved. In other articles and books, Bales has written widely on this subject.

21. Alex Bavelas has investigated "Communication Patterns in Task-Oriented Groups." See Shepherd, pp. 89–90.

shifting from one person to another and occasionally a couple of conversations are going on at the same time.

Even when a small group is made up of people who do get along well, things can happen *during* the interaction to block or hinder success. Somebody becomes offended at some imagined or real slight; somebody "goes into his or her shell" because of resentment at not getting a chance to speak; somebody feels that the chairman is "running" the conference and decides not to cooperate; somebody is trying to make a good impression on somebody else in the group; or somebody engages in a contest with someone else to see who can make the greatest number of "contributions." *There is often a great deal going on in a conference which has nothing to do with the problem being discussed.*

It is apparent, then, that each of us comes to a group with a kind of dual personality. One side of us works *on the problem* and on finding a solution for it; how well we work at it depends on how much we know about the problem and on how much we know about the steps and procedures in problem-solving. The other side of us works *on the people* in the group; we try to cooperate with them most of the time, but for a variety of personal reasons we sometimes hold back, and on other occasions we may not cooperate at all. How well we succeed in our people relationships depends on how much we know about getting along with and understanding others; it also depends *on how much we want to get along with them* in the interests of solving a common problem.

It follows that all those taking part in a group need to be considerate of the feelings of the others in the group. A supervisor who notices a steady increase in the number of employees arriving late for work won't make any points by opening a conference with "What do I have to do to get you people here on time?" He or she could do much better with "What can we do to get off to a better start in the mornings?" A smile, a pleasant word, or a compliment is the positive way to set the stage for a productive conference. If people are given encouragement to discuss a common problem, they are usually willing to "give it a try." In doing so, they discover that the "people difficulties" they encounter are more than balanced by the advantages and pleasures they get out of working together.

Your effect on a group will be increased by

1. . . . constant, sensitive, sympathetic attention to what members are saying and doing . . . .
2. . . . constant aware[ness] of his/her own feelings and ideas.
3. an aware[ness] of procedure.[22]

22. Shepherd, p. 117.

SUGGESTIONS FOR GROUP LEADERS

The leadership function should be regarded as resting with the group as much as with the leader.[23] The extent to which group leadership is possible depends, of course, on the experience and attitudes of the individuals participating in the group. If the members of a group are relatively inexperienced in conference methods and procedures, a designated leader or chairperson is going to have to assume primary responsibility for getting the conference off to a good start and for keeping it moving toward its objectives. On the other hand, if the members of the group know the routine and are disposed to cooperate, the leader has very little to do as "leader." He or she has essentially the same responsibilities as every other "member." To put it another way, the "effective leader is one who can create the conditions by which he will actually lose the leadership."[24]

How does the leader try to reach that point? By a friendly approach to the others in the group, by consideration for the feelings of others, by sensitivity in understanding others and by actively listening to them, by conveying to the members of the group that he or she accepts what *they* think and what *they* want to do, and by linking the ideas of one member to those of another in order to call attention to the relationships existing between them.

Assuming that the leader exercises leadership functions only to the extent necessary, and assuming further that each member of the group is expected to assume "fair share" of responsibility for leadership, the suggestions below are intended not only for the designated chairperson or leader but also for each member.

1. *Decide on the goals to be reached.* The goals of information-sharing groups are normally clear; they stem from the reason or reasons for getting together in the first place. Writing them down and announcing them at the beginning of the meeting still serve the useful purpose of helping those taking part to keep the discussion centered on the subjects at hand. In nursing-care conferences, for example, the primary goals are usually (1) to collect and exchange all available information and observations on a given patient, (2) to interpret what that information means in terms of the patient's physical and mental state, and (3) to arrive at conclusions on ways and means of relating to the patient as an individual facing personal problems of anxiety, insecurity, and a complete change of surroundings.

If the purpose of the conference is to go beyond information-sharing and the conclusions to be drawn from that activity, the group may follow the four-step formula on page 196. If the "committee" is interested only in determining what

---

23. See Thomas Gordon, "Group-Centered Leadership and Administration," in Carl R. Rogers *et al., Client-Centered Therapy* (Boston: Houghton Mifflin, 1951), pp. 320–383.

24. Ibid., p. 334.

the problem is and how serious it is, proceeding through the first two steps will suffice. If solutions are the only concern, step 4 will suffice. If the group is undertaking full-scale analysis of a problem along with recommendations for its solution, all four steps are obviously necessary.

2. *Prepare the agenda.* In many groups, this blueprint for activity can be a relatively general plan reflecting the steps in reflective thinking. We feel or observe a difficulty, examine various solutions to the difficulty, select one of the solutions, and put that solution into operation.[25]

In many occupational settings, members of a group will already be aware of a difficulty or it will be brought to their attention by management. Defining the exact nature of that difficulty or problem is a critical step in group process. It is not uncommon for the effectiveness of a group to be reduced because of a failure to determine what the real problem is. If a mother takes a child's temperature and finds that the child has a fever, she may give aspirin to reduce the fever and ignore the problem, that is, what is causing the fever. The same is true of groups. It is not uncommon for groups to respond to the symptoms of a problem rather than the problem itself.

As the complexity of a group's task increases, the group will want to prepare a more thorough agenda. Phillips and Erickson, for example, list five categories:[26]

1. Specification of the problem.
2. Fact-finding
   a) Factual statement of the problem
   b) Factual analysis of causes
3. Goals and criteria for solutions
4. Evaluation of solutions
5. Implementation of best solution

In your case, following the five steps will ensure that your group "covers all the bases."

3. *Keep the group on track.* This suggestion goes hand in hand with the one above; there is no point in having any kind of step-by-step procedure unless the members of the group try to adhere to it. Comments, ideas, and questions typically occurring in a discussion are not always "on target." Some skipping, cir-

---

25. For a discussion of these steps, traditional since ancient times, see John Dewey, *How We Think* (Boston: D. C. Heath, 1933), p. 107.

26. Gerald Phillips and Eugene C. Erickson, *Interpersonal Dynamics in the Small Group* (New York: Random House, 1970), pp. 22–23.

cling, jumping ahead, and backtracking is to be expected and in fact is necessary; unless a "contribution" is totally beside the point (proposing a solution, for instance, in the first five minutes), there is no reason to take corrective action. By "keeping on track" we mean *maintaining a general progression* through the steps required to reach the goals decided upon.

These are some of the things a leader and his or her assistant leaders could say to help maintain that progress:

> Are we all satisfied that we have a good basic statement of our goal or problem?
>
> Does anyone have anything to add to the facts?
>
> At this point, *let's summarize the facts.*
>
> Do you feel that we have enough information now to evaluate the facts and try to pin down causes?
>
> Or should we adjourn now to get additional information?
>
> Is the fact just stated actually a fact? Or is it an opinion?
>
> How important to us do you think fact *A* should be? Fact *B*?
>
> Do you feel that fact *C* could be one of the causes of our problem?
>
> Do you think we've talked about this topic long enough? If so, let's move on to another item.
>
> Is this line of thought directly related to our discussion?
>
> *Let's summarize what we have accomplished so far* in our attempt to find causes.
>
> Are you ready now to move on to a discussion of possible solutions?
>
> Is it possible that the last option suggested would cost too much?
>
> Has this idea been tried anywhere else? Is it practical?
>
> Are we ready to write up our suggestions for solving the problem?

The questions and comments above serve as gentle prods to help the group make progress in a reasonable way. You will note that all questions and comments are aimed at the group in general; no one individual is directly asked to make a statement. Note also that from time to time—and especially at the conclusion of work on a major step—a summary is in order; it serves as a review of what has been done *and* as a transition to the next step.

4. *Encourage everyone to participate.* Kron[27] suggests that tactful questions and comments like those below can be used to keep the "contributions" coming:

---

27. Thora Kron, *The Management of Patient Care,* 4th ed. (Philadelphia: Saunders, 1976). In an excellent chapter on the nursing-care planning conference, Kron discusses participation. pp. 141–143. (Some questions in the present text are examples used in a Purdue Nurses Training course.)

"Would anyone like to comment on that last statement?"

"Do any of you have anything further to add?"

"And?"

"Let me reword the question this way."

"Let's approach the problem from this angle."

"Could you explain that idea more fully?"

"Could you amplify that suggestion?"

"Let's talk about that further."

"What has been your experience?" (Especially useful when addressed to a nonparticipator)

. . . to set aside any misinformation:

"Most of what you say is correct, but I wonder about . . . ?

"Do all of you agree with that statement?"

"I wonder if you misunderstood the question?"

"Could you tell us the source of your information?"

"Where can we find that information?"

"Would someone volunteer to look that up?"

. . . to encourage and modify suggestions:

"Do you mean that . . . ?"

"Do you suppose we could . . . ?"

"Would it be better to . . . ?"

"Would it be possible to . . . ?"

"Your suggestion may work, but. . . . "[28]

5. *Summarize at regular intervals.* In an information-sharing conference, the chairperson, leader, or someone designated as the "recorder" jots down notes on the information provided, on the interpretations discussed, and on the approaches adopted or conclusions reached. At various stages of the discussion, the recorder is in a good position to summarize what has been said. When the meeting is getting near its close, the usual procedure is for the leader to handle the final summary.

In a problem-solving group, summaries are equally important. Examples of the kinds of comments leading into a summary appear under suggestion 2 above.

---

28. See also the probes under "The Corrective Interview" in Chapter 8.

As any group moves from one major step to another, a summary helps set the stage for the move and, as pointed out earlier, provides a useful transition.

SUGGESTIONS FOR GROUP MEMBERS

Earlier in this chapter you read suggestions on the steps required for efficient information sharing and problem solving. How to relate *personally* to others in order to set up a supportive "people atmosphere" is the primary focus of the suggestions that follow.

Be Willing To Cooperate. "We are all in this together" is a cooperative attitude that makes for success in conferences. When you agree with someone, indicate your support in some way (comment, smile, etc.). If you disagree, make clear that you are in disagreement with the idea, not with the person affected. (Make an enemy of that person and he or she will disagree with you from that point on.) If a moment of tension arises over some hotly contested point, do what you can to keep the emphasis on the point at issue and not on the people. Here again, a ready smile, a humorous remark or a quick move to another topic will release tension and help the group over the occasional rough spot in interpersonal relations.

Encourage the shy or reserved type to take an active part in the proceedings. The shy person should be seated where it is easy for the leader or someone else to give him or her both verbal and nonverbal encouragement to speak up.

Be Ready to Compromise. The whole idea behind a conference is to apply "collective brain power" to a problem. The emphasis should be on cooperative thinking, not competitive jockeying for advantage. The assumption is the more heads involved, the better the final result or decision. Each of us, because of background and experiences, does have something special to offer to the group; at the same time, no one of us knows everything. Don't be timid about saying something, but be prepared to accept reasonable modification and correction.

Respect the Views of Others. People say things because they believe them. If you don't go along with someone's statement of fact or opinion, your saying "That's not true!" won't win you any friends or change any views. A more reasonable and less offensive approach: "Could you tell me where those figures came from?" or "What are your reasons for taking that position?" As a member of the group, you have as part of your job the task of helping the group maintain an all-ideas-are-welcome atmosphere, in which every member feels comfortable and free to take an active part in the discussion without worrying about being criticized or contradicted. It is possible to have healthy differences of opinion and a good conference atmosphere at the same time; all that is necessary is that the members of the group have an honest regard for each other as human beings and co-workers.

Listen Actively. In Chapters 2 and 6, it was pointed out that you can communicate with a speaker by really listening to him or her. On the other hand, if you're looking at the ceiling while somebody is trying to make a point in a conference, he or she will take the cue from you and do some ceiling-inspecting when you're doing the talking. Listening, always important, is especially so in groups, where there are at least as many distractions as there are people.

SUMMARY

We began the chapter by defining a *group* as "a collection of individuals who have relations with one another that make them interdependent to some significant degree." We emphasized the element of interdependence and noted that, particularly in an occupational setting, workers share goals, the realization of which often benefits both worker and employer. We underlined the importance of the *team* in occupational groups and the increasing reliance placed on them in our modern society. Additionally, we offered an explanation of why groups succeed in occupational settings.

Next, we examined the inner workings of a group and explained the concepts of *cohesion*, *norms*, *roles*, *sentiments* and *internal* and *external* systems. This was followed by a discussion of the individual's role (your role) in a group and, more specifically, how that individual (you) might effectively function in (1) an information-sharing group and (2) a problem-solving group. We also presented guidelines for participation.

10
Communicating Publicly: One to Many

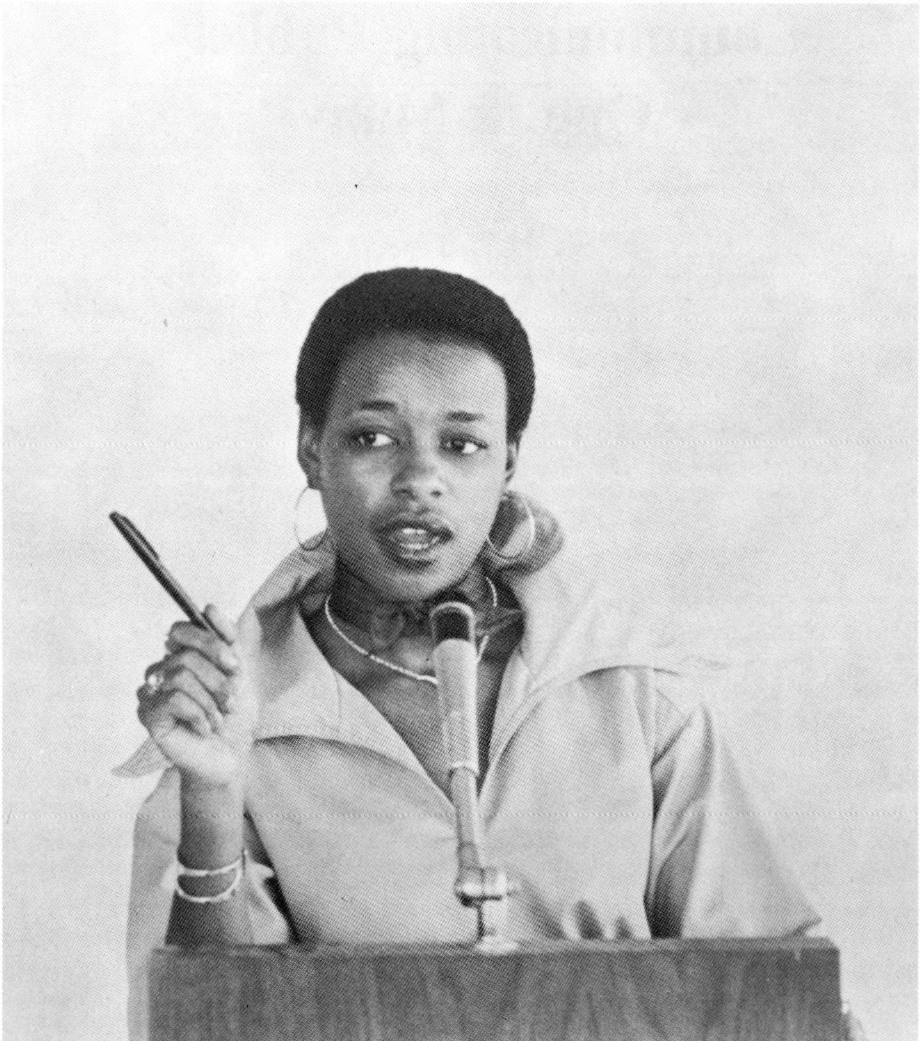

10
Communicating Publicly: One to Many

"Never be afraid to feel a little lonesome."

Adlai Stevenson II

At first glance, the advice of the late U.N. ambassador and former presidential candidate may not seem at all applicable to a public speaking situation, much less to public speaking in an occupational setting. Adlai Stevenson, however, was well known for his ability as a speaker, and he had a clear understanding of situations when you alone possess information that others do not have or you alone hold a view which you wish others to accept. His remark emphasizes the importance of believing in yourself and of being willing to put yourself on record in public.

Our aim in this chapter is to focus your attention on communication procedures and practices especially appropriate in speaking "one to many"—and also helpful in building up your confidence and reducing the "public loneliness" you may sometimes feel.

Here's where we're going

Study of the materials in this chapter should enable you to:

1. Approach audience analysis in a way that will help you be more effective in a presentational work setting.

2. List, define, and demonstrate the value of four types of organizational plans.
3. Be aware of the value of audiovisual aids and be able to list six "rules" that make the use of such aids more effective.
4. Demonstrate an understanding of the suggested parts of an information briefing by explaining the purpose of the introduction, conclusion, and transition and by explaining how to prepare those elements.
5. Explain how certain attitudes might enter into an occupational setting and how they require an individual to employ persuasive techniques in order to respond to those attitudes.
6. Prepare and present an 8- to 10-minute information briefing by employing the preparation steps suggested in this chapter.
7. Prepare and present an 8- to 10-minute persuasive proposal by employing the preparation steps suggested in this chapter.

PART I—PRESENTATIONAL SPEAKING: GENERAL CONSIDERATIONS

The Place of Public Presentations

We want to begin this chapter by emphasizing the fact that you will probably be called upon to speak publicly and that the place in which you will do much of this speaking will be your work setting. There are those who contend that skill in public speaking is no longer necessary and that the average person is seldom, if ever, expected to speak in a public setting. The problem is that many people think of public speaking as being limited to those occasions when you put on your best clothes, enter a large auditorium, step up to a massive walnut lectern, and then speak to thousands of listeners about issues of international magnitude. It is true that few persons face very large audiences to discuss major issues. However, thousands of individuals stand up every day to present information and proposals to small audiences. You and your teachers engage in some public speaking in almost every class, and public speaking situations are equally common in other occupations. The law enforcement officer presents materials on bicycle safety to the fourth grade. The juvenile officer makes a presentation concerning drugs to a parent-teachers group. The dental hygienist talks about good dental habits to second graders. Indeed, in all but the most solitary occupations, there are occasions when persons are called upon to make presentations to groups of other people. Because public speaking does occur and because it also reflects subtle changes in the message settings that we have already described, we devote this chapter to that kind of "communication to many."

In preceding chapters, we have identified three message settings. In chapter 2, we concerned ourselves with *intrapersonal* communication—that communication in which you are personally both the source and receiver of the message. In that communication activity, you develop a sense of yourself and of your place in relationship to others. In our subsequent discussion of interview relationships in the occupational setting, we focused on communication interaction between *two* persons, *interpersonal* communication. In that kind of interaction, there is a constant interchange of behavior with an opportunity to ask and answer questions and to monitor and alter your communication effort on the basis of feedback from the other person.

In the third category, *group* communication, the complexity of the communication is increased by the inclusion of several others in the effort. The chapter on this subject emphasized the word "with" in communication *with* others. The constant interchange that was present in the interview remains, but that interchange is not limited to one other; it is shared with several others. The group's communication efforts still require and reflect constant monitoring, but that monitoring is complicated by the dynamics resulting from the added *others*. In the group there is a sharing of information and an equal access of each person to all the other participants.

The public presentation offers a fourth message setting. In the public speaking situation, the "with" changes to "to." One individual emerges as the primary source, a presenter of information or an advocate of a particular position. The individual speaks to the others in an effort to convey that information or to move them toward the speaker's position. The speaker will still solicit feedback, will still look for and listen to questions, and will still monitor his or her communication behavior. At the same time, the speaker will seek to maintain control and a position as "the central source" in order to successfully convey his or her message.

There is no magic size of audience to determine whether or not you are engaging in a public presentation, nor do physical elements such as spotlights and lecterns establish that you are a public speaker. If you search your memory, you will recall situations in which an individual lectured to you as an "audience" of one person or to a very small "audience" of four or five persons.

As your work responsibilities increase, the size of the group or audience may grow, and as the size of the group increases, you will need to employ the techniques of public presentation with increasing effectiveness. However, it is important to remember that it is not the size of the audience that determines whether you are engaged in public presentation; it is the central role you have assumed and the "talking to" relationship you have with the listeners.

Clearly, when one assumes the role of primary message source, special communication behaviors will be required. In this chapter we are first going to present general procedures applicable to the kinds of public presentations you will encounter, namely the *informative briefing* and the *persuasive proposal.* Then some additional theory and detail on each of the two types of messages will be provided.

By way of preamble to taking up the subject of general procedures, we would emphasize Drucker's contention that any kind of "communication . . . always makes demands. It always demands that the recipient(s) become somebody, do something, believe something."[1] The point of significance in this statement is that if you are "demanding" (no matter how modest that demand my be) you must persuade the recipient(s) of the value of meeting your demand. To a greater or lesser degree, then, all communication involves persuasion.

It is in this context that we want to examine two types of public presentation; the informative briefing and the persuasive proposal. In an *informative briefing* you urge upon your listeners whatever body of information you are presenting to them; you want them to believe you and you take steps to achieve that goal. In a *persuasive proposal*, you generally want the members of the audience to consider and act upon the reasons (backed by information) presented to justify a certain course of action. In other words, there is normally a degree of persuasion in the presentation of information and, on the other hand, facts and figures (information) appear to advantage in the persuasive proposal.

Recognizing, then, that there are elements of information in persuasion and elements of persuasion in information, we offer these definitions:

> The informative briefing is a presentation in which the speaker's primary objective is to induce in the audience an *understanding* of a certain body of knowledge.
>
> The persuasive proposal is a presentation in which the speaker's primary objective is to induce in the audience an *acceptance* of his or her proposal for the solution of a problem.

Many discussions of public presentations begin with a segment concerned with selecting a topic. We will proceed on the assumption that choosing a topic will not be a major problem for you when you decide or are called upon to make a presentation in your work. The need for that presentation will have grown out of the job or, at the very least, will be job related. The police officer who explains police work to a group of high school seniors offers an example of the job-related situation. The officer may not be required to give the presentation as a matter of duty, but if it weren't for the fact that he or she is an officer, the invitation would never have been extended. The briefer knows the subject very well either through training and experience or is well enough acquainted with it to know where to find material. (It is also a good idea to have a librarian help you discover just how

1. Peter F. Drucker, *Management: Tasks, Responsibilities, Practices* (New York: Harper & Row, 1974), p. 487.

much information can be found in your library.) This is the case in most presentational speaking—you will be called upon to speak because you know something or you will seek out the opportunity to speak because you have something to say, something that you want others to hear.

General Procedures in Public Presentations

Determine your purpose Let us assume that you've either been asked to make a presentation or you have decided to give one. In either case, the first question to ask yourself is "Exactly what do I want the listeners to do as a result of this presentation?" Until you know precisely what it is you want to accomplish, there is very little you can do to proceed. Your answer to this initial question might be: "I want workers to be aware of four new provisions in the retirement system."

Once you've made that decision, the second question to ask yourself is "Why?" If you answer the question honestly, you may discover some of the factors that get in the way of communication. If, for example, your answer to the question "Why?" is "Because," or "The boss told me to," or "It's in the book," you will have an indication of why certain informational briefings go so badly. If you don't have a good reason for making the presentation, the listeners will find no good reason to respond to it.

The third question to ask yourself is, "If I am successful, so what?" or "Is this briefing really necessary?" There is little to be gained from a presentation of any sort when a successful presentation is clearly impossible. An extreme example: If the mayor of a large city were to go into the most impoverished area of that city and present information to "make the citizens aware of the ten most active stocks on the New York Stock Exchange," even the best prepared and carefully delivered presentation would have very little meaning to persons who are much more concerned about tomorrow's meal than blue chip stocks.

Let us consider another more direct example and the three questions leading out of it:

What do I want the listeners to do?

The first of these situations relates to the earlier statement of purpose "I want the workers to be aware of four new provisions in the retirement system." Imagine that your company officers and representatives from the labor force have negotiated changes in the retirement system which give the workers a number of options, such as increasing the amount of money deducted from pay checks for investment in the system, and making it possible to allocate different percentages of deductions to mutual funds. Very few take advantage of the changes, even though they represent some real gains for the workers. As the personnel officer or union leader, you consider briefing small groups of employees in order to gain acceptance of the new system.

Why?

1. Very few workers are aware of and understand the changes.
2. The dollar value of the changes represents a real saving to the workers.
3. The company believes that a general understanding of the changes would result in a raise in worker morale.
4. You personally hate to see the workers pass up a benefit that could mean so much to them.

Certainly, you seem to have an adequate answer to the question "Why?"

If I'm successful, so what?

1. The workers will realize a 5% increase in their pension benefits.
2. The company will profit from increased morale.

A successful presentation will bring about real benefits, both for the workers and the company. There is clearly a need for the briefing.

Moving on to a second example, let us imagine a speaker responding to another set of circumstances. Suppose that you are supervisor of a department for a family owned manufacturing company. It comes to your attention that several good people have recently left your department. You have made a point of asking people who leave to give you their reasons for doing so, and you've come to the conclusions that about three out of four leave because they feel there is little chance of advancement in a relatively small family controlled operation. You consider the possibility of giving a briefing on the chances for advancement in the company. However, you do some checking of the figures and find out that there is practically no opportunity for advancement and that, in fact, you're one of the few supervisors not connected with the family in question. You drop the idea of a presentation (and decide to try to hold people by making working conditions more pleasant). The need for a briefing of some kind may still exist, but there clearly is no need for one on advancement possibilities within the company.

To summarize, in determining the purpose of any type of message, you need to answer these three questions:

1. What do I want the listeners to do as a result of this message?
2. Why do I want them to do it?
3. If I'm successful, so what?

Try this

Put yourself in the place of a real person in the community who has a special ability in or a knowledge about a field of work that would be of interest to the class. On a sheet of paper, write the following information:

1. His or her full name.
2. His or her field of expertise.
3. A statement of purpose for an informative briefing which would be appropriate for presentation by that person to the class. Begin this statement with the words "As a result of this presentation I (the suggested speaker) would like you to. . . ."
4. An answer to the question "Why?".
5. An answer to the question "If I (the suggested speaker) am successful, so what?"

Analyze your audience Far too often we decide what it is that we want to accomplish and then we transfer our own attitudes, values, knowledge, and interests to our audience. We conclude that the listeners will want the same questions answered that we would want answered—that the listeners will be able to understand the things that we understand—that they will become excited, or troubled, or involved by and in the same things that we will.

When you are the speaker, rather than simply transferring your feelings to the listeners, you should empathize with your listeners; that is, determine how the listeners feel about and what they know about the issue. The more you can determine about the listeners, the more effectively you can determine what you need to say, what questions you must answer if you are going to be successful in achieving your purpose. The need for adaptation to your specific audience is crucial. Here is a short form aimed at helping you work more closely and efficiently with the specific listeners who will be sitting there in front of you.

What reason or reasons do the listeners have for attending the meeting? _______

To what specific listener needs and desires can appeals be made? ___________

What group pressures or influences may be operative in the audience? To what extent can they be used? ____

Why should they listen to *me* on this subject? What is their relationship to me or to my organization? ____

How willing are they to accept new ideas?

Very eager_____Eager_____Neutral_____Resistant_____Strongly resistant_____

What do they probably know about the subject?

Much_____Some_____Little_____Nothing_____

What can be predicted about their *attitude* toward my purpose?

Very favorable_____Favorable_____Neutral_____Hostile_____Very hostile_____

About their attitude toward me and/or the organization I represent?

Very favorable_____Favorable_____Neutral_____Hostile_____Very hostile_____

If feelings of hostility are known or thought to exist, what can be done to overcome or neutralize them? Can an early emphasis be placed on advantages that may accrue to listeners who hear me out? What are these advantages? __________

____

Are they in any position to take action or follow my proposal? __________

____

(If the answer is "no", you should reconsider your purpose. How can that purpose be modified so that the group can react? Should you aim simply at conveying information?)

What can be assumed about the vocabulary level of this group on this subject?

Extensive_____Limited_____Technical_____Nontechnical_____

What techniques of presentation or argument are likely to get a negative reaction from this group? __________

____

What techniques of presentation or argument are likely to get a favorable reaction from this group? __________

____

Finally, is there anyone from whom I can get an analysis of his experience with this audience or group? __________

____

____

____

You may think of some additional questions or variables which will help you tailor your remarks to fit a specific audience. However, those above will serve to remind you that the listeners normally ask themselves some of the same questions.

1. What do *we* have to gain from this talk? (It is critical that a speaker realize that the willingness to listen and respond is directly related to the listener's ability to see that what the speaker is saying is important to that listener—that he or she has something to gain.)

2. What makes *this* speaker an expert?
3. Does the speaker recognize that we already know a lot about the subject? Or nothing? Or that we are some place in-between?
4. Does the speaker recognize that we are technicians who understand the jargon of the field? Or that we are not technicians? Or that we are beginning technicians with a limited vocabulary? Does the speaker define the terms most of us don't know?

We would emphasize one last, important point about audience analysis. It comes *after* your determination of purpose. You decide what it is you want or need or have to communicate, and then you examine your audience in order to determine how you can increase the likelihood of success. Don't give up with a comment such as "They won't want to listen to that," or "They won't care." Instead, proceed on the basis of "This is important—how can I convince them of its importance?"

Up to this point, the advice in this chapter will remind you of the discussion of communication theory in earlier chapters. Nevertheless, let us emphasize again that your potential for communicating effectively is always enhanced by your being very much aware of *why* you are communicating. Similarly, you increase your chances for success by being sensitive to the specific needs of your listeners.

Select your materials A careful analysis of your audience serves the purpose of identifying for you the kinds of questions that you will have to answer in your message. As we said before, selecting a topic is seldom a serious problem in work-related presentations. It is also possible that a great amount of material will be readily available to you; if it is not, you will have to dig for it.

We noted above that your knowledge and experience are two reasons why you will be asked or why you will choose to speak. The first natural step in finding materials is to inventory yourself. List the things you know about the subject or about the issues. This inventory process will give you a clearer sense of (1) what you really know about the topics at hand and of (2) what you don't know about them. You will thus identify your areas of weakness, areas in which you will have to do additional research.

We will not try to include a course on research techniques, but let us emphasize three possible sources of information. First, check with those persons in your company or organization who might be able to supply you with information. The longer you work in a particular organization, the more familiar you will become with those persons. A second significant source, and one that we have mentioned before, is the library. Professional librarians are skilled in finding materials and usually enjoy the opportunity to help. Finally, do not neglect the large quantity of information available through the federal government. Here, too, the librarian can be a source of help. He or she will be able to direct you to appropriate agencies and addresses.

Nothing contributes more to a successful presentation—and, incidentally, to a feeling of security—than knowledge. Read and observe as broadly and carefully as time and conditions permit. When you have gathered information, you are still faced with the problem of selecting precisely what information you should employ in a particular presentation. Here, we return to the audience analysis. You will remember that one of the things we suggested was that, if you were the listener, you would want certain questions answered. Ask yourself that same question: "If I were a listener, what questions would I want answered—what information would I want furnished before I would react as the speaker desires?" This question gives you an indication of the specific information that you should include in your presentation. When you have decided what questions your listener will probably want answered, you know what information to provide.

Organize your materials At a later point in this chapter, we will offer suggestions on the specific details of organization. For the moment, it is enough to note that effective public communication calls for three broad divisions: (1) the introduction, (2) the body of the presentation, and (3) the conclusion. All three have within them, and between them, connecting elements called transitions.

The Body. It may seem strange to begin this discussion with the body of the message, but we do so for two reasons. First, while we do recognize that the introduction and conclusion are indispensable, it makes sense to decide what you're going to say before worrying about the introduction and conclusion. If you have nothing to say, little is to be gained by a brilliant beginning and an impressive close. Second, in the process of identifying questions that must be answered for your listeners, you have already begun work on the body of the message. In fact, one way to look at the body is to regard it as consisting of the answers to those questions. Listeners are looking for answers, and a major part of your speaking responsibility is to provide those answers to the audience's satisfaction. In the discussions of the informative briefing and the persuasive proposal which follow later in this chapter, we will discuss the body of the message in much greater detail. That greater detail will serve to offer additional emphasis to the importance of the body. At this point, however, let us turn to those elements which have common qualities in both the informative briefing and the persuasive proposal: the introduction, the conclusion, transitions, and visual aids.

Introductions and Conclusions. You've heard speakers who extended their introductory remarks at the expense of the subject at hand. You've also heard some who didn't seem to know how to bring a talk to an end. These people were in trouble because they did not recognize the need to plan opening and closing remarks. The planning can take place at a relatively late stage in the preparation of the talk, but it cannot be omitted.

When you begin to speak, your purpose is (1) to get the attention of your listeners, (2) to convince them that you know something about the subject, (3) to let them know what you are trying to accomplish, and (4) to point out why it is in their interests to listen to you. If attention is already at a high level, the first point is not needed in your introduction. The second point can be left out if you are known to be knowledgeable in the field. The fourth is unnecessary if possible benefit to the listeners is too obvious to require comment. In other words, you use the four points as a kind of check list to be sure that your introduction has in it those elements required by the listeners you face in a given situation.

How do you get attention? Six different ways are suggested below, and others will occur to you.

1. Recount an incident, example, illustration, or anecdote. Be sure that the relation to your subject is direct.
2. Tell a joke or story bearing directly on the subject. (However, be honest with yourself; if you don't tell jokes or stories well, avoid this kind of introduction.)
3. State a startling or shocking fact.
4. Make some remarks about the occasion which brings the listeners and you together.
5. Quote some authority or expert who has said something noteworthy about the subject.
6. Ask a question, either rhetorical or actual.

The conclusion of a talk can also be left to a late stage in the preparation process. It usually consists of (1) a summary of the main points leading up to a restatement of the main idea of the speech and/or (2) a final statement or appeal in accord with the purpose for which the talk was given. Try to leave your listeners with something to remember and, at the same time, make it clear that you have come to the end of your presentation.

Transitions. In any conversation, discussion, or other form of speech communication, there is a need for transitions—devices that indicate a "going across" or a "passing over" from one major idea to another. For example, when a speaker introduces a sentence by saying "Second," you normally understand that his or her intent is to move to a second point. The use of

"Second" helps you keep track of the development of the talk. Ordinarily, a speaker relies on more than just numbers to emphasize movement.

In practically any talk, you will also find signpost words and phrases like these leading into a succession of related ideas: *another concern, then, after, in any event, another method, while, in addition, furthermore, not only, also, besides,* and *too.* Such words show movement through time, space, and from topic to topic *within* the broader framework of the talk.

In addition to the verbal indicators which tell listeners where you are, nonverbal indicators (gestures, facial expressions, changes in stance, etc.) provide reinforcement for transitions. For example, if you move physically as you mention moving to another main area of the talk, the listeners are given that much added notice of your intention. No matter how well prepared a speaker may be, his work is not finished until suitable transitions have been worked out.

What do you think?

Do you use transitions in everyday conversations? What forms do these transitions take? Can you cite a few? When someone says, "I didn't notice but you seem to have changed the subject," is that person also saying, "If you had given me warning of a change in subject, I would be in a better position to understand you"? Is "That reminds me of a story" a transition? "To come to the point"? Have you noted any nonverbal reinforcement of transitions? Or transitions that were entirely nonverbal?

Why does a speaker sometimes begin a talk with a joke? Do you remember any such instance which could be reported to the class? Why should a joke be related to the subject under discussion? Wouldn't an unrelated joke also help to win over and relax an audience? Is everyone equally able to tell a joke? If you're not good at telling jokes, should you try to tell one in a talk?

If the introduction comes first in a talk, why not prepare it first? This text discusses four elements that are usually found in an introduction. If in doubt as to whether or not you should make clear your competence to discuss a subject, should you just leave that element out? What element of the four should never be left out? Under what circumstances do you believe the summary could be left out of the conclusion to a talk?

1. Bring to class the introduction to a speech, editorial, or article from any source, excluding this textbook. Be prepared to read it aloud and point out one good or bad feature in it as an introduction.
2. Do the same with a conclusion drawn from the same sources.
3. Listen to a conversation and take mental note of the verbal and/or nonverbal transitions used. Afterward, jot them down and bring them to class for inclusion in a composite class list of "conversational transitions."

4. Bring to class a list of five transitions you found in any source, including this textbook. Be prepared to cite them as your contribution to a class discussion of transitions.

Plan your visual aids Almost any kind of interpersonal communication may be helped along with visual aids. They are used in conversations (not content with describing an engagement ring, a girl *shows* it to her friends), in small-group discussions, and in speaking-listening situations of all kinds.

As the term implies, a visual aid is something which can be seen and which helps the speaker get his or her ideas across. The types most readily available or most easily prepared are (1) actual objects (like the girl's ring) of a size permitting convenient handling and display, (2) models or mock-ups of such objects, (3) drawings, (4) diagrams, and (5) graphs. Items in the first two classifications can usually be borrowed; for example, if you want to explain how a carburetor works, it should not be too difficult to get one for a few days from a local garage or car dealer, and people in business often have lightweight models or mock-ups of various kinds which they are willing to lend on a short-term basis in return for the free advertising obtained through a demonstration. Drawings or tracings of drawings, diagrams, and graphs can be made by any student willing to spend a little time on the preparation of posters or charts. (Sometimes these units, too, can be borrowed.)

Let us examine each of the five types enumerated above:

Actual Objects. The student in Fig. 10.1 is discussing the features of a new instrument designed to prevent drunken "drivers" from starting a car. He is showing it to a relatively small group; if his audience were large, he would have to resort to some other kind of visual aid. The student in Fig. 10.2 is talking about the parts of a camera and, at the moment, is pointing to the lens. Actual objects can be used to good effect if the units displayed are big enough to be *easily* seen by everyone in the room.

Models or Mock-ups. The speaker in Fig. 10.3 is explaining the forces affecting a plane in flight. With model in hand, he can demonstrate factors of lift, gravity, thrust, and drag. (If he were to attempt discussion of aircraft controls, his audience would be handicapped because control details would be hard to see.) In Fig. 10.4 the speaker is holding a cutaway mock-up of a differential gear assembly. He is explaining how differential gears make it possible for wheels to turn at different rates as equal power is transmitted through the gears to those wheels. When you are using models or mock-ups, it is wise to ask yourself if the person in the back row can see the details to which you will refer.

Drawings. The poster on "Stages of the Four-Stroke Cycle Engine" (Fig. 10.5) is self-explanatory. Although these drawings are professional in appearance, you could draw acceptable copies of them or of other drawings for use

Figure 10.1

in a talk to a small audience. Figure 10.6 shows how an overhead projector can be used to project a drawing on a screen.

Diagrams. As you move away from accuracy in detail to more generel representations, you move to diagrams. For example, the poster on the aircraft fuel indicator system (Fig. 10.7) shows no details of physical appearance; it simply indicates units and their functions. Note that the captions appear *next to* or *on* the elements to which they refer.

Figure 10.2

Figure 10.3

Figure 10.4

Graphs. You've seen any number of *bar* graphs. The one in Fig. 10.8 is constructed horizontally; others are handled vertically. Graphs add interest to statistics and, more important, make it easier for an audience to understand them. Some bar graphs achieve a more striking effect by substituting drawings of people or other symbols for the plain bars; an example is shown in Fig. 10.9. You might not be able to reproduce buildings in that detail but, with outlines only, you could still produce the same effect.

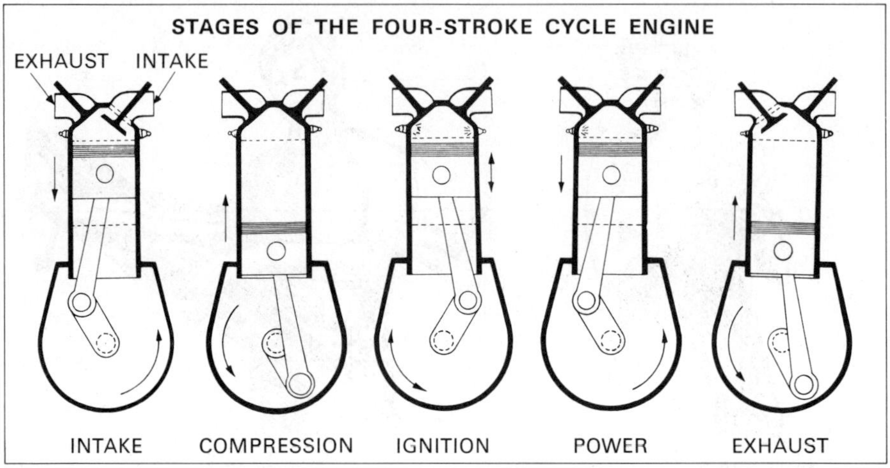

Figure 10.5

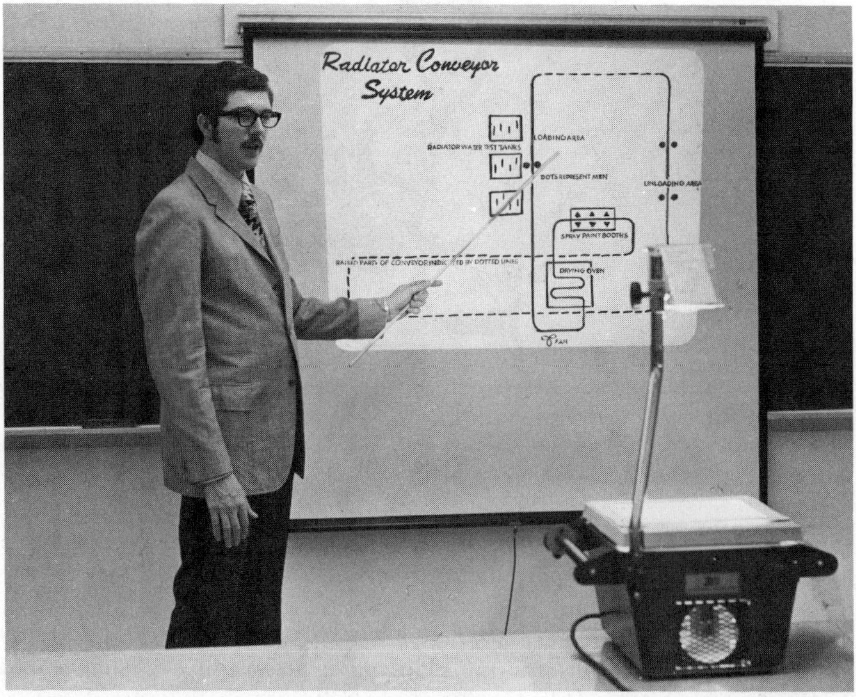

Figure 10.6

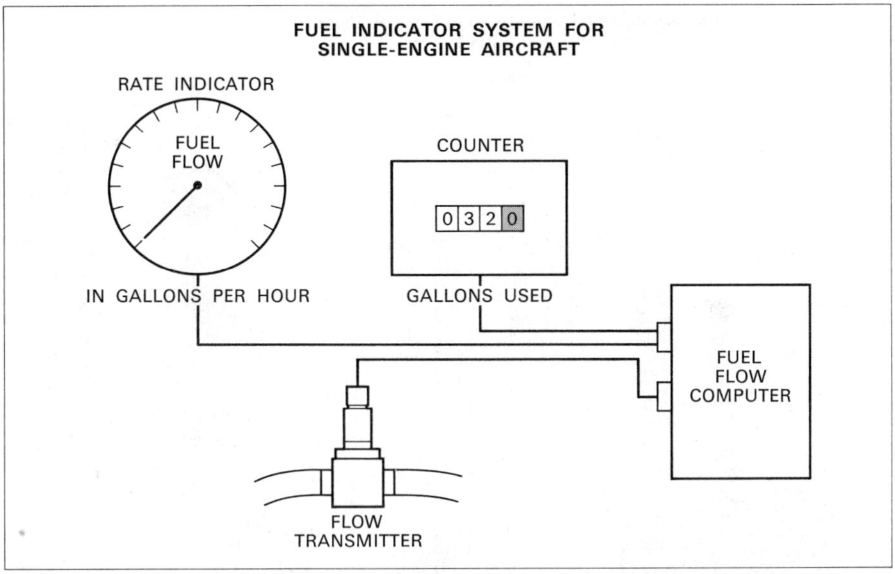

Figure 10.7

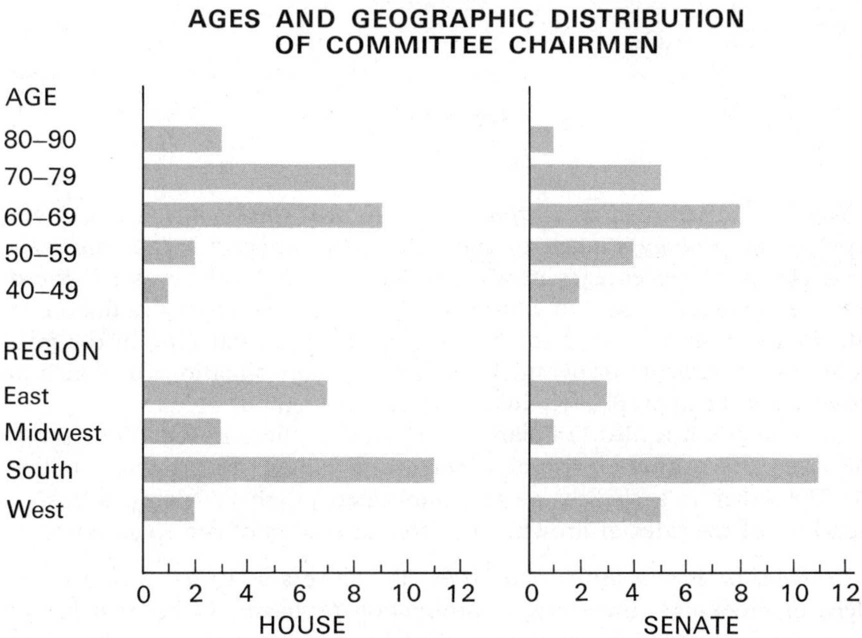

Figure 10.8

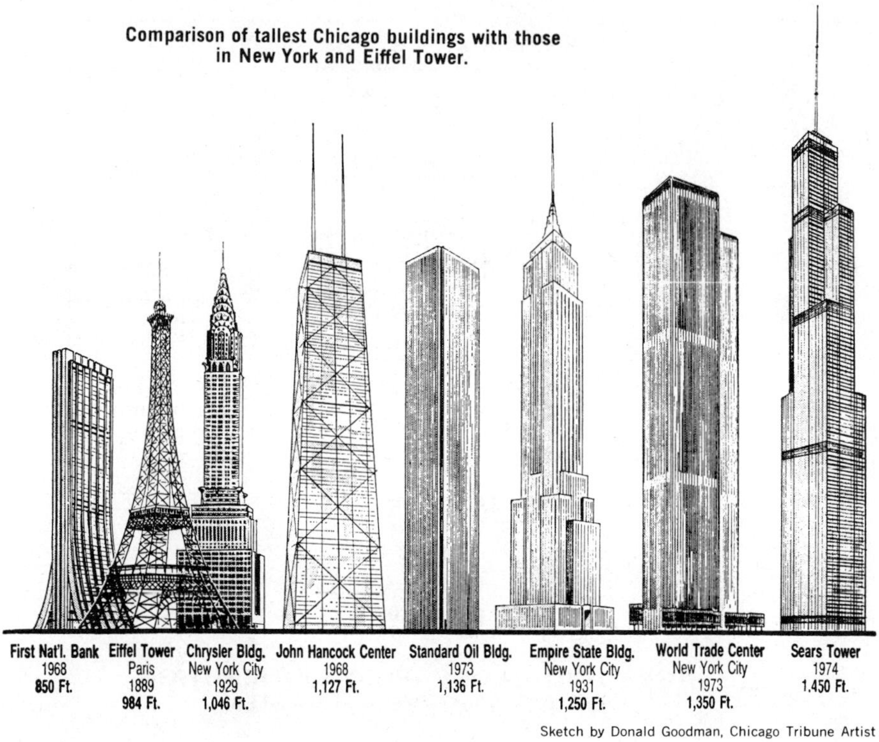

Figure 10.9

You have often seen *pie graphs,* too. The two shown in Fig. 10.10 could be used by an ecology student to show that litter appears on the highway in roughly the same percentages in which it turns up in "solid waste." Pie diagrams are frequently used to illustrate sources of tax money and how it is spent. They can also be used to show certain kinds of batching in the mixing of concrete, ingredients in livestock feed, and in any situation for which *proportioning* can be appropriately indicated by this method.

The *line* graph is also familiar to you. One of those in Fig. 10.11 shows a single line pattern of the projected increase in billions of passenger miles by 1980. The other is a slightly more complicated graph providing a basis for comparison of the rates of growth for different sectors of general aviation.

The Problem of Producing Visual Aids. If you're able to use actual objects, models, or mock-ups, there are no production problems. Either you have the item or items in question, or they can be borrowed for the occasion. Drawings, diagrams, and graphs are harder to come by. However, students and

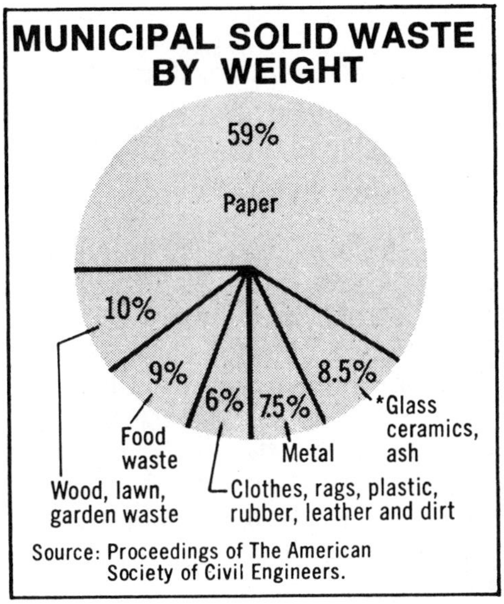

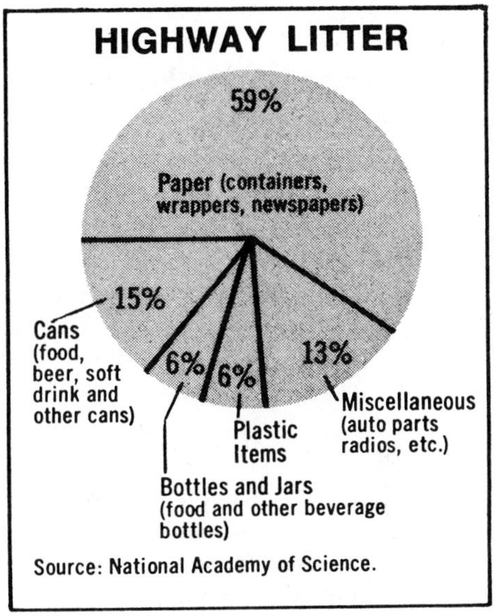

Figure 10.10

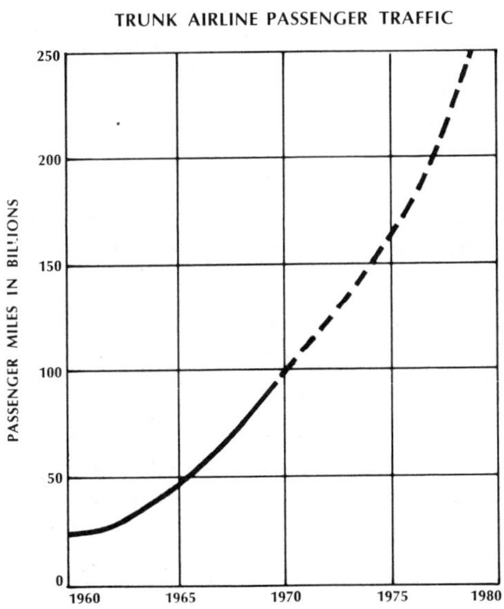

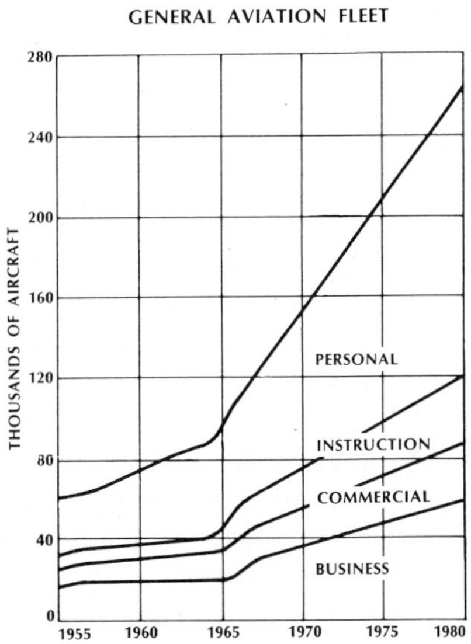

Source: Federal Aviation Administration

Figure 10.11

others usually feel capable of doing the necessary art work, especially since no high degree of sophistication is expected by the average audience. Others call on friends or professional draftsmen or artists for a more finished job. Whatever route you take, you will want to review the "production requirements" below:

1. If you plan to use objects, models, or mock-ups:

   a) *They must be large enough to be easily seen.* Trying to show an audience the details of tooth construction in a gear would be close to impossible, even if the gear itself was easily visible. (A supplementary poster drawing of tooth detail could serve this purpose.)

   b) *They must light enough in weight* to suspend from available hangers or to hold up in the hands for as long as necessary. A casting so heavy that it must remain on a desk or table throughout the talk is not going to be of much use. A mock-up made of plastic, cardboard, or other lightweight materials is occasionally available. Such a demonstration unit can be a completely satisfactory substitute for the real three-dimensional item.

2. If you plan to use posters or flip charts (Fig. 10.12):

   a) *Make them big.* For use in the average classroom, a poster should measure at least $2\frac{1}{2} \times 3$ feet. Sometimes one poster will suffice; if you need more than two or three, use standard "tablets" of chart paper of approximately the same size or larger. As you finish with a page of the chart, you tear it off or turn it over to show the next page.

   b) *Keep them simple.* Cluttering them with detail makes them more difficult to see and understand. Complicated designs and elaborate artistic drawings do little to clarify a talk and can have the opposite effect. Place your labels directly on, next to, or connected by arrows to the diagrammed elements involved.

   c) *Use bold diagrams and lettering.* Thin-line drawing and lettering cannot be easily seen and often cannot be seen at all from the rear of the room. Use *dark* inks, crayons, paints, or pencils on light backgrounds. (Unless you are an art student, the reverse—light colors on dark backgrounds—is seldom successful.) Plastic lettering and drawing aids are inexpensive; their use almost guarantees the neat appearance of a poster or chart.

   d) *Plan the display system.* Is a stand available for posters and/or charts? (Trying to hold a poster or a chart in hand is tiring and awkward.) Are any hooks or clasps available from which you can suspend your visual aids? You will ordinarily find that "standing" them in the chalk rail of a blackboard is impractical; such rails are usually too

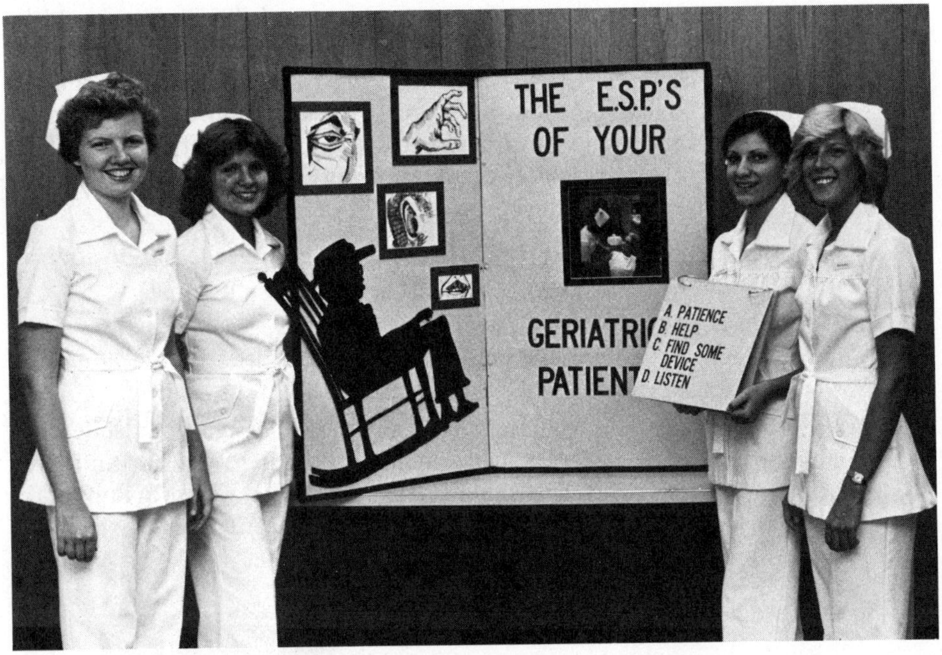

Figure 10.12

low, and even when they are high enough, posters seem to delight in bending and falling from them. Masking tape can be used to attach certain kinds of poster materials to a blackboard or wall. Do some preliminary prospecting in the room for which the aids are planned. The effect of good visuals is easily lost if they are not high enough to be seen.

e) *Test the effect in advance.* Take your visual aids to the room in which they are going to be used, and between classes or at some other time, set them up and check them for easy viewing and reading from a seated position in the back row of the room.

f) Double check "minor" details such as spelling and addition.

3. If you plan to use an overhead or slide projector, do not lose the natural advantages provided by these aids. The overhead projector allows you to magnify and add to or alter diagrams or drawings during the presentation, and you can do this without turning your back to the audience. Generally, it is wise to do all of your pointing and marking on the stage of the projector while you continue to face your listener. Also, do not block your listeners' view by standing between them and the projected image.

The slide projector allows you to picture places and things that would be difficult to visualize with words alone. If possible, either have a friend operate the projector or employ a remote control so that you are able to remain at the front of the room during your presentation. The problem of size and many other things must also be faced in the use of slides. As you may know, you can have slides made from any art that you make available to a slide maker or local photographer. Some rules for slides:

a) As already suggested, *keep them simple.* The audience has to look at the slide and listen to you at the same time.

b) *Use only a few of them.* Except in travelogues, the slides should not be the center of interest. They should be regarded strictly as *aids* to what the speaker has to say.

c) *Be sure that they can be easily seen and read.* Design your slide on a standard sheet of paper (8½ × 11 inches), tape it to a wall, and back off about six feet.[2] If you can read it, the design will probably make an acceptable slide. (Figure 10.13 is an example of a slide which can be easily read.)

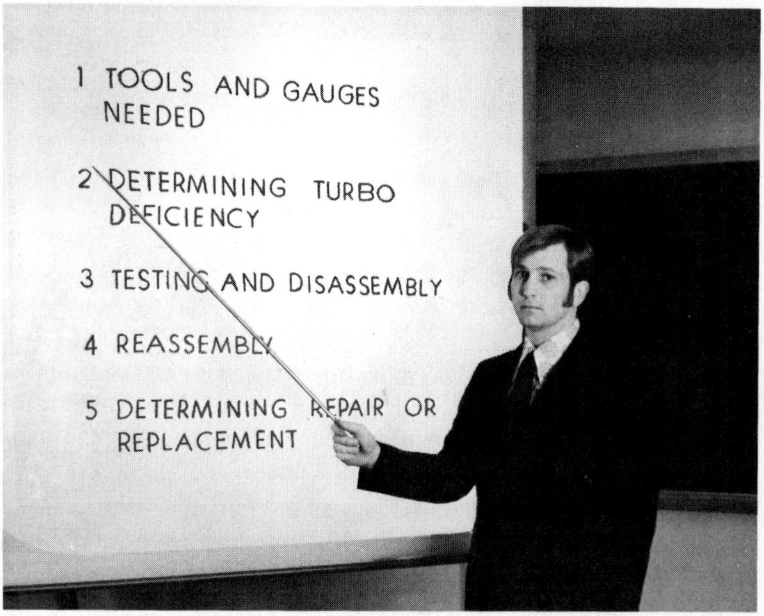

Figure 10.13

2. Prescription given in the *Journal of the Acoustical Society of America* **44** (1968), p. 836.

   d) When in doubt, *consult the experts.* There are people in every community who regularly work on or with slides.

4. Test the equipment ahead of time. Your audience may be willing to tolerate equiment failure, but they will not be so generous if you demonstrate ignorance about the equipment itself. Anticipate what you will do if the equipment, despite all your precautions, fails to work.

5. Feel free to use any other types of aids if they will help your presentation.

   a) Audio aids can add an effective dimension to a presentation, and some points may be most easily made by using audio aids. If, for example, you want your listeners to be aware of sounds that might signal an equipment breakdown, a taped set of the sounds can be most helpful.

   b) Look into the possibility of aids that aim at other senses. If you want the audience to be aware of an odor, it may be possible for you to use an "olfactory" aid—bring the smell to them. As we noted earlier, chemists are now able to duplicate certain smells chemically. The Northern Illinois Gas Company recently included a chemical scratch strip in the monthly bill so that customers who were not familiar with the odor that indicates leaking gas would learn to recognize it.

   c) Consider the possibility of using a videotape recorder for demonstrations, examples of complex subjects, or magnification of small actions or items.

What do you think?

Many meeting rooms have a permanent or portable chalkboard as a part of their standard equipment. Why not make plans to use writing or drawing on the chalkboard as a visual aid to a talk? What problems might be encountered? What would you do if you planned to use the chalkboard and the meeting was suddenly switched to a room without one? There's an old adage about pieces of equipment like slide projectors, motion picture projectors, tape recorders, amplification systems, and other equipment depending on electric power and/or an operator: "If something can go wrong, it will." Have you had any unfortunate experiences with such equipment? What did you do? Have you seen any? What did the speaker do?

Prepare your delivery

Rehearsal. We urge you to rehearse your presentation carefully and thoroughly. This does not mean that you should memorize your message; word-for-word memorization is a waste of time. As you run through the briefing a few times, you can assume that you will never give the talk twice in exactly the same words. When you give the talk before members of a group, you will communicate with them in a way that is different in some respects from your rehearsal experiences.

Well, then, why rehearse? Simply to establish a sequence of patterns and relationships that will make it easier for you to concentrate on communicating with your listeners instead of trying to remember what comes next. Furthermore, it's asking for trouble if you attempt to use a visual aid without having practiced handling it; you'll find yourself talking to the aid instead of to your audience.

If you prepare carefully (and preparing includes rehearsal), you will find it impossible to forget your main ideas and what you want to say in elaborating on them. If you think you'll feel more comfortable with some memorizing, limit that activity to gaining control over your opening and closing sentences; knowing exactly how you're going to begin and how you're going to close will make it easier to get started and will make for a more polished conclusion.

Use of Notes. Many persons are concerned with the question of whether or not to use notes in a presentation. The concern is well taken, but the question implied by that concern is a difficult one to answer. You would do well to keep the following things in mind.

The use of notes will have an effect on your audience. If you use too many notes and are locked to them, the audience may interpret that dependence as a lack of knowledge or an indication of insecurity. As the earlier comment indicated, problems grow out of memorization, but these problems are no greater than the problems that grow out of heavy dependence on notes. If you feel a need to use them, we would recommend that you limit your notes to key words or key ideas—those things that you see as critical to the success of the message. Beyond these few notes, you should depend upon your practice and your basic knowledge of the materials.

There is a major exception to this advice. If you are presenting either complex statistics or direct quotations, we believe that your audience will be more comfortable if they see you referring to a note. This demonstrates that you are not making the comment up.

Incidentally, one way to reduce your need for notes is to make greater use of audiovisual support. Many of the items that you present in this manner will not only be clearer to your audience but also to you as the audiovisual materials serve to jog your memory and help you maintain organization.

Eye Contact. In our discussion of nonverbal behavior, we identified a number of behaviors which will affect your audience's perceptions of and reactions to you. It is important to emphasize that eye contact is one of the most critical of these. In the United States we place particular importance on it. As a speaker, you should make an effort to make frequent visual contact with the members of your audience. In small and medium-sized groups, the contact should be direct and long enough to establish that you really see the person. Avoid scanning your audience's faces—instead, let them know that you see them as individuals.

The Lectern. Far too many speakers have come to believe that the lectern is a necessary part of a public presentation. They appear to feel as if remaining behind it will protect them from all critics and guarantee success. Don't let the lectern use you—you use it. When you come around the podium and move toward your listeners, you give them a point of visual reference. They know you are coming closer, that you are secure, that you care. When you return to the lectern, they see it as a physical transition or, depending on the circumstances, as a return to a more formal relationship. The lectern can be a part of your presentation or you can hide behind it and allow it to become a major source of distraction.

Voice and Gestures. This is the place to say that few people ever talk too loudly and many talk too softly. Turn up the volume high enough so that you're *sure* you are reaching those sitting farthest away from you. If you're not sure, ask them if they can hear you; they'll be glad to answer. The problem of being heard is less acute when a microphone is available. However, if it's the fixed-base type or one built into a lectern, your volume will slide every time you turn to look at or comment on one of the visual aids—another good reason to be so familiar with the visual aids that you don't have to spend any time talking at them. In addition to making certain that your volume is adequate, you will also want to make an effort to vary the tone, rate, and pitch level of your voice.

On the subject of gestures, all that need be said here is that *gestures can be planned.* In the process of practicing a presentation, you have an opportunity to work some appropriate gestures into the talk rather than wait to let them happen spontaneously on the occasion of the talk. The speaker who counts on injecting gestures at that late date often stands there as though he or she were made of wood.

Timing. You will seldom get an opportunity to present a briefing or any other type of talk without a time limit, either stated in advance or implicit in the situation. There is no excuse for using more than the specified time or more time than is reasonable if no time limit is specified. Getting your timing down pat is another advantage of rehearsing. If you find that you're consistently running overtime, cut out some of your material, or cut down on the breadth of the subject you're trying to cover. For example, if a report on "street-paving methods" in your community is taking too long, you can move down progressively from that subject to "asphalt street-paving" to "emulsified asphalt street-paving'' to ''emulsified-asphalt cold-mix street-paving.'' Practically any subject can be limited once and then again and again. On the other side of the coin, when you don't have enough material to fill out the time slot you're expected to fill, don't hesitate to add some.

Provision for Questions. The informative briefing, as you would expect, is a type of communication that is likely to raise some questions in the minds of the listeners. You should plan to give your listeners a chance to ask questions, either as you finish what you have to say on a particular point or at the end of the talk. If questions are encouraged at specified times during the briefing, be careful not to be stalled by unlimited questioning at any one point. The safer practice, especially for speakers with little experience, is to announce that there will be a ''question-and-answer period'' at the close of the briefing.

Feedback ''in Advance.'' You may have a tape recorder or access to one. Recording a rehearsal will give you an opportunity to check the vocal side of your presentation. Some institutions have videotape recorders available for this purpose; they have the added advantage of telling you how well you're handling nonverbal aspects of the talk, including the visual aids. Having a couple of friends on hand for a practice session is another way to get some suggestions for improvement; they can also tell you if they feel that your choice of language is appropriate for the intended audience.

What do you think?

Individuals who use notes in a talk have a variety of ''systems.'' Some speak with their eyes fixed on a succession of note pages. Some use a small card or two carrying a sentence or phrase outline. Some use only a listing of main points on a card or on one of their visual aids. Some use no notes at all. How do you account for these differences in approach? To what extent do you feel a speaker should rely on notes? How do listeners react to a speaker who seems very dependent on notes?

Is there any particular merit in giving a talk—in practice or at any other time—in exactly the same way twice? Are there any good reasons not to give it the same way twice?

In this book we take the position that gestures can be consciously worked into a talk. Would there be any dangers you would want to avoid in doing so? Are there some listeners who might react negatively to gestures during a talk? Who? Is it possible to tailor gestures to fit a set of listeners? How?

Sometimes you hear this comment: ''I just couldn't do a good job on that subject in the time available.'' What do you think of it?

Establish your credibility So far in this chapter we have suggested that your effectiveness in public communication will be enhanced by following certain standard procedures. In addition, you will find that your listeners' view of you personally has much to do with their acceptance or rejection of what you have to say. Listeners must see you as a person to believe. This factor, important as it is in one-to-one and small-group communication, is crucial in one-to-many audience situations, where feedback is not so direct or so easily interpreted.

There are a number of ways to establish this source credibility. *Knowing what you're talking about* is one. An audience of one or many is quick to sense ignorance or carelessness. If you are a *recognized* authority in a field and the audience accepts you as one, a part of your credibility problem is solved. Perceptive listeners will still expect a well-ordered series of good reasons for following your advice. Uncritical or emotional listeners may accept your proposal "on faith," but not too many present-day audiences are made up of those who blindly follow "authoritative pronouncements." That is why it is sometimes necessary to tell an audience something about your qualifications to speak on a particular topic. The listeners will make judgments of their own after you begin to speak.

In addition to knowing what you're talking about, you should believe in the position you're taking. A lack of conviction and insincerity are hard to hide. Listeners must feel *your* confidence in the worth of your proposal; *they must trust you.* If they begin to suspect that your only interest is personal profit or some other strictly personal goal, your credibility will evaporate.

There are other standards, some of them superficial, by which listeners take the measure of a speaker. You are probably aware of some of your own biases. And certainly you've heard comments like these: "She looked so honest." "I just don't believe a salesman with a moustache." "That fellow is someone to trust—he has a good firm handshake and is not afraid to look you straight in the eye." Further, most of us are aware that there is a natural inclination to accept ideas from a forceful, dynamic speaker. We might disregard or reject the same ideas presented by a meek, soft-spoken type. Some people are lucky enough to have "winning personalities." Others have to work hard to make a favorable impression. Whatever your personality may be, honest regard to listener feelings and views is usually paid back in kind by the members of any listening group.

In our earlier chapters, we identified qualities that establish trust, that make you a more credible individual. Here we would emphasize that many of the nonverbal behaviors have great impact on the level of credibility that the audience attributes to you. It is important that you believe in what you are saying, but it is equally important that the audience recognizes that you believe—that you care about the material. It is important that you know about and understand the issue you are considering, but it is also important that the audience believes that you know about and understand the issue. Perhaps the most important steps in acquiring these sorts of audience responses are those of preparation and practice.

PART II—PRESENTATIONAL SPEAKING: SPECIFIC TYPES

Let us now examine in some detail the two techniques of public presentation commonly encountered in the work-setting: the *informative briefing* and the *persuasive proposal*.

The Informative Briefing

As we have already seen, the informative briefing is a presentation in which the speaker's primary objective is to induce in his or her listeners an understanding of a certain body of knowledge. A briefing differs from small-group communication (Chapter 9) in that *one* person now takes full responsibility for presenting information and for interacting with any number of persons from two to 20 or 100 or more.

Determining your purpose If your general purpose in giving a briefing is (1) *instruction*, your emphasis will be on instructing others in how to do something, how to use something, or how to teach something. If your general purpose is (2) *reporting*, your emphasis will be on bringing others up-to-date on a situation, development, or campaign that they are already familiar with. If your general purpose is (3) describing, clarifying, or explaining, your emphasis will be on *general explanation* of the kind, for example, that new students get at the beginning of a semester or that new employees get to acquaint them with a company. All three of these general purposes (instructing, reporting, explaining) present essentially the same problems to speakers and listeners.

Each of the following situations would call for an informative briefing: a corrections officer explaining routine cell block duties to new officers; a supervisor explaining work rules to a group of new employees; a credit manager describing a new credit-application form to members of his or her staff; a consumer-goods expert telling a consumer group how to get the most for a dollar; a senior police officer explaining a football game traffic-control plan to officers assigned to the game; a factory representative giving newspaper pressmen instructions on operating and maintaining a new press; a safety expert explaining the latest accident-prevention methods to a group of supervisors; and a Parks Service guide describing rock formations to a group of tourists.

Similarly, you have encountered informative briefings in the courses you're taking. And if you report to a corrections class what your city or town is doing about drug control, you are providing information. Or if you describe the steps in the process of preparing an income tax return, you are presenting an informative briefing. A professor in a nurses' training program who spends a period or two talking about concepts in counseling is providing information. In the informative briefing, then, the speaker's primary aim is to create or increase audience understanding—to transfer new information.

As in all communication situations, the speaker may also have some additional intentions. For example, when called upon to make a report on the plant safety program, the speaker may try to do an especially good job because he or she sees the occasion as a chance to make a favorable impression leading to a promotion. The fire chief explaining the operation and maintenance of some new equipment may also be trying to persuade his men to handle that equipment properly. The county agent talking about a new method for insect control can be expected to throw in a few words urging an audience of farmers to adopt the new system.

Analyzing your audience The series of audience-analysis questions provided earlier in the chapter will help you here. As always, your task is to begin where the listeners are and take them to another point in their understanding of your topic.

Choosing the organizational pattern As we have seen, organizing a presentation is primarily a matter of following through on what you have decided is your specific purpose by (1) *choosing the main ideas* you want to get across and (2) *determining how you're going to back them up* with explanations, statistics, illustrations, etc. Your analysis of the audience can help you in both operations.

The Step Pattern. One of the most common and useful outlining plans consists of the steps in a process.

If, as a result of your presentation, you want a group of student visitors to know the steps in making paper from wood pulp or the steps in photography, there are two questions you will have to answer. First the listener will want to know why he or she should know the steps, and, second, the listener will want to know the steps. Sometimes the *why* question is answered in your introduction or opening comment, sometimes it is the initial part of your presentation, and sometimes it is a question that you allow your entire presentation to answer. In any case, it *must* be answered at some point. The second question, "What are the steps?" is best answered in the order in which the steps occur. The steps become your main points and the explanation of what goes on in each one becomes your back-up or support. If there are more than five steps in the process, try to telescope them into that number or even into two, three, or four. If you give the listener too many ideas to remember, that listener is like the rest of us—he or she will forget a few. Instead, limit yourself. Share five or six ideas and make it easier for your listener to remember and to react. For example, the processes of paper-making and photography are quite complex; each could easily be discussed under 10 separate and distinct steps. Each could also be discussed under five, as we see in the following examples:

STEPS IN MAKING PAPER FROM WOOD PULP

1. Procurement of raw materials	1. Procurement of raw materials
2. Debarking	
3. Beating	2. Preparation of fibers
4. Grinding	
5. Digesting	3. Formation of fiber sheets
6. Screening	
7. Bleaching	4. Moisture removal
8. Milling	
9. Moisture removal	5. Finishing operation
10. Coating or sizing	

STEPS IN PHOTOGRAPHY

1. Choice of camera	1. Initial choices of equipment
2. Choice of lens	
3. Choice of film	
4. Exposure of film	2. Taking the pictures
5. Fixation of film	3. Developing the film
6. Washing of film	
7. Drying of film	
8. Printing	4. Making the prints
9. Fixation of print	
10. Washing of print	
11. Drying of print	
12. Finishing touches	5. Finishing touches

If you wanted to do some further simplifying of structure, it would take no great ingenuity to see that in each case you could do some further telescoping by planning to take care of the first point in the introduction; other points could also be merged without creating problems. So, then, the original ten steps could become:

Steps in Making Paper from Wood Pulp

1. Preparation of fibers
2. Formation of fiber sheets
3. Finishing operation

Steps in Photography

1. Taking the pictures
2. Making the prints

Of course, the short phrases above are not yet phrased as "main points." To set up the main elements of a skeleton outline, we continue with the photography example. For this, we have to assume that you are a journalism student who has been asked to talk about your specialty, photography, to another journalism class with only one or two students in it who know anything at all about the process. Your purpose may be stated this way: "As a result of this presentation, I want the members of this class to be aware of the steps in the process of photography."

IN THE INTRODUCTION

[Opening sentence:] As some of you may have noticed, I took two of the news photos appearing in the last issue of the campus paper.

[Personal competence:] I have been taking and developing pictures since the age of 10. My father is a free-lance photographer, and photography has always been "big" in our family.

[Purpose of talk:] As you may have already guessed, I'm going to talk about photography. My primary purpose is to introduce you to the basic steps in photography. To do that, I'll be pointing out, first, that taking good pictures is no accident and, second, that making good prints is equally demanding.

[Reasons to listen:] As future journalists, you ought to know something about the elements of photography, because much of your work will be closely related to news photos. You're also aware that, in a tight job market, the reporter who can report a story *and* do the necessary photography has a better chance for a job. By the time I'm finished, some of you may be encouraged to look into the possibility of taking a course in photo-journalism; at the very least, I hope, all of you will have a better understanding of the photo skills which are so much a part of modern journalism.

IN THE BODY

I. Taking good pictures is no accident.

- A. Handling equipment.
- B. Principles of composition.
- C. Shutter speeds.
- D. Proper exposure.

[Transition:] As you can see, anyone willing to pay some attention to detail can become a reasonably good photographer. However, taking the photos is only half the battle.

II. Making good prints is a very important step.

- A. Developing the film.
- B. The process of printing.
- C. Finishing the print.
    1. Retouching.
    2. Cropping.

IN THE CONCLUSION

[Summary:] So we see that there is more to photography than just aiming the camera; good pictures depend on attention to detail, first, in taking the pictures and, second, in making the prints.

[Final comment:] Finally, let me add that there is always room for good reporters in the world of journalism. Those who also know something about photography have an edge over those who do not. I hope that you will end up among those who do.

As you examine this outline, remember that those persons who are most successful at presenting information are successful because they (1) have that information and (2) are able to persuade the listeners that they need the information and that the speaker is the proper source for the information.

You should note that the introduction includes a sentence or two on "Why should they listen to *me*?" (personal competence) and another sentence or two on "What do these listeners have to gain?" (reasons to listen). Those comments are meant to promise answers to those very critical questions.

As for the other parts of the skeleton outline, the opening is intended to get attention and arouse interest; the body of the presentation is supposed to answer the listener need pointed out in reasons to listen; transitions are used to smooth the way for movement from one point to another; the summary reminds the listeners of what has been said; and the final comment brings the message to a reasonable close.

For another example of an informative briefing, we assume that you are the supervisor in a plant area where a battery of new machines has been installed for stamping out a metal base for parking meters. Your problem is to tell a dozen workers how to operate the new equipment. In other words, you are the technician planning to talk with a group of nontechnical employees about the operation of those machines. Shop noise makes it necessary to hold the briefing in a corner of the cafeteria. The outline might look something like this:

IN THE INTRODUCTION

[Opening sentence—with light touch:] The company wanted to make life a little easier for you; that's why the new stampers are being installed to replace the old models.

[Personal competence:] They had me attend a couple of factory demonstration sessions, and you'll be glad to know that it *will* be easier on you to operate these machines.

[Purpose:] First, we'll talk about what this machine is like. Then, we'll cover how to start it, how to operate it, and how to shut it off.

[Reasons to listen:] If we can keep these machines in good operating order, piecework production will go up and so will your pay. But there's the usual safety problem with stampers; unless you watch the score, you have a good chance of losing a finger or two.

IN THE BODY

I. This is what the machine looks like. [Using visual aids.]

   (There follows a discussion of physical characteristics, power requirements, limits of operation, etc.)

   [Transition:] So much for general information. We'll move on to how it works.

II. This is how you start this stamper. [Using visual aids.]

   (Discussion of control positions prior to starting and during warm-up. Mention of necessary adjustments at various stages of operation. Warning of dangers to operator.)

   [Transition:] Any questions about starting?

III. This is what you do in production phases. [Using visual aids.]

(Step-by-step procedures under normal conditions. What to do if something goes wrong. What to look for in diagnosing difficulties.)

[Transition:] Any questions about production operation?

IV. This is how you shut off the stamper. [Using visual aids.]

(Need for fast shut-down under emergency conditions, overheating, etc. Procedure for routine shut-down.)

[Transition:] Any questions about shutting down?

IN THE CONCLUSION

[Summary:] If you have any problems, call me to your station right away. Otherwise, I'm going to assume that you fully understand how to handle this equipment.

[Final comment:] And as I said before, it's in our best interests to keep these machines running full-speed—but let's not take any chances with safety. You won't enjoy the pay if you have to spend some time in the hospital.

Both of the preceding outlines have been examples in which a speaker's plan for organization, except for necessary simplification, depends on the natural sequence of steps in the process being examined.

The Spatial Pattern. The spatial pattern is similar to the step pattern insofar as there is a natural relationship among the materials to be presented. The natural relationship is one of space. You might, for example, take your listeners on a verbal tour of your plant. If the plant is an assembly plant, it would be natural for you to describe the several stations on the assembly line as one encounters them in the assembly process.

The Chronological Pattern. On certain occasions it is natural to organize things on the basis of time. A speaker might describe a task by listing the steps of that task on the basis of when they occur in time. This is an especially appropriate method when the task will span a considerable length of time. For example, if the speaker is informing the listeners of a company's construction plans, it would be natural to describe those plans in the order in which the construction will occur.

The Cause-and-Effect Pattern: When you are called upon to inform an audience of a problem or potential problem, the cause-and-effect method of organization is effective. In the case of an informative briefing on plant safety, you might describe a set of dangerous behaviors and then show what might happen to the listeners if they do not avoid those behaviors and instead observe safety precautions. Occasionally the effects may be so dramatic that you might want to reverse the pattern; that is, show your audience the effects of careless behavior and then enumerate the specific kinds of behaviors that might lead to the effect.

The Topical Pattern. If the informative briefing does not fall into the step, spatial, or chronological classifications, it usually deals with a series of topics and is called *topical.* In this pattern, the speaker determines what order of topics seems most natural and convincing. For example, if you are a social worker appearing before a service club to describe what the community is doing in terms of social services, *you* have to decide what comes first, second, third, etc. You might want to establish this topical order:

I. Our town gives practically no help to individuals in need.

II. Our town gives some help to families in distress.

III. Our town gives considerable help to organized community projects.

Or you might decide that your listeners would prefer the reverse of the order above:

I. Our town gives considerable help to organized community projects.

II. Our town gives some help to families in distress.

III. Our town gives practically no help to individuals in need.

The point is that the order of main ideas in a topical pattern is decided upon by the speaker; the decision is based on what order he or she believes will be most effective with a given group of listeners. What should they hear first, second, third?

For another example of the topical pattern, let's assume that a lecturer in nurses' training is talking about the different ways in which patients may respond to illness. In this particular lecture, she or he may choose to state main ideas in this way:

I. The patient may respond to illness with threats.

II. The patient may respond with frustration.

III. . . . with lack of cooperation.

IV. . . . with expressions of dependency.

V. . . . with complaining behavior.

The order of the ideas above is clearly the choice of the speaker. The presentation could begin with the mildest form of reaction and move to the most violent, or it could start with the violent and move toward the mild. If it appears that the audience would prefer a particular order, it is wise to adopt it. Otherwise, the order which seems most sensible is best.

Perhaps you've noticed a certain similarity in the phrasing of main points or ideas in the examples given for both the step and the topical patterns. Many speakers feel that it is a good idea to aim at making such points as short, as simple, and as generally similar as possible. Those qualities make the main ideas easier for listeners—and the speaker—to remember.

What do you think?

Does setting up a step or topical pattern for a talk have any real advantages? What are they? Some people use the pattern or outline as a guide for writing out a talk word-for-word; they feel that even if they do not memorize the talk, writing it *in oral style* points up gaps in information, forces the composition of transitions, and aids in the timing. Does this make sense to you? What are the advantages of experimenting with a number of ways to organize ideas? Is it possible that one method would be "right" for one audience and another "right" for another?

Typical complete outline: Informative briefing After (1) deciding what your purpose is, (2) reviewing what you know about the listeners, and (3) choosing an appropriate organization plan, what is your next step in preparing for an informative briefing? The following sample outline should serve to provide a summary of the suggestions offered in this chapter. For visual aids, in this case, the speaker would use small pieces of lumber showing (1) various types of knots and (2) various grades of lumber.

IN THE INTRODUCTION

(Purpose) I want to show the listener how to select lumber.

(Interest) A. Right after Christmas vacation, my roommate came back with a cut finger.

1. (Story of his cutting himself while doing some remodeling at home)
2. We then got into a discussion of the lumber that he was using.
   (Account of roommate's not knowing anything about lumber he was using)

(Reasons to listen) B. I am sure that at some time most of you have done some work with wood or have done some remodeling.

1. Chances are good that you went to a lumberyard and just asked for a piece of wood. . . .

2. Afterwards, you realized that the wood you bought was not right for the job, or it was too expensive.

(Experience) C. For the past two years I have worked at Pioneer Lumber Yard, Ottawa, Illinois, and I have become acquainted with the various grades of lumber.

(Purpose) D. Today I am going to pass on some of what I've learned by discussing

1. what factors enter into the grading of lumber, and
2. how these factors determine the grading of lumber.

IN THE BODY

I. Four factors enter into the grading of lumber.

A. Knots

1. As the size of the knot increases, the quality decreases.
2. As the number of the knots increases, the quality of the lumber decreases.
3. The more knots that are close to the edge, the quality of the lumber decreases.
4. Kinds of knots

a. Spike knot—a long thin knot that is extremely hard and becomes loose when the lumber dries out, causing weak spots in the lumber.
b. Ingrown knot—a knot in which the grain has grown into the knot, thus making it a part of the wood.
c. Encased knot—a knot in which the grain of the wood has grown in such a manner that the knot is encased. When the lumber dries, the knot becomes loose and falls out.

B. Pitch pockets—as the number and size of pitch pockets increase, the quality of the lumber decreases.

C. Decay—as the amount of decayed portion on a piece of lumber increases, the quality decreases.

D. Effect of defects on appearance and general utility—if the defects make the board look crude and rough, the quality decreases.

Transition: So we have four factors affecting grading—*knots, pitch pockets, decay,* and *the effect* of those defects on appearance and utility. Let's move on now to what the grades actually are.

II. The factors we've been discussing are used to divide lumber into two broad classes, *select-grade* lumber and *common-grade* lumber.

   A. There are four classes of *select-grade* lumber; all of them have a generally good appearance and finishing quality.

      1. Grade A is lumber that is practically clear with no defects.

      2. Grade B

         a. A few small defects—minor imperfections in manufacturing and seasoning.

         b. Minor pitch defects.

         c. Small hard knots up to ½ inch in diameter.

      3. Grade C

         a. A few small defects that can be covered with paint.
         b. Smooth hard knots up to 1 inch in diameter.
         c. The number of defects per board is about twice that of Grade B.

      4. Grade D

         a. Any number of defects as long as they do not detract from finished appearance when painted.
         b. A few knots more than 1 inch, slightly soft and rough.
         c. The number of defects usually 3–5 times that of Grade B.

   Transition: From the four classes of select-grade lumber, we now move to the next broad classification.

   B. There are five classes of *common-grade* lumber; all have defects that detract from a finished appearance but are suitable for construction purposes.

      No. 1 common

         a. Tight knots.
         b. Limited size of defects.
         c. Watertight.
         d. Contains pitch defects.
         e. ½–¾ inch intergrain knots which will not usually come loose.

      No. 2 common

         a. Larger or coarser defects.
         b. Some pitch pockets or decay.
         c. About 10 percent of the knots are loose.
         d. Maybe some knotholes, but of restricted size.

      No. 3 common

         a. Larger and coarser defects than in No. 2.
         b. Occasional knotholes.
         c. Larger portions of split, decays, and holes than in No. 2.

No. 4 common—extremely low quality of lumber with coarse defects.

No. 5 common—bottom of the heap—mostly good only for scrap.

IN THE CONCLUSION

(Summary)	In this I have tried to explain (1) what factors enter into the grading of lumber and (2) how those factors enter into grading lumber into four select-grade classes and five common-grade classes.
(Closing remarks)	I hope that you now have a fairly good idea of how lumber is graded, and the next time you go to buy lumber, you should have a pretty good idea of what you need for the job you have in mind.

In review, then, the informative briefing is a talk in which the speaker tries to bring his or her listeners to an understanding of a certain body of knowledge.

The preparation steps are:

1. Determining your purpose.
2. Analyzing your audience.
3. Selecting relevant materials.
4. Choosing an appropriate organizational pattern.
5. Planning your visual aids.
6. Preparing your delivery.
7. Establishing your credibility.

Planned talks take time, but the planning pays dividends. The organizational patterns described in this chapter, along with the suggestions on transitions, introductions, and conclusions, can help you present a briefing and also make it easier for an audience to listen to you. Planning and organization will help *you* in talking with an audience and will also give the listeners confidence that you know what you're doing. The speaker's self-confidence and audience's confidence in the speaker usually go hand in hand; they are reason enough to plan one's remarks.

Typical briefing topics The following "typical briefing topics" will give you an idea of the kinds of items that individuals might need to address in the job setting:

General information on:

1. A new method for locating men trapped in a coal mine
2. The use of a computer in billing procedures
3. New developments in turbine engines for cars
4. A new method for controlling auto combustion fumes
5. How the Forestry Service preserves your forests
6. How a particular commodity (tobacco, lumber, eggs, etc.) is graded
7. How a dispatcher keeps track of trains
8. How a corn picker operates

Maintenance and repair procedures for:

1. Envelope sealer
2. Assembly-line conveyor belt
3. Cable-testing machine
4. Burglar alarm
5. Sump pump
6. Parking meter
7. Electric dishwasher
8. Bowling pin-setting machine

Operating instructions for:

1. Tube-bending machine
2. Fork lift
3. Coil-winding machine
4. Stamp-cancelling machine
5. Overhead crane
6. Roto-tiller
7. Screw-making machine
8. Arc welder

The Persuasive Proposal

The persuasive proposal is a presentation in which the speaker's primary objective is to induce in the audience an *acceptance* of his or her proposal for the solution of a problem.

We have already asserted our belief that some degree of persuasion is a part of any communication. If nothing else, the speaker must persuade listeners that he or she (the speaker) is worth listening to. How then does the persuasive proposal differ from an informative briefing? In our minds, it is a matter of degree. As you ask your listener to make a bigger change or take a larger risk, you must concern yourself more with the elements of persuasion. When you want your audience to *know* something, you are asking only a modest change. It is possible that they can come to know something and still will not *do* anything differently as a result of that knowledge. Large numbers of workers *know* that certain work behaviors are dangerous, but they go right on taking risks. If you decide that you want them to *stop* those same procedures, you are asking them to make a significant change, a change that may alter 10 or 12 years of habit. In the latter situation, you may still describe the presentation as informative but elements of persuasion are clearly involved—and if the primary purpose of the talk is *acceptance* of certain safety practices, the talk could be classified as a persuasive proposal.

For a more clear-cut example of a persuasive proposal, let's now assume that you have an idea for a safety training program. You are confident that your program could reduce the accident rate by 20 to 30 percent. The challenge you now face is that of proposing your plan to three persons in upper management. In this instance, you are not only trying to bring about a significant change, but your proposal is directed upward to those superior to you in your organization. At the time of the presentation, you will be speaking to persons in higher positions who can actually make the recommended change, and at the same time that you are calling upon them to take risk, you are taking the greater risk; you are addressing persons who have the power to affect your future.

When you are working on a persuasive proposal, you enhance the chances of your success by paying careful attention to the general procedures discussed earlier in this chapter and to four additional elements: attitude change, group influences, message strategy, and proposal preparation.

Changing attitudes, beliefs, opinions In a persuasive proposal, the speaker wants a listener not only to understand a message but also to change an attitude or take some kind of action. *Action* is a concept that is self-explanatory, but *attitude* may warrant further clarification.

In Chapter 6, you will remember, we defined attitude as a predisposed response to people, ideas, and things that we encounter. If you feel strongly that "controlling prices is bad policy," you have an overall attitude toward such controls that would presumably stand in the way of your supporting them. Over the years, you have learned what you know about the economy; your position is based on what you have learned; you feel strongly about your position, and the way you feel about it predisposes you to react unfavorably whenever the subject of price control comes up.

Your beliefs are close to being in the attitude category; in fact, the word *belief* could often be substituted for attitude. However, a belief statement is considered to fall short of attitude status in that a belief does not indicate *an overall view* of the item or items under consideration. You could have a number of beliefs that a political office holder was (1) handsome, (2) courteous, (3) unsophisticated, (4) honest, (5) conservative, (6) careless in dress, and (7) a good family person. Your general evaluation or attitude toward this person could be favorable. (If it became known that you went out and voted for him or her, there would be behavioral evidence to the effect that your attitude was favorable.)

You are also familiar with a special kind of attitude, namely *prejudice;* it is an overall evaluation or attitude based on a number of mistaken beliefs. A religious bigot may be totally honest; the problem is that he or she believes too many myths and untruths about another religious group. And all those myths and untruths are reflected in the following unfavorable attitude toward the other group: "I don't have any use for those people." Of course, it is also possible to have an unfavorable attitude based on beliefs which you have good reason to hold.

Below the level of strongly held beliefs and attitudes is the level of *opinions, tastes,* or *preferences.* Maybe you have preference for a certain brand of cola or other soft drink; you like it (taste) and it is your present view (opinion) that it is as good as any other such product on the market. Other things being equal, you may continue buying that brand for some time. However, you would seldom feel so strongly about "brand allegiance" that someone with a good argument couldn't convince you that you should make a change. (And even farther down the scale, we come to the neutral or no-position situation, in which you have no views at all, one way or the other; for instance, if you haven't ever considered running for office, people trying to get you to do so might have to overcome initial surprise and inertia, but the presumption is that you would have an open mind, at least in the opening phases of the discussion.)

At the opposite end of the continuum is the *value.* When all or practically all the members of a group, organization, or society very strongly hold the same general view or attitude, that very broadly accepted view is commonly called a value (or common premise). For example, if the great majority of U.S. citizens feel that "American industrial know-how is superior to that of any other country," that view is a basic position or value shared by most of our people. Other typical American values: equality of opportunity, generosity toward the poor and afflicted, faith in hard work, and optimism about the future.[3] When you know that a particular group holds a value in common, you can set up that view as a target for change or, more likely, take advantage of it as support for your persuasive line of argument.

In summary of the ideas above (and of those in Chapter 6), it may be helpful to you to think of the word *attitude* as representing a wide variety of "predispositions to think and act," which range from the less stable individual opinions, tastes, and preferences through beliefs and belief clusters or attitudes to the more stable general values accepted by the community at large. If you go to a restaurant with a friend who doesn't have a taste for fish, you may be able to talk him or her into trying broiled fresh salmon. If someone tells you that he or she believes the state in which you live is behind other states in needed social legislation, you may be able to change or weaken that belief by citing the growing numbers of progressive bills being passed by your legislature each year. If someone says he is against large corporate farms, you may undertake to ask him for his reasons (beliefs), and after suggesting that there may be some weaknesses in them, you may try to sell him on your reasons (beliefs) for adopting a different stance (attitude). Lastly, someone may point to another person as an example of the American ideal or value, "the self-made man." In other words, a person of humble background is generally admired for having achieved fame and fortune within the framework of our system of free enterprise. You may personally hold that happiness comes not from piling up dollars and possessions but from living "the simple life" away from the drives and competitions that produce ulcers. As you would expect, changing or even modifying a widely shared value is exceedingly difficult and seldom attempted.

It would be nice to be able to say at this point that experts on the definition of persuasion have also worked out some effective persuasive formulas. Unfortunately, about all they agree on is the fact that knowing your listeners or receivers is fundamental to success. You have to know as much as possible about their individual or collective (in a crowd) background and current thinking. Then, even if they do what you are trying to persuade them to do, you cannot assume that you were persuasive. They may have been planning the action long before you appeared on the scene, and you may have irritated them almost to the point of not doing it; they may be doing it only because they like you personally; they may be doing it because they have a matching favor to ask of you in the near future; someone else may have persuaded them to do it; or they may have wavered several times between doing it and not doing it, and you just accidentally stopped talking when they were on the "doing" wavelength.

3. For a longer list, see Edward D. Steele and W. Charles Redding, "The American Value System: Premises for Persuasion," *Western Speech* **26** (Spring 1962), pp. 83–91.

In other words, persuasion *followed* by action does not necessarily mean that persuasion *caused* the action. Nevertheless, it is only by action that you can really do any measuring of persuasion; for someone to *tell* you that you have been persuasive means little unless it is followed by some kind of activity demonstrating that they have changed (adopted or abandoned, weakened or strenthened) a known attitude.

Recognizing group influences Some of the ways in which people react in a communication situation have nothing to do with their individual views, nothing to do with the message, and nothing to do with the speaker. Earlier in this chapter it was pointed out that group-held views or values could be the target for change or could be used, directly or indirectly, as support for your case. Among the stronger bases for such attitudes or values are the "institutions" to which one belongs or to which one professes allegiance. We are also influenced by the smaller informal groups to which we belong or want to belong and by the individual leaders to whom we look for advice and guidance. To refresh your memory on the influences of group consensus, group pressure, and group leadership, you may want to review the section in Chapter 6 on "The Listener and Group Influence." A speaker cannot afford to ignore situational influences of those kinds. Likewise, a speaker can take advantage of one other group phenomenon, that of group participation.

There is no faster way to enliven the proceedings in a speaker-audience situation than to make provision for some kind of active participation on the part of the listeners. Many a "lost cause" has been rescued by a question-and-answer period or by some other device offering active involvement to those present (e.g., having listeners move into a number of small discussion groups).

What do the observations above mean to you as one who may be making a persuasive proposal? In some situations, you will want to enhance and highlight the association of a person or persons with a particular institution, group, or leader, and in others you will want to minimize or ignore such an association. Second, you will note that, no matter how strong group-anchored attitudes may be, change can be effected through introducing evidence that others in the group have already changed their views in the direction advocated. Third, you will recognize that the influential member or members of a group should, under certain circumstances, be the prime targets of the persuasive message because of the influence they exert on other members of the group. Finally, you will be aware that there are some inherent advantages in fostering audience participation.

Adopting a message strategy Once you know as much as possible about the attitudes of your prospective listeners and about the group influences at work among them, you are ready to anticipate reactions as you work on the content of the proposal you intend to make. In other words, you are in a position to make adjustments in the basic message from the standpoints of strategy and structure.

Advertising is a kind of persuasive message that you see and hear every day. In some ads, the message is a simple reminder of one or more of your needs and desires; for example, "Write today and we will send you information on how you can get a high school diploma or a college degree by correspondence only." The self-concept, of course, is always a primary target of any approach: "You'll be proud of yourself when you finish one of these courses." In other ads, the message is a threat accompanied by a ready solution: "Is your hair dry and unattractive? Try Lubo-Charm, the perfect shampoo, and see what a difference it makes!" If this is a television ad, the first shot shows a girl looking anxiously at her dry and stringy hair; in the second shot, she radiates happiness as, with hair beautifully done, she basks in the eyes of an admiring male. Some ads just concentrate on the solution, because the problem is so well known. For instance, "Buy this handy gadget for easy and quick dicing of potatoes, vegetables, and fruits."

In the persuasive setting, then, the listener is concerned with questions like these: What does this proposal mean to me? Personal gain? A boost to my *ego*? Satisfaction of some need or desire? Avoidance of pain or discomfort? Why should I go along with the idea or course of action suggested?

To convince the listener that he or she should indeed go along with your proposals, your first decision is necessarily one of choosing the overall strategy which you feel will cause the listener to do something or change his or her attitudes in some way.

Determining the persuasive angle of attack The tension-and-release or the need-and-solution approaches are generally considered basic to persuasion. We have seen that people are always concerned with their self-concept and with the satisfaction of the needs and desires supporting those views. Every human being responds to someone who shows him or her how to attain those needs and desires, whether they are real or imagined. Every human being also responds to perceived threats or blocks to the attainment of those goals. In either case, having wants or being prevented from attaining them creates tensions. Stated differently, an effective tactic in persuasion is to make people aware of their needs and then relieve them of the anxieties that accompany those needs, or, if they are already anxious, try only to dispel their anxieties. For example, the insurance salesperson often uses the technique of inducing worries about the lack of adequate protection and then shows you how easily those worries can be resolved by buying a particular policy. If you say that you're worried about being able to pay the premiums at a time in life when your earnings are relatively low, *that* problem is easily solved with a delayed-payment program.

Perhaps you are familiar with the idea of tension-and-release under the heading of the *need-for-a-change* proposal. Whatever terms you use, it is clear that in some instances you could concentrate on *need* or *tension only;* for example, pointing out the features of a particular multispeed bicycle (tension) until the prospective purchaser buys it. To put it another way, you provide the tension and the listener provides the relief from it. In other instances, you offer *relief from an existing tension;* you convince people who are worried about future food shortages that the coastal areas of the seas can be sucessfully "farmed."

We're assuming that you will not say one thing in one part of a talk and contradict it in another; in other words, your message must be consistent. All of us want to be consistent and are uncomfortable or tense when we are not. So it is that listeners faced by the effort of someone to change their attitudes will: (1) modify those attitudes to relieve the conflict with the new ideas; of (2) try to resolve the difficulty by justifying and reaffirming their old attitudes; or (3) try to dodge, distort, or attack the incoming messages. As a speaker, of course, you hope that your listeners will be in group 1, and that they will change their attitudes or follow your advice on a particular action. Nevertheless, they may be in group 2 and may be stubbornly insistent, for instance, that "the old ways are the best ways." (If you believe that the listeners may be in that group, plan your approach so that it can be quickly modified on the spot to one that will be more acceptable to the listeners.) Finally, if you have any reason to believe that the majority of an audience may "try to dodge, distort, or attack the incoming messages," change your approach to one which that particular audience will find less threatening and more acceptable. For instance, people who smoke *know* that smoking is inconsistent with good health; you can badger a few into quitting, but it is generally better strategy in talking with a group to suggest only a reduction in smoking. In other words, plan the purpose of the proposal and the proposal itself with the idea of *keeping as many as possible of the audience in group 1.*

Preparing the proposal Many of the suggestions previously offered on general procedures and on the preparation of the informative briefing have application to the persuasive proposal. However, the proposal is clearly a greater challenge and obviously more complex; consequently, you will want to expand the procedural steps to cover that increased complexity in planning and structure:

1. *Determine your purpose* along the lines already suggested in this chapter.
2. *Analyze the problem to be solved.* For this purpose, follow the problem-solving procedure suggested in Chapter 9, in the section on "The Problem-Solving Group," or the alternative approach below.
    a) *Is there a need for a change?*
        1) What is wrong with the present method or situation?
        2) What evidence is there that the present method is unsatisfactory?

b) *What is the solution to the problem?*
Has it been worked out in detail?

c) *Will the solution meet the need?*
(A plan that only partially meets the need will not solve the problem.)

d) *Will the solution create any new problems?*
(A solution which creates new problems is seldom acceptable.)

3. *Analyze the audience.* Use the audience analysis pattern described in this chapter. Add other questions which you consider appropriate.

4. *Construct the message.* Make use of both analyses (2 and 3 above). Follow the recommendations in this chapter on organizational pattern and on the use of visual aids. Take into account what has been said about attitude change, group influences, and message strategy.

5. *Plan to do what you can to enhance your credibility.* Know what you're talking about, take an honest stand, and try to "win friends" as well.

6. *Try to anticipate questions* which listeners may ask. Prepare answers for them in advance.

7. *Rehearse your proposal* until you are confident that you have full control of every phase of it.

Typical outlines The following outlines provide, first, an overview of the general structure of the persuasive proposal and, then, a specific example of one such proposal.

IN THE INTRODUCTION

A. Begin with an attention-getting sentence.

B. State your purpose, namely, to obtain the approval of the group for your proposal. Explain how you are going to go about it by first discussing the problem and then suggesting the solution.

C. Cite whatever advantages the listeners stand to gain from listening to you.

D. Tell the listeners how you happen to know something about the problem in question.

IN THE BODY

I. Describe the *problem* in detail (use visual aids).

A. Open with evidence that there is, in fact, a problem; point to "undesirable effects" which are obvious or which can be shown to exist.

B. Try to pin down causes of the problem.

C. Set up criteria a good solution must meet. (If you have found three major causes of the difficulty, you will probably have to find at least three "cures.") You can plan your criteria along the following lines.

1. What must the solution do?

2. What must it not do?

II. Describe the *solution* in detail (use visual aids).

A. State your overall approach to the solution.

B. Present its main features.

C. Show how your solution meets the criteria set up in your discussion of the problem phase. A good way to do this is to take up the criteria one by one and show how a part of your solution handles each criterion.

D. Meet objections.

1. If you know of objections to what you are proposing, try to meet them by showing how proposal advantages outweigh the objections.

2. Show workability. Discuss success of proposal undcr similar conditions or under test conditions.

IN THE CONCLUSION

A. Summarize the main elements of your talk—major details of the problem and major details of the solution. *Emphasize the advantages to be gained from it.*

B. Conclude with an appeal for approval of your proposal. Ask for questions on any part of your analysis of the problem or on your solution.

Typical Complete Outline Persuasive Proposal:

Purpose: To obtain group approval for a new forage weight and dump mechanism. (Talk given by student technician who sees opportunity to improve forage harvesting methods.)

Listeners: The Farm Director, the Farm Superintendent, and the forage research department heads of a Farmers' Forage Research Cooperative. Their attitude toward new methods is one of cautious interest.

Visual aids: Slides showing old and new procedures.
Charts showing comparative costs of old and new procedures.

IN THE INTRODUCTION

(Attention) It's a good many years since harvesting on our research farms has been done with a hand scythe. At the same time, there's a danger that we get to thinking our "modern methods" are so good they can't be improved upon.

(Reasons to listen) All of you know that our harvesting costs have been going up, and, in a period of very tight budgets, any harvesting method that will be more efficient and will also cut costs is worth investigating.

(Purpose) I am going to review the costs of our present harvesting system. Then a new system with lower costs will be presented for your consideration.

(Experience) Most of you are aware that I have been working for you during the summers since 1975. I have been a part of the harvesting crew for the local farm, so the present harvesting method is very familiar to me. The new method was first tried here last summer, and I spent much of my spare time last winter working on refinements for it.

IN THE BODY

I. The problem is that our harvesting costs are high and going higher.

A. Let me review for you the costs of our present method.

1. For two men on a trip to Orange, Virginia, 15 hours of driving time one way, two days for travel, one day for harvest, at $6.00 per hour per man with overtime for travel days, Wage cost: $540.00.
2. Three extra hands hired on location for eight hours at $2.50 per hour per man, Wage cost: $60.00.
3. Meals for two men, three days at $12.00 per day per man. Food cost: $72.00.
4. Housing for two men for two nights at $24 per night, Motel cost: $48.00.

Total cost for harvesting the 600 test plots at Orange: $720.00, or *$1.20 cents per plot*.

B. In view of the costs above, it is quite expensive to harvest a remote site with the five-man crew required to handle current equipment.

C. Any good solution, then, would have to
   1. Be cheaper than $1.20 per plot harvested.
   2. Cover any added depreciation costs for equipment.
   3. Cut down on the manpower required.

Transition: Since we know what our costs are and also know what requirements a solution would have to meet, we can now move on to the discussion of a solution.

II. I am proposing a new combination of equipment operated by one man only.
   A. The new equipment combination consists of these elements:
      1. An easy-to-empty basket device to catch the chopped forage as it is directed from the harvester chute.
      2. A load cell and scale attached to the basket to weigh the forage from each plot.
      3. A clipboard holder mounted close to the operator to record the forage weight for each plot.
      4. A modified corn elevator conveyor to convey the emptied basket contents to the cart.
      5. As you see in this last slide [Fig. 10.14], a four-foot wide metal cart with a volume of 32 cubic feet.

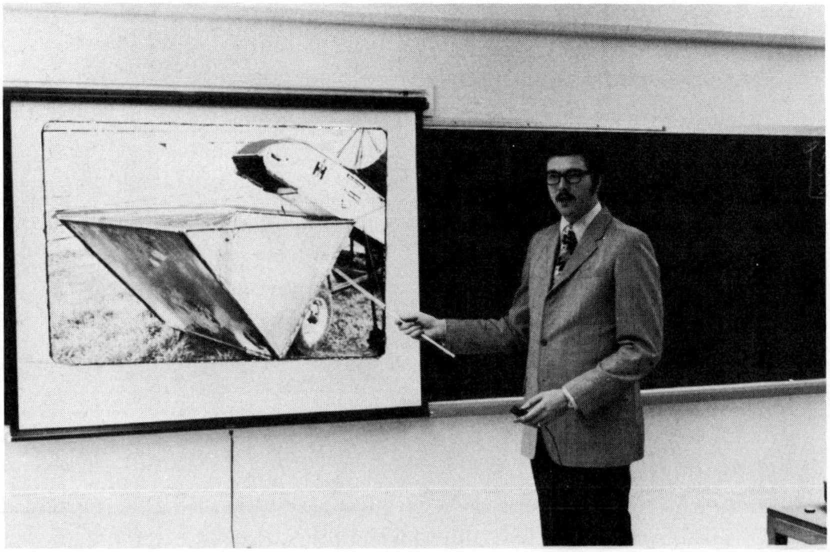

Figure 10.14

Transition: If you have any questions about the equipment which I have been showing you [slides], I'll be glad to answer them at the close of this presentation. For now, let's move right on to costs of operation.

B. What are the costs involved in one-man operation of this equipment?

   1. The superintendent of the local farm had the equipment you've been looking at constructed or modified for a total of $1,800.

   2. If one man took this equipment on a trip like the one to Orange, Virginia, the costs would be these:

      a. Wage cost: 5 days of 8 hours at $6 per hour $240

      b. Food cost: 5 days at $12 per day 60

      c. Motel cost: 4 nights at $18 per night 72

   Total cost would be $372, or *62 cents per plot.*

C. How does the new plan meet our criteria for a good solution?

   1. Is it cheaper per plot harvested? Yes, by approximately 60 cents per plot.

   2. Does it cover depreciation of the equipment?

      Amortized over five years, the equipment costs only $360 per year; this cost is more than covered by the savings we can make in manpower.

   3. Is there a cut in the manpower required?

      The reduction in manpower from five to one results in a saving of $350 per trip to Orange, Virginia. We have four such trips per year for an annual saving of $1400.

D. Is this plan workable?

   1. It was tried last summer and failed.

      The oil pressure system of the scale mounting on the harvester was subjected to so much vibration that the readings were inaccurate.

   2. The bugs have now been worked out.

      a. The only connection between harvester and cart is now the point of the hitch and the hydraulic lines.

      b. A recent test in heavy grass showed a high degree of accuracy in the scale readings.

IN THE CONCLUSION

A. The forage harvesting plan I have been describing is easily transported and handled by one man instead of five. The equipment costs are more than covered by the manpower savings. All the bugs have been worked out, and the system is completely reliable.

B. Because of the savings we can make and because using this equipment will free both manpower and money for other assignments, I hope that you will adopt this new harvesting method. You undoubtedly have some questions on this proposal; I will be glad to try to answer them now.

Typical proposal topics This list of topics is intended to give you some examples of ways in which proposals fit into job settings:

1. A police lieutenant might propose to his superiors the adoption of the "team approach" to patrolling the community.
2. A department store salesperson might propose to a group of department managers a new approach to handling cash refunds, one which sales employees believe will exert better controls over those refunds.
3. A perceptive supervisor might propose a reordering of the assembly process in order to increase production of the units being manufactured.
4. A personnel manager might propose to the company board of directors that it adopt a new health and life insurance program for the employees.
5. The leader of a research team might propose to the directors of a research foundation that they support the team with a financial grant substantially higher than in past years.

SUMMARY

Everything we have said about general procedures and about preparing the informative briefing is true about preparing the persuasive proposal . . . and much of what we've said about the proposal is also applicable to the briefing. What makes persuasion more difficult is that the speaker is trying to bring about a change in attitude and/or an observable action. Attitudes represent views held and positions taken *before* the proposal is made. When attitudes are known to stand in the way of acceptance of a proposal, the speaker must make the effort to change them, modify them, or at least take them into account. This means that if an influential listener is opposed to cartoons, you don't use cartoons. It means that if your listeners are opposed to spending more money for equipment, overcoming their attitudes on costs will not be easy. However, it also means that if your proposal is sound, a way can be found to present it in a reasonable and effective way.

In terms of overall theory and practice, this chapter covered (1) the place occupied by the public presentation in the work setting, (2) general procedures common to all presentations, (3) specific procedures designed for the informative briefing, and (4) special elements and procedures demanding attention in the persuasive proposal.

Epilogue

"My personal feeling is that this is how any further improvement of the world will be done: by individuals making Quality decisions and that's all."

Robert Pirsig in ***Zen and the Art of Motorcycle Maintenance***

In the course of this book, we have examined the role that communication is playing or will play in your career, and we have shared information with you that we believe can help you increase the effectiveness of your communication efforts.

We leave you with Pirsig's thought because the single, most important bit of advice that we can offer you concerning your communication efforts is that they are yours—you are responsible for them. *You must make the decisions.* You will decide what to communicate, when to communicate, and how to communicate. Truly, it is only through individuals accepting the responsibility for making "Quality" decisions that we can hope to meet the challenges of the future.

Be like Fireman Tom Patrick, in Studs Terkel's *Working*—be able to "look back and say . . . I did something on earth."

Bibliography

Besides books and articles used in the preparation of the text, this bibliography includes selected books and articles which may have immediate application to speech communication in a career context.

American Business Communication Association Bulletin (December 1975).

Anastasi, Thomas E., Jr. *Face to Face Communication.* Cambridge, Mass.: Massachusetts Management Center of Cambridge, 1967.

Anastasi, Thomas E., Jr., and Sidney A. Dimond. *Listening on the Job.* Reading, Mass.: Addison-Wesley, 1972.

"Back to School for Better Speech Making," *Business Week* (August 11, 1973), p. 58 ff.

Bales, Robert F. "In Conference," *Harvard Business Review,* **32** (1954), pp. 44–50.

Balinsky, Benjamin. *The Selection Interview: Essentials for Management.* New York: Martin M. Bruce, 1962.

Balinsky, Benjamin, and Ruth Burger. *The Executive Interview.* New York: Harper & Row, 1959.

Banaka, W. H. *Training in Depth Interviewing.* New York: Harper & Row, 1971.

Barnlund, Dean C., and Franklyn S. Haiman. *The Dynamics of Discussion.* Boston: Houghton Mifflin, 1960.

Bassett, Glenn A. *Practical Interviewing: A Handbook for Managers.* New York: American Management Association, 1965.

Beebe, Steven A. "Eye Contact: A Nonverbal Determinant of Speaker Credibility," *Speech Teacher* **23** (January 1974), pp. 21–25.

Birdwhistell, Ray L. *Kinesics and Context: Essays on Body Motion Communication.* Philadelphia: University of Pennsylvania Press, 1970.

Black, James M. *How to Get Results from Interviewing.* New York: McGraw-Hill, 1970.

Blake, Robert, and Jane S. Mouton. "A 9,9 Approach for Increasing Organizational Productivity," *Personal and Organizational Change Through Group Methods: The Laboratory Approach,* Edgar H. Schein and Warren G. Bennis (eds.) New York: John Wiley & Sons, 1965, pp. 169–183.

Bolles, Richard Nelson. *What Color is Your Parachute*? Berkeley, Cal.: Ten Speed Press, 1977.

Bowles, Jerry. "I Improved My Image," *Esquire* **82** (August 1974), pp. 66–69 ff.

Bowman, Lee. "Executives As Public Speakers," *Dun's* **103** (January 1974), pp. 71–72A.

Breth, Robert D. *Dynamic Management Communications.* Reading, Mass.: Addison-Wesley, 1969.

Broadwell, Martin T. *The Supervisor and On-the-Job Training.* Reading, Mass.: Addison-Wesley, 1969.

Buys, William E., Charles V. Carlson, Hite Compton, and Allan D. Frank. *Speech Teacher* **17** (November 1968), pp. 307–310.

Cartwright, Dorwin, and Alvin Zander (eds.). *Group Dynamics, Research and Theory,* 3rd ed. New York: Harper and Row, 1968.

Deutsch, Morton. "Field Theory in Social Psychology," *The Handbook of Social Psychology.* Gardner Lindzey and Elliot Aronson (eds.) Vol. I. Reading, Mass.: Addison-Wesley, 1968, pp. 412–487.

Dewey, John. *How We Think.* Boston: D.C. Heath, 1933.

Dickson, Paul. *The Future of the Workplace.* New York: Weybright and Talley, 1975.

Doob, Anthony N., Alan Gross. "Status of Frustrator as an Inhibitor of Horn Honking Responses," *Journal of Social Psychology* (December 1968), pp. 213–218.

Doyle, James J. "Outstanding Managers are Myths from Textbooks, Consultant Says," UPI *Elgin Daily Courier News* (July 17, 1977).

Drucker, Peter F. *Management: Tasks, Responsibilities, Practices.* New York: Harper & Row, 1974.

Duker, Sam (ed.). *Listening: Readings,* Vol. I. New York: Scarecrow Press, 1966.

Duncan, Starkey. "Nonverbal Communication," *Psychological Bulletin* **72**, pp. 118–137.

Endicott, Frank S. *A College Student's Guide to Career Planning.* Chicago: Rand McNally, 1967.

Fenlason, Anne F. *Essentials in Interviewing.* New York: Harper & Row, 1962.

Fenn, Margaret. "Factors in Interpersonal Relations," *Journal of the American Hygienists' Association* **42** (1968), pp. 138–146.

Goffman, Erving. *Behavior in Public Places.* New York: Free Press, 1963.

Goffman, Erving. *The Presentation of Self in Everyday Life.* Garden City, N.Y.: Doubleday, 1959.

Gordon, Raymond L. *Interviewing: Strategy, Techniques, and Tactics.* Homewood, Ill.: Dorsey Press, 1969.

Gordon, Thomas. "Group-Centered Leadership and Administration," in Carl R. Rogers *et al., Client-Centered Therapy.* Boston: Houghton Mifflin, 1951, pp. 320–383.

Gulley, Halbert E. *Discussion, Conference, and Group Process.* New York: Holt, Rinehart and Winston, 1968.

Hall, Edward T. *The Hidden Dimension.* Garden City, N.Y.: Doubleday, 1966.

Haney, William V. *Communication and Organizational Behavior.* Homewood, Ill.: Richard D. Irwin, 1973.

Harral, Stewart. *Keys to Successful Interviewing.* Oklahoma City: University of Oklahoma Press, 1954.

Hays, Joyce S., and Kenneth Larson. *Interacting with Patients.* New York: Macmillan, 1963.

Hennig, Margaret, and Anne Jardim. *The Managerial Woman.* Garden City, N.Y.: Anchor Press/Doubleday, 1977.

Hoff, Ron. "What's Your Presentational Quotient?" *Advertising Age* (January 16, 1978), pp. 93–95.

Holtzman, Paul D. *The Psychology of Speakers' Audiences.* Glenview, Scott, Foresman, 1970.

Homans, George C. *The Human Group.* New York: Harcourt, Brace & World, 1950.

Hoppock, Robert. *Occupational Information,* 3rd ed. New York: McGraw-Hill, 1967.

Johnson, Lyndon Baines. *The Vantage Point.* New York: Holt, Rinehart and Winston, 1971.

Journal of the Acoustical Society of America **44** (1968).

Kirkham, George L. "What a Professor Learned When He Became a Cop." *U.S. News and World Report* (April 22, 1974), pp. 70–72.

Knapp, Mark L. *Nonverbal Communication in Human Interaction.* New York: Holt, Rinehart and Winston, 1972.

Kron, Thora. *The Management of Patient Care.* Philadelphia: Saunders, 1971.

LaBenne, Wallace D., and Bert I. Greene. *Educational Implications of Self-Concept Theory.* Pacific Palisades, Cal.: Goodyear, 1969.

Laird, Dugan, and Richard C. Grote. *Solving Managerial Problems.* Reading, Mass.: Addison-Wesley, 1971.

Leavitt, Harold J. *Managerial Psychology.* Chicago: University of Chicago Press, 1958. Second and third editions appeared in 1964 and 1972.

"Living in: Relations Between Chicanos and Police in Riverside," *Time* (April 21, 1975), pp. 33–34.

"Manager's Memo," *Chicago Daily News* (June 21, 1977), p. 31.

Martin, John Bartlow. *Adlai Stevenson of Illinois.* Garden City, N.Y.: Doubleday, 1976.

Maslow, A. H., and N. L. Mintz. "Effects of Esthetic Surroundings: Initial Effects of Three Esthetic Conditions Upon Perceiving 'Energy and Well Being' in Faces," *Journal of Psychology* **41**, pp. 247–254.

Maslow, A. H. *Motivation and Personality.* New York: Harper & Row, 1970.

McCroskey, James C. *Introduction to Rhetorical Communication.* Englewood Cliffs, N.J., 1968.

McGinniss, Joe. *The Selling of the President, 1968.* New York: Trident, 1969.

Mehrabian, Albert. *Silent Messages.* Belmont, Cal.: Wadsworth, 1971.

Merton, R. K., *et al., The Focused Interview.* Glencoe, Ill.: Free Press, 1956.

Mills, Theodore M. *Group Transformation: An Analysis of a Learning Group.* Englewood Cliffs, N.J.: Prentice-Hall, 1964.

Miner, John B. *Personnel and Industrial Relations.* New York: Macmillan, 1969.

Minor, Ed. *Simplified Techniques for Preparing Visual Instructional Materials.* New York: McGraw-Hill, 1962.

Molloy, John T. "Looking Right!" *Chicago Daily News* (November 30, 1976), p. 15.

Morrisey, George L. *Effective Business and Technical Presentations.* Reading, Mass.: Addison-Wesley, 1968.

Morrison, James H. *The Human Side of Management.* Reading, Mass.: Addison-Wesley, 1971.

Muchmore, John. "The Uniform: Its Effect," *Police Chief* (January 1975), pp. 70–71.

Nichols, Ralph G., and Leonard Stevens. *Are You Listening*? New York: McGraw-Hill, 1957.

New York Life Insurance Company. *Making the Most of Your Job Interview.* New York: New York Life Insurance Company. A booklet available through New York Life agents.

Payne, S. L. *The Art of Asking Questions.* Princeton: Princeton University Press, 1951.

Peters, Herman J., and James C. Hansen (eds.). *Vocational Guidance and Career Development.* New York: Macmillan, 1971.

Pfeiffer, J. William, and John E. Jones. *A Handbook of Structured Experiences for Human Relations Training.* Iowa City: University Associates Press, 1969 (Vol. 1), 1970 (Vol. 2), 1971 (Vol. 3).

Phillips, Gerald M. and Eugene C. Erickson. *Interpersonal Dynamics in the Small Group.* New York: Random House, 1970.

Pope, LeRoy. "Accountant Claims Ability to Type, Shear Sheep," UPI *Elgin Daily Courier News* (April 4, 1977), p. 9.

Rogers, Carl R., *et al. Client-Centered Therapy.* Boston: Houghton Mifflin, 1951.

Rogers, Carl R. *Counseling and Psychotherapy.* Boston: Houghton Mifflin, 1942.

Rogers, Carl R., and F. J. Roethlisberger. "Barriers and Gateways to Communication," *Harvard Business Review* **30** (July–August 1952), pp. 46–52.

Ruesch, Jurgen, and Weldon Kees. *Nonverbal Communication.* Berkeley: University of California Press, 1970.

Schein, Edgar H., and Warren G. Bennis (eds.). *Personal and Organizational Change Through Group Methods: The Laboratory Approach.* New York: John Wiley and Sons, 1965.

Sheehy, Gail. *Passages: Predictable Crisis of Adult Life.* New York: E.P. Dutton, 1974.

Shepherd, Clovis. *Small Groups: Some Sociological Perspectives.* San Francisco, Cal.: Chandler, 1964.

Skipper, James K., and Robert C. Leonard. *Social Interaction and Patient Care.* Philadelphia: Lippincott, 1965.

Steinmetz, Lawrence L. *Interviewing Skills for Supervisory Personnel.* Reading, Mass.: Addison-Wesley, 1971.

Stewart, Charles J., and William B. Cash. *Interviewing: Principles and Practices.* Dubuque, Iowa: Brown, 1974.

Tacey, William S. *Business and Professional Speaking.* Dubuque, Iowa: Brown, 1970.

Terkel, Studs. *Working.* New York: Pantheon Books, 1974.

Toffler, Alvin. *Future Shock.* New York: Bantam Books/Random House, 1970.

Wall Street Journal (February 8, 1977), p. 1.

Wambaugh, Joseph. *Blue Knight.* Boston: Little, Brown, 1972.

Weaver, Carl H. *Human Listening: Processes and Behavior.* New York: Bobbs-Merrill, 1972.

Weeks, Francis. "Data Sheets and Resumes," *American Business Communication Association Bulletin* (December 1975), pp. 13–14.

Webster's Seventh New Collegiate Dictionary. Springfield, Mass.: G. & C. Merriam, 1970.

Weinstein, Deena, and Michael Weinstein. *Roles of Man.* Hinsdale, Ill.: Dryden Press, 1972.

Wiksell, Wesley A. *Do They Understand You*? New York: Macmillan, 1960.

Wilcox, Roger P. *Oral Reporting in Business and Industry.* Englewood Cliffs, N.J.: Prentice-Hall, 1967.

Winter, Ruth. *The Smell Book: Scents, Sex and Society.* Philadelphia, Pa.: Lippincott, 1976.

Wolfe, Tom. *The Electric Kool-Aid Acid Test.* New York: Bantam Books, 1969.

Work in America: Report of a Special Task Force to the Secretary of Health, Education, and Welfare. Cambridge, Mass.: MIT Press, 1972.

Young, P. *Interviewing in Social Work.* New York: McGraw-Hill, 1935.

Young, Richard. *Recruiting and Hiring Minority Employees.* New York: American Management Association, 1969.

Index

This Index is a select guide to primary discussion areas for the topics noted; it is not an exhaustive list covering secondary or incidental occurrences of those topics.

A book or article by more than one author is entered under the name of the senior author, and only the last names are listed (e.g., Anastasi and Dimond). In a reference to the work of one author, his or her name is given in full. The complete citation for a book or article appears in a first footnote and in the Bibliography.